41/2

THE HOLE TRUTH

THE HOLE TRUTH

Determining the Greatest Players in Golf
Using Sabermetrics

BILL FELBER

UNIVERSITY OF NEBRASKA PRESS | *Lincoln and London*

Library of Congress Cataloging-in-Publication Data
Names: Felber, Bill, author.
Title: The hole truth: determining the greatest players
in golf using Sabermetrics / Bill Felber.
Description: Lincoln: University of Nebraska Press,
2019. | Includes bibliographical references and index.
Identifiers: LCCN 2018011999
ISBN 9781496206541 (cloth: alk. paper)
ISBN 9781496212740 (epub)
ISBN 9781496212757 (mobi)
ISBN 9781496212764 (pdf)
Subjects: LCSH: Golfers—Rating of—Statistical
methods. | Golf—Statistics.
Classification: LCC GV964.A1 F45 2019 | DDC
796.3520922 [B]—dc23 LC record available at
https://lccn.loc.gov/2018011999.

Set in Minion Pro by E. Cuddy.

Contents

Acknowledgments

I would like to take this opportunity to thank Pete Palmer for his invaluable advice on the preparation of this book. Pete is the preeminent expert on statistical analysis in baseball. The concepts transfer.

Introduction

In June 1914, amid open discussion of the imminent prospect of war, Charles Carlos Clarke—a respected member of the London Stock Exchange—put pen to paper in a letter to the editor of the *Times*. Mr. Clarke was alarmed that the young men of Great Britain might prove incapable of the tasks so certainly to be demanded of them. "We all know what the Duke of Wellington said about the Battle of Waterloo being won upon the Eton playing fields," he wrote. "There was no golf then, and I do not think that boys and young men playing golf only and neglecting cricket, football and, if possible, riding to hounds is likely to lead to the winning of the V[ictoria] C[ross]."[1]

Aside from being erroneous—golf significantly predates Waterloo—Mr. Clarke's complaint about the threat to the nation posed by the game is hardly original. The sport has at times been termed slow, unathletic, the province of the rich, sexist, environmentally wasteful, and—supposedly by Mark Twain—a good walk spoiled. Whatever truth is contained in that indictment, it and Mr. Clarke overlook plenty of evidence mitigating in golf's favor, not least of which is its competitive nature.

This book is about golf's competitive nature.

It is one of many golf books on the shelves today. Generally, they follow one of three models. The most common are instructional, written by expert teachers or popular touring pros. You will find within these pages not a whit of instruction on how to hit a golf ball.

A second category includes the pretty picture books. They feature photos, maps, and illustrations of famous and fascinating golf holes the world over. For $75 or $100, they will take you vicariously to the institutional layouts of the United States, England, Australia, and elsewhere. No pictures in this book . . . just charts.

Finally, there are the bio books. John Daly wrote one about how he screwed up his remarkable talent. Alice Cooper wrote another about how golf nearly derailed his renegade musical career. John Feinstein wrote several, stealing the title of one from Twain. This book confesses to being interested in golfers—at least the best of them—but it is in no sense a diary.

This book is about the ways and means of answering a seminal question regarding golf performance: Who was the most dominant golfer of all time and why? For as long as people have been playing golf—back into the seventeenth century and professionally since the mid-nineteenth century—nobody's ever actually attempted a statistics-based analytical approach to providing that answer.

As with many questions pertaining to golf success, subjectively answering such a question isn't terribly difficult. It's asked and answered often—not necessarily correctly—in taverns, fairways, and locker rooms across the nation. The subject came up during a dinner table argument of which I was a participant a while back at an exclusive Georgia golf locale—no, not that one, the place on the state's western border. (And let me take this occasion to offer a delayed apology to any who might have been within earshot for the increasingly strident tone of that particular discussion. Such topics do tend to be argument starters.)

My verbal adversary adopted the position that various advances—in the physical nature of man, in technology, in equipment, in course design, in training—meant that the question essentially answered itself. The best golfer of all time, he contended, was the winner of the most recent tournament. It's a superficially logical position, if subject to change on short notice.

The basis for this book—which I argued at that conversation—is for a more relativistic consideration of the answer, acknowledging (indeed embracing) the game's changing nature. Obviously, if Bobby Jones were returned to life and health and then given his old hickory-shafted mashie, persimmon-headed driver, and rubber-core ball in a match against Jordan Spieth, the outcome would be foreordained. But what if the impact of the training, clubs, balls, courses, and traveling conditions could be normalized in order to create a condition-neutral measurement of Spieth in his prime against Jones—or Hagen, Palmer, or Hogan, in their primes? What if the question were viewed as one of individual dominance against their contemporaries? Who would win then?

And could any of those men achieve a greater dominance over their peers than Annika Sorenstam, Mickey Wright, Nancy Lopez, or Kathy Whitworth—again assuming a condition-neutral and nature-neutral outcome? There is no reason such an inquiry needs to be pertinent to one gender and one only. Nobody asserts that the best woman could be expected to beat the best man head-on in a contest over the same course length and using the same equipment. The pertinent question is which player has come closest to maximizing the inherent ability of the human species under the times and conditions in which he or she actually played. That would represent a true and honest measurement of the best golfer of all time.

The bulk of this book pursues the answer to that question by way of a largely statistically driven analysis of the careers of seventy of the best-known and most successful players in the professional game's history. Those seventy do literally span that history, from Old Tom Morris, the first recognized "great" tournament player of the 1860s, to Dustin Johnson and Spieth, the numbers 1 and 2 players in the Official World Golf Ranking as of the conclusion of 2017. For each of the seventy, there is a basic career outline that is followed by a three-part synopsis of the player's rating: a chart of each player's best major tournament performances during his or her "peak" seasons, a career summary of major tournament performances, and a line graph showing the player's development across the length of his or her career. If the player ranks among the top twenty-five players of all time based on either peak or career value, that fact is noted at the outset of the analysis. The above sentence contains several words or phrases requiring definition; the full explanations are found in chapter 3 and also in the appendix.

Unless otherwise cited in the text, the data forming the basis for the rating of each player are not particularly mysterious or exotic. Golf is a results-driven game; it's measured by a score, and those scores are a matter of public record. The trick lies in how one views those scores. Historically, golfers have viewed scores as a counting exercise, which during any given tournament is precisely what they are. Low score wins. That assumption breaks down, however, when one attempts a cross-era comparison, influenced as such comparisons are by developments over time. For such cross-era work, one is forced to abandon an attachment to raw scores in favor of a measurement that one might term *relative dominance*. That is to ask, "How much better was Player A than all the other players against whom he or she was competing?" In that context, the question of one golfer's superiority over another—irrespective of eras, gender, equipment, weather, or other factors—becomes answerable.

1 The 3 Percent Game

The role of statistical analysis in golf can be explored to a reasonable degree of certainty. But to do so, one must first recognize and then adjust for the impact of a variety of natural changes that have occurred to golf—and, for that matter, to almost every other form of human endeavor—over a period that covers centuries. The groundwork to do so has already been laid—not in golf but in baseball. In a 1989 essay titled "The Changing Game" published in *Total Baseball*, I noted the ways that changes over time in numerous aspects of life—the numbers of people available to fill rosters, improved equipment, technological and sociological advances, educational level, and strategy—affected the national pastime. "By what context does one measure [Rogers] Hornsby's feats of the 1920s relative to [Wade] Boggs's of today?" I asked at that time, answering, "By the context of the technological, strategic, societal and cultural changes that have wrought both of them."[1]

Even more so than baseball, golf suits itself to this sort of statistical approach because while baseball is substantially a statistical game, golf is almost entirely so. In baseball the team-wide object may be victory, but individual players contribute in varying and disparate ways, some by hitting, some by pitching, some by fielding. Each skill requires a separate technique of measurement and a separate field of reference, and those can be imprecise, even unquantifiable. A batter may contribute to victory even by making a well-placed and well-timed out. There are many career .125 hitters in the Hall of Fame; they generally had 95 mph fastballs and great control of that pitch. But because the tasks performed by members of a baseball team are often different, the difficulty with baseball analysis lies in determining how all those disparate aspects can be merged into a single accurate and meaningful expression.

That's the easy part in golf, where one is measuring just one player with just one goal. The goal is called his or her score. The task is merely to relativize and, if possible, explain it.

Such statistical analysis is also a lot more important to the under-standing of golf than other sports for the simple reason that golf is more competitive. The gap between the determinable talent level of golf pro-fessionals is smaller than it is among those in other sports. Nor, among other sports where such a thing can be quantified, is there an especially close second.

In a typical modern Major League Baseball (MLB) game, the aver-age winning team scores about 5.5 runs; the average losing team scores about 3.5. In other words, one would expect the winning team on any given day to score runs at a rate about 22 percent above the average and expect the losing team to score runs at a rate about 22 percent below the average. That's subject to wide variation in the particulars, but it's accurate as a generalization.

In other popular professional sports, similar results emerge. In profes-sional football, an average modern score is about 27–15. That means the winning team scores points at a rate about 29 percent above the league average, while the loser's score rate is correspondingly reduced. The score of an average National Hockey League (NHL) game is about 4–2, mean-ing that the winning and losing teams over- or underperform league averages by about 34 percent. Because National Basketball Association (NBA) games are by their nature higher scoring, the differential between winning and losing is smaller as a percentage. But it still amounts to about 5.2 percent (10 points). One sees even more striking disparities when looking at individual skills. As measured by batting average and considering all those with enough plate appearances to qualify for con-sideration, the difference between the best (.348 D. J. LeMahieu) and worst (.209, Danny Espinosa) hitters in baseball during 2016 was 67 percent. Measured by yards per game, the difference between the best passer in the National Football League (NFL) in 2016 (Drew Brees, 325.5) and the worst (Brock Osweiler, 197.1) was 65 percent.

Such distinctions are unfathomable in golf. On the 2016 Professional Golfers' Association (PGA) Tour, the difference between the lowest stroke average per round (Jordan Spieth, 68.85) and the average (70.93) was 2.08 strokes, or about 2.9 percent. The difference between Spieth and the worst player (Steven Bowditch) was just 7.46 percent. The spread on the Ladies Professional Golf Association (LPGA) Tour was a bit higher (Lexi

Thompson, 69.02, average 71.62, worst Ssu-Chia Cheng 76.00), but the differences still amounted to 3.6 percent and 9.2 percent, respectively.

Reduced to tabular form:

League	Average team/ individual score	Winning team/ individual score	Percentage difference
NHL	3	4	33.3
NFL	21	27	28.6
MLB	4.5	5.5	22.2
NBA	101	106	5.2
LPGA	71.62	69.02	3.6
PGA	70.93	68.85	2.9

Because both games are so statistically oriented, many of the sabermetric techniques developed for baseball are easily translatable to golf. The question becomes: What does one want to learn? There may be an infinite number of answers to that question, but two should suffice to begin the dialogue. The first: What tangible skills are most important to success on the professional tour? The second—can one compare and rank the greatest professional golfers of all time?—is set aside for succeeding chapters.

As is the case with virtually every professional sport today, the by-product of sabermetric research many years ago spilled over into golf. More than a decade ago, the PGA Tour's website began making available second-level or third-level statistical tools. Initially, there were fewer than a dozen such measurements. Today it is possible to study 60 different measurements related to the striking of the ball by a driver alone. The tour offers 97 statistical measurements related to play from the fairway or rough, 29 analyzing play from around (but not on) the green, and 95 related to the seemingly simple act of putting. That's an obsessive 281 stats designed to analyze performance that during an average round probably encompasses only about seventy strokes.

The basic tool for quantifying relationships between sets of numbers— say, scoring average and any of the 281 available statistics—is called regression analysis. You can think of it as correlation. It asks a fundamental question: How strong is the relationship between the two numbers? In other words, if one goes up (or, in the case of scoring average, down), is the other likely to follow? Correlations can be thought of as running from 0.0 to 1.0, with zero indicating no correlation whatsoever and 1.0 indicating a perfect correlation. When comparative sets of data normally flow in opposite directions—does your score get lower as you drive the ball farther?—correlations are calculated negatively, with –1.0 indicating the strongest correlation and 0.0 indicating no correlation. For purposes of simplicity in this analysis, all correlations—even naturally negative ones—will be expressed on a 0.0 to 1.0 basis. The significance of the findings will be unaffected.

As one talks about correlation, honesty compels acknowledgment of a mathematical axiom: correlation may or may not indicate causation. The stereotypical illustration of this is the fact that an extremely high percentage of those convicted of violent crimes brush their teeth every day. It does not, however, follow, that tooth brushing causes violent crime. In correlation studies, as elsewhere in life, logic must be allowed to intervene.

An important cautionary note, though, is merely that if everyone can do it, correlation studies may not point to causation. Regarding golf, that forces some questions: Can everybody hit a 300-yard drive? Can everybody stick a 5-iron within 5 feet of a 4.25-inch hole from 200 yards away? Can everyone make a good percentage of their 20-foot putts? No, no, and no. So if strong correlations exist between those abilities and a player's final score, one is safe in giving at least some weight to the causal prospects of them.

The table that follows lists the correlations between scoring average and six measures of player performance during the 2017 PGA Tour season, one in which 195 pros played enough rounds to meet tour minimums for analysis. Again, the average score of a qualifying PGA Tour player during 2017 was 71.05. Here are the results, showing the skill, the average performance, and the strength of the correlation. Because one is more used to seeing correlations expressed as percentages rather than decimal points, that's how it will be done henceforward. Just keep in mind that 0.0 percent is meaningless and 100 percent is perfect.

Skill	Average	Correlation
Driving distance (yards)	292.77	44%
Driving accuracy (percentage)	60.60	12%
Greens in regulation (percentage)	65.39	59%

Proximity (feet)	36.74	10%
Scrambling (percentage)	58.74	52%
Total putts	29.07	20%

The data appear to suggest that only a couple of the six aspects of play correlated to any meaningful degree with a player's stroke average. The strongest correlation, with percentage of greens hit in regulation, measured only about 59 percent. The only other correlation above 50 percent involved scrambling ability, measuring 52 percent. The correlation between scoring and driving distance, surely the most discussed aspect of tour play, registered 44 percent.

It is not only possible but confirmed by analyzing additional data back to 1980. Here are the correlations for each of those six categories for every fifth year dating to the beginning of record keeping. Where a space is blank, data for that season were not kept. The final column shows the average for all since the statistic in question was first kept.[2]

	1980	1985	1990	1995	2000	2005	2010	2015	Average
Distance	13%	26%	14%	35%	31%	19%	15%	33%	19%
Accuracy	53%	46%	48%	30%	35%	08%	17%	17%	32%
Greens in regulation	66%	77%	66%	59%	66%	59%	38%	55%	61%
Proximity						46%	23%	17%	36%
Scrambling				60%	61%	51%	69%	46%	58%
Putting	25%	34%	34%	32%	30%	16%	42%	24%	30%

On average, two of the six skills—greens hit in regulation and scrambling—correlate with a player's score to a level above 50 percent. The rest appear to have a modest to insignificant historical relationship to scoring, although in saying that, a caveat is in order with respect to distance off the tee. For the past four seasons, the correlation between driving distance and scoring has basically shot directly up, from just 14 percent in 2013 to 24 percent, then 33 percent, then 35 percent, and finally to an all-time high of 44 percent in 2017. More on that in a few paragraphs.

If that is all one had, one would conclude that winning on tour is more a matter of artistry than talent, that there is no formula for excellence. It is not, however, all one has; there are the 281 categories mentioned earlier. The data push has come in several stages. Between 2001 and 2004, the PGA Tour accelerated its use of lasers to measure player distance and accuracy. A select couple of categories became 30, then 50. In 2007 the tour first measured the actual mechanics of ball flight, giving us such micromeasurements as clubhead speed, spin rate, launch angle, carry and hang time . . . basically, the same things your sporting-goods retailer use to sell you a new driver.

Statistically, however, the most important of those new categories was made possible in 2003. That is when tour officials began utilizing a system they called ShotLink to more precisely and more thoroughly record every shot actually hit on tour. They did more than that; they made the data available to researchers. A few years later, Mark Broadie, research director of the program for financial studies at Columbia University, took the tour up on its data availability, eventually developing a performance measurement system that came to be called Strokes Gained.

The Strokes Gained system is sufficiently intricate that it cannot be explained to any level of detail here. Suffice to say, it analyzes each shot against the average result of all shots taken from similar circumstances in order to attach a positive or negative value. In that sense, it is similar to baseball's wins above average, an offshoot of the better-known wins above replacement, which measures the relative contribution of each game-related act. In both cases, a zero-based norm results, which is a good thing. The second good thing is that Strokes Gained improves the correlational relationship between skills and scoring. Here are the correlations for the four major "Strokes Gained" categories for five-year increments since the formula's application dating back to 2004:

	2005	2010	2015
Strokes Gained off the tee	46%	46%	52%
Strokes Gained approaching the green	76%	60%	64%
Strokes Gained around the green	31%	49%	31%
Strokes Gained putting	37%	46%	42%

If one compares the strength of those correlations with the strength of correlations of the six basic tasks already examined, the comparison generally favors the "Strokes Gained" approach. This is true in the most significant category—greens in regulation (GIR) versus Strokes Gained approaching the green—but is also true in Strokes Gained putting versus putts per round and in the emerging category, driving distance versus Strokes Gained off the tee. Since its inception, the correlation between Strokes Gained approaching the green and scoring has never fallen below 59 percent and has averaged 70 percent. That is a noteworthy correlation indeed, and it is also noticeably stronger than either the 47.5 percent correlation between GIR and scoring or the 37 percent correlation between proximity and scoring over the same years. Since 2004 the average correlation between Strokes Gained off the tee and scoring has been 49 percent; the average correlations for distance and accuracy for that same period are 19 percent and 15 percent, respectively. The average correlation between Strokes Gained putting and scoring has been 38 percent; substitute putts per round, and the correlation falls to 26 percent.

Where the Strokes Gained approach does less favorably than the tried-and-true method is in assessing a player's work around the greens, chiefly his ability to scramble for par or better. Since 2004 the average correlation between Strokes Gained around the green and scoring has been a relatively modest 38 percent, measurably less than the 52 percent correlation between basic scrambling ability and scoring. There are two possible explanations for this: first, Strokes Gained doesn't work particularly well the closer you get to the green, and, second, success around the green doesn't correlate well to winning.

Back to putting . . . what's going on here? In 2017 tour pros averaged 29.07 putting strokes, 41 percent of their average score. Yet neither the correlations between Strokes Gained putting or putts per round and scoring have measured higher than 50 percent in thirty years, and in 2017 those correlations were just 25 percent and 20 percent, respectively.[3] If one particular skill amounts to 41 percent of the game, shouldn't its correlation to score be something beyond incidental? The explanation is probably pretty logical, if one thinks about it. In 2017 the average pro hit his approach shot 36.74 feet from the hole. For all putts longer than

25 feet, the best putter on tour in 2017—Xander Schauffele—made just 5.6 percent . . . but that only amounted to 30 makes in 540 attempts. Three-putts are even more rare. There were 7,846 of them in 2017, but that's across more than a quarter-million holes, amounting to just 2.2 three-putts in an average player's seventy-two-hole tournament.

Speaking broadly, in other words, tour pros pretty much always two-putt from any significant distance. So, no, putting isn't as broadly decisive as one might think. (That does not rule out it's being decisive on an event-by-event basis; more on that shortly.)

To this point, the book has been dealing only with general, season-long data sets. When working from the general to the specific, a host of variables come into play. Those include, but are not limited to, the depth or quality of a tournament field, the playing conditions, weather, and innumerable idiosyncratic factors. Jordan Spieth may be the best putter on tour, but how's his tummy feeling this morning? Did a contender celebrate a good round with a late night on the town? And by far the biggest variable, not at all idiosyncratic, is the competitive closeness of the field . . . in a word, *luck*.

What all of that means is that on an event-by-event basis, the relationships between skills and scores may be more meaningful. Is there a correlation between excellence in certain skills and scoring that may come and go over time but may influence results on a week-to-week basis?

Here's a secret to fantasy players: Given the competitive nature of the tour, predictive analysis of a golf tournament is almost impossible to do in a statistically reliable fashion. That in turn means even excellent data are essentially worthless for predictive purpose. Sorry, Draft Kings fans. If those data make any sense at all, it is only retrospectively, which is how they are used here.

The difficulty with predictive analysis is even more challenging on the women's tour. That's because LPGA data-collection techniques are primitive for this data-driven age, generally encompassing just six rudimentary skills and only dating back to 1993. The six are driving distance, driving accuracy, greens in regulation, sand saves, putting, and putts per GIR. Here are the correlations for the four most pertinent in 2017:

	Correlation
Distance	0.30
Accuracy	0.30
Greens in regulation	0.86
Putting	0.37

And here are the LPGA Tour correlations in five-year increments dating to 1995, along with the seasonal average since the data were first kept:

	1995	2000	2005	2010	2015	Average
Distance	48%	37%	33%	29%	23%	36%
Accuracy	33%	31%	35%	36%	35%	36%
Greens in regulation	86%	83%	74%	81%	81%	83%
Putting	38%	36%	53%	36%	44%	42%

To the extent the LPGA data suggest anything—and their sparseness somewhat undermines that premise—they appear to suggest that women take an even more mechanical approach to the accuracy game than men do. Look at the line representing the correlation between greens in regulation and scoring, a relationship that for the women is consistently above 80 percent. That's 10 percentage points higher than the men's 70 percent correlation for Strokes Gained approaching the green and 20 points higher than their 60 percent GIR correlation. In short, the world's best women's players tend to be mechanics; the world's best men's players, while also showing distinct mechanical aspects, mix more artistry into their winning equation.

The following analysis, drawn from 34 PGA Tour and 28 LPGA Tour events played during the 2014–15 season, includes all the majors as well as all the FedEx Cup and CME Globe events—in other words, all the big ones. Because Strokes Gained data are not generally available on an event-by-event basis, they use driving accuracy, driving distance, greens in regulation, and number of putts. Here are the highlights:

1. The average rank of the men's 34 event winners in putting was 8.85. Generally, that would have been out of a field of about 70

who played all four rounds. Four of the tournament winners led their fields in putting, 15 ranked among the top 5, and 20—that's nearly 60 percent of the winners—ranked among the top 10. None ranked lower than 34th.

2. The average rank of event winners in hitting greens in regulation was 17.68. Three winners led their fields in GIR, 11 ranked among the top 5, and 20—again nearly 60 percent—ranked among the top 10. Only four ranked outside the top 40, the lowest being Chris Kirk, who ranked 62nd in greens in regulation while winning the 2015 Colonial.

3. The average rank of event winners in driving distance was 25.24. The disparities in this category were wide. Five winners—Dustin Johnson at the Cadillac, Rory McIlroy at the Wells Fargo, Jason Day at the BMW, J. B. Holmes at the Shell, and Bubba Watson at the Travelers—led their fields. At the same time, 8 won despite ranking outside the top 50 in driving, among them Jim Furyk, who won the Heritage while ranking 75th out of 76 in driving distance.

4. The average rank of event winners in driving accuracy was 33.88. Only 3 winners ranked among the top 5 in driving accuracy, only 6 among the top 10, but 8 ranked outside the top 50.

5. In two important respects, women performed differently from men. The average rank in putting of the winners of 28 women's events was 19.39, 11 spots worse than the average rank of the men's winners. On the other hand, the average rank in greens in regulation of those female winners was 7.50, 10 spots higher than the men's winners. Six of the 28 women's winners also led their fields in greens in regulation, 16 ranked among the top 5, and all but 1 ranked among the top 13. (The exception, ANA Inspiration winner Brittany Lincicome, ranked 65th in greens in regulation that week. She offset that by ranking 1st in both driving distance and putting.)

6. The average rank for winners of women's events in driving distance was 23.68; for driving accuracy, it was 30.50. Both figures are roughly identical to the men.

On an event-by-event basis, the correlation data suggest some significant relationship between putting and scoring. That's true for the full field. For winners, the relationship appears to be even stronger. Of the 33 men's tournament winners for whom there are season-long putting data, 27—that's 80 percent—regularly beat the tour average of 29.08 putts per round. So putting well is an aid to winning. The difficulty of actually using that information on a predictive, week-to-week basis lies in the fact that putting skill seems to come and go.

Jordan Spieth, a five-time winner in 2015, was also the best putter on tour, averaging 28.82 putts per round. Still, when Spieth won, he generally outputted even himself. In his five 2015 victories, Spieth averaged just 27.68 putts per round, a performance that's even more exceptional than it sounds since Spieth won the U.S. Open at Chambers Bay despite needing 31.5 putts per round. In his other four wins, Spieth averaged just 26.7 putts per round, just 91.8 percent of the tour's season-long average and just 93 percent of Spieth's own season-long average.

Other instances were even more dramatic. Davis Love usually needed 29.67 putts per round in 2015, but at the Wyndham he got around in 29.0 putts per round, and he beat Jason Gore by one shot. Justin Rose averaged 29.17 putts per round for the season, but at the Zurich Classic he averaged just 25.8, just 88 percent of his season-long putting requirement. Guess who won?

In fact, winners of 30 of the 34 tour events examined from 2015 bettered their season-long putting averages on the way to those victories, and they did so by an average of 4 percent. At 29.9 putts per round, Robert Streb was one of the worst putters on tour in 2015. Yet at the McGladrey Classic he averaged only 28.3 putts per round and won. Bubba Watson needed 29.8 putts per round on average, but when he won the 2015 Travelers he required just a field low 26.8 putts per round. Jim Furyk required 29.7 putts per round on average, but won the RBC by taking just 26.5 putts per round. Guys get hot from week to week.

In raw numbers, tour winners needed 27.46 putts per round when they won, contrasted against a season-long average for those same players of 28.59 putts per round—one stroke. In case you're wondering, 20 of those 34 events were decided by one stroke or in a playoff, so, yes, that single stroke of week-to-week performance improvement was decisive. For the PGA Tour as a whole, the 2015 average number of putts per round was 29.08.

As noted earlier, putting was a less decisive factor in winning among the ladies, where the key ingredient was the ability to hit a green in the regulation number of strokes. Of 25 2015 tour winners for whom there are both season-long and individual event data, 60 percent beat their seasonal GIR averages during their wins, and 11 did so by more than 10 percent. At the Walmart event, Chella Choi hit 90.7 percent of greens in regulation on her way to a playoff victory over Ha Na Jang. That was a 20 percentage point step up by Choi, who for the season hit only 69.3 percent of greens in regulation; the women's tour average in 2015 was 66.7. For the season, Inbee Park averaged 74.6 percent of greens in regulation, slightly better than the tour average. But during her five victories, Park hit greens 79.44 percent of the time, about 12.5 percentage points more often than the field.

As with the victorious men on greens, the women victors were naturally predisposed toward their specialty. For the year, those women averaged hitting 73.56 of greens in regulation, about 7 percentage points more than their opponents. But on the weeks they won, the women victors did even better, averaging 79 percent.

Obviously, the disparity between the two tours' fondness for statistics is not driven by technology, so the obvious alternative factors are interest and cost.

2 Dominance and Chance

There is a widely held and mistaken view in armchair sports analysis that the great teams separate themselves from the merely average ones in their ability to win the close games. If a baseball team is in first place in early July and is also winning a disproportionate number of one-run games, media analysts are guaranteed to point this canard out repeatedly. It's a belief based on the gut-level assumption that most games are decided by a run or two. Ergo, teams that triumph over the long haul must necessarily do well in those close games.

In fact, as those who study baseball closely have realized for some time, the actual relationship between winning close games and winning a lot of games is surprisingly casual. The reason is as evident as it is overlooked: outcomes of close games are more likely to be determined by chance occurrences. When one says a team is winning the close games, what it means to some extent is that they're lucky. Luck is not much of a strategy.

Far stronger than the relationship between winning close games and winning a lot of games is its opposite, the relationship between winning routs and winning a lot of games. The best teams don't squeak by their opponents; they pound them. The worst teams don't get edged out at the margins; they get hammered. In 2017 eight Major League Baseball teams averaged at least a half run per game more than their opponents. Those eight had a .596 winning percentage. At the other end of the spectrum, ten teams averaged at least a half run less than their opponents. The winning percentage of those teams was .428. Of the eight teams that excelled in run production, seven fared worse in one-run games than they did generally with a combined .555 winning percentage in those close games, 41 percentage points below their collective season-long average. The ten teams at the extreme negative end of the run-production scale had a combined .454 winning percentage in one-run games, 26 percentage points better than their season-long winning percentage. Eight of the ten did better in one-run games than they did generally.

There is no reason to believe that in other sports—and notably for this book's purposes in golf—the statistical axioms are different. You don't excel by winning the close ones; you excel by dominating. But as one examines the role of dominance in top-level golf, one would be well served to take a brief detour into recent history.

In 2007, encompassing fourteen medal-play tournaments, Tiger Woods averaged 67.79 strokes per round. The tour as a whole averaged 70.94 strokes. Put another way, the field needed 100 strokes to play the same number of holes Woods could play in 95.5. That means Woods was 4.5 percent better than the average player.

As with any other carbon-based life form, Tiger had his good weeks and his bad weeks, although in Tiger's case the bad weeks weren't very bad. What one might consider his "normal" performance range over that period—mathematicians refer to this as the first standard deviation of his performance—was about 19 percentage points, meaning that about two-thirds of the time Tiger's score fell between 93.6 and 97.4 percent of whatever the field was doing in a given week.

Most of the remaining one-third would be encompassed by a second standard deviation. That would encompass about 97 percent of all events, in Tiger's case extending his predictable performance range to a maximum of 99.3 percent and a minimum of 91.7 percent of the field average. Any Woods performance above 99.3 percent of the field average or below 91.7 percent of that same number, while possible, would be freakishly rare. In fact, there were none in 2007. His worst effort came at the Players Championship, an even-par 288 that was good for a tie for thirty-ninth (his score being 98.9 percent of the field average). His best was 93.0 percent at the PGA Championship, which he won by three shots. A simple graph illustrates the percentage likelihood of a Woods performance at various levels relative to the field average for the 2007.

There was a 99 percent likelihood that Woods's score would exceed the field average (point A), approximately a 50 percent likelihood that it would be 95 percent or less than the field average (point B), and at least a measurable chance that it could go as low as 92 percent of the field average (point C). On tour, 95 percent is often a winning range, so you can readily understand why Woods won seven tournaments in 2007.

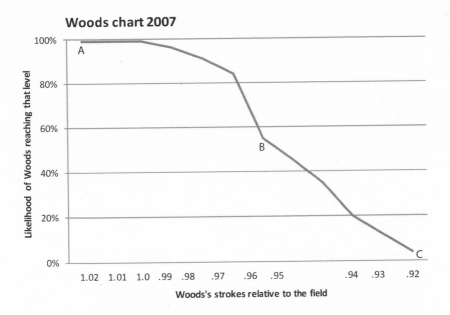

Woods chart 2007

Since Woods does not play in isolation, these numbers really need to be interpreted in the context of his competitors. On the 2007 PGA Tour, approximately two dozen golfers averaged 99 percent of or below the field average for the events in which they played. That is to say, their average was consistently within two standard deviations of the top of Tiger's predicted range of 99.3 percent, giving them at least a plausible chance of matching him on one of their good weeks. Although literally anybody on tour is good enough to conceivably win a tour event, those two dozen constitute the most likely challengers to Woods. Consequently, the most meaningful way to assess Tiger is to compare him to them.

Of those nearly two dozen, the most consistently dominant in 2007 was Ernie Els, whose scores averaged 98.1 percent of the field average for the fifteen medal-play events in which he competed. Els's normal variation—his first standard deviation performance—was 2.5 percent, which is wider than Woods's 1.9 percent. (He's not alone in that; only Chris Riley matched Woods's performance variation in 2007, and Riley's average score, 99.7 percent of the field average, was far higher than Woods's. The average variation among the top men's pros was about 2.5 percent.) The bottom line is that Els could expect to use between 95.6

percent and 1.006 percent of the field-average number of strokes, with a prospect that his performance could fall as low as 93.1 percent or rise as high as 1.031 percent.

Chart the 2007 Els against the 2007 Woods, and Ernie's problem beating Tiger comes into focus.

In other words, 90 percent of the time, Tiger 2007 would shoot what Ernie 2007 would shoot about half the time. Conversely, Ernie shot Tiger's 50th percentile score only about 15 percent of the time. From this, roughly estimating Ernie's prospects for actually beating Tiger is simply the product of Ernie shooting at a certain level multiplied by the prospect of Tiger not doing so. Let's assume, for illustration, that Tiger shot his 50th percentile score. The chart estimates that there was about a 15 percent chance in 2007 of Els scoring at that same level. Fifty percent times 15 percent is 7.5 percent. Ergo, when Tiger played his normal game in 2007, Els had approximately a 7.5 percent chance of beating him. In reality, Ernie did a bit better than that, besting Tiger twice in the fourteen 2007 PGA Tour events in which they both competed and matching his score two other times. In the remaining ten tournaments, Tiger beat Ernie.

One can make the same estimates up and down the performance range. It is known that Ernie's normal score was about 98 percent of the field average. It is known that there was about a 90 percent prospect that Tiger would shoot within 98 percent of the field average—which means there was a 10 percent chance he wouldn't. So if Ernie merely shot his normal round, his prospects of beating Tiger were 50 percent times 10 percent, or about 5 percent.

Thus far, the task of beating Tiger in 2007 sounds pretty much hopeless, which it would have been if the contest were simply between Woods and any single competitor. But a typical PGA Tour field consists of about 150 entrants, whose range of talents is remarkably compressed. Among the nearly 200 players who competed in at least ten tour-certified tournaments in 2007, the scoring average range between the very best (Woods, 67.79 strokes) and very worst (Todd Hamilton, 72.83 strokes) was less than 7 percent. Given the potential week-to-week variance for so many bodies, that is as inconsequential as it is possible to get.

Even so, during his fourteen 2007 medal-play starts, Woods was bested by only 68 different players, a fascinatingly small number considering

Woods vs. Els

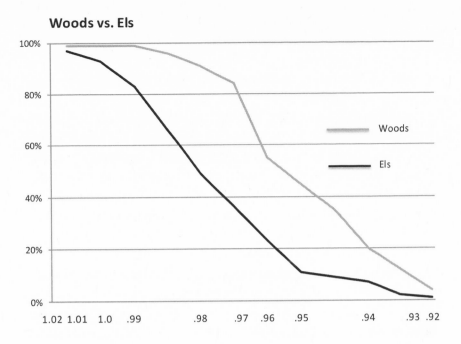

that fourteen tournaments, each consisting of about 150 competitors, amounts to roughly 2,100 opponents. The news was actually worse than that for Woods's pursuers, because 33 of the 68 did it in the two tournaments where Tiger played poorly (by his standards), the Palmer and the Players. In the other dozen tournaments in which Woods competed, just 35 players managed to finish in front of him even once. Only 3 men—Stewart Cink, Sergio Garcia, and K. J. Choi—beat Woods as many as three times.

It has already been established that the upper end of Tiger's expected performance range in 2007 was 99.3 percent of the field average. In 2007 only 13 men's tour players produced a dominance rating of .993 or lower, and those 13 can probably be characterized as the guys Tiger needed to pay attention to. Listed from most dominant to least dominant, those 13 included:

98.1: Els
98.3: Justin Rose
98.4: Vijay Singh

98.7: Jim Furyk, Sergio Garcia

98.9: Arron Oberholser

99.0: Steve Stricker

99.1: K. J. Choi, Zach Johnson, David Toms, Adam Scott

99.2: Rory Sabbatini

99.3: Padraig Harrington

As demonstrated earlier, none of these guys individually posed a consistent threat to Woods, since in 2007 he was likely to shoot their midpoint score about 90 percent of the time. But considered as a pack, they were a more legitimate force. Their average dominance rating was about 98.8, and the average variance of their performance was about 2.5 percent, setting the low end of the first standard deviation of their predicted performance at about 96.3 percent. That number, not far from Tiger's own 95.5 percent midpoint, meant that in any given week, the question of Tiger versus this particular field of most likely pursuers was fundamentally a toss-up, an assertion borne out by Woods's seven victories in his fourteen starts. His seven defeats came to Choi (the Memorial and the AT&T National), Singh (the Palmer), Harrington (the British Open), Johnson (the Masters), Phil Mickelson (the Deutsche Bank and the Players), and Angel Cabrera (the U.S. Open).

In addition to their wins head-to-head against Woods, those 13 players won six of the thirty-two events in which Woods did not take part. Again, that proportion of wins makes sense because when Tiger was removed from the picture in 2007, the talent spread among all other golfers was so small that what developed was pretty much a fair fight. While the average dominance rating—about 98.9 percent—of the 13 most likely challengers was definitionally better than the 100 percent dominance rating for the "field," the "field" had one huge advantage, size.

To this point, largely for purposes of simplicity, the analysis has hinged on the prospect of Tiger 2007 shooting his midpoint score. There is no law stipulating that he would do so, and when he posted a score in the lower third of his personal range, the fact that his range was so much lower than anybody else's made him essentially invulnerable. His performance chart suggests that in 35 percent of his 2007 tournament competitions, Woods should have put up a four-round total that was 5.4 percent lower than the field average for the tournament in question. (In fact, he did even better, with very low scores six times in fourteen medal-play starts, or 42.9 percent of the time.) Even among the 13 tour players identified as Woods's most legitimate threats in 2007, only 2—Els and Furyk—had even a 10 percent statistical chance of separating themselves from the field by 5.6 percent. That puts their individual likelihood of matching Woods when he goes low at 35 percent times 10 percent, or 3.5 percent. And in real life, Tiger's statistically improbably good season made the likelihood just 4.7 percent. In real life, Tiger played eight events in which his score was better than one standard deviation below the average dominance rating of his plausible pursuers—that is, below 96.3 percent—and he won seven. Combined, Els and Furyk had twelve opportunities to beat Woods when he was playing at that level, and they went a collective zero for twelve. Here's the full table, with the lowest dominance rating in boldface.

Event	Woods	Els	Furyk	Other
Buick Invitational	**96.0**	DNS	DNS	
Doral	**95.2**	97.6	100.4	
Wachovia	**93.8**	98.2	102.3	
Bridgestone	**93.4**	98.6	DNS	
PGA	**93.0**	94.0	99.9	
Deutsche Bank	96.2	DNS	101.2	95.5[a]
BMW	**93.9**	99.3	98.9	
Tour Championship	**94.0**	102.4	99.9	

Note: DNS = did not start. a. Phil Mickelson.

Fast-forward now to 2015. The most dominant player on the PGA Tour was Jordan Spieth, with an average of 97.9 percent and a standard deviation of .024. That means the first standard deviation of Spieth's expected performance range—a performance he could be expected to deliver about two-thirds of the time—was between 95.5 percent and 100.03 percent of the field average. In fact, Spieth made twenty-three starts on the PGA

Tour in 2015, of which eighteen landed in the first standard deviation and two within the second standard deviation. The remaining three represented the three times Spieth missed the cut.

Spieth won five times on tour in 2015, two fewer than Woods in 2007, but perhaps even more remarkable given the difficulties Spieth faced that Woods did not. As noted above, Woods faced 13 competitors who could reasonably project to score within two standard deviations of Woods's upper performance range, 99.3 percent. The upper limit of the second standard deviation of Spieth's performance in 2015 was 1.027 percent. Aside from Spieth, there were 147 players on tour in 2015 who compiled dominance ratings of 1.027 or lower. Repeat: Woods had 13 significant challengers in 2007; Spieth had 147 in 2015.

Not only was the competition deeper in 2015 than 2007, it was far closer. Recall that in 2007, the runner-up to Woods's 95.5 dominance rating was Els at 98.1. That's a spread of 2.6 between first and second. In 2015 the spread between Spieth and the runner-up, Jason Day (98.0), was just 0.1. The third most dominant player, Henrik Stenson, was at 98.2, followed by Rory McIlroy and Bubba Watson, both at 98.6. Within the 2.6 spread that separated Woods in first and Els in second during 2007, Spieth faced 46 competitors in 2015.

Beyond that, whereas the first standard deviation of Woods's performances was 1.9, it was 2.4 for Spieth. That means Spieth was less predictable than Woods—witness his three missed cuts.

Let's repeat the Woods 2007 chart, this time substituting Spieth and his 147 significant challengers for 2015. This time the low end of the first standard deviation of the performance of Spieth's challengers is 0.8 with a group average of 1.000, meaning that all events in which Spieth's dominance rating was 99.2 or below will be studied. There were eighteen such events, Spieth winning five. Here's the comparison of his dominance rating in each event to that of his 2 closest competitors, plus all others in the group of 147. (Winners' dominance rating are in bold face.)

Event	Spieth	Day	Stenson	Other
Waste Management	97.8	DNS	DNS	**96.3**[a]
AT&T Pro-Am	98.4	98.0	DNS	**96.1**[b]
Northern Trust	97.4	DNS	DNS	**97.0**[c]

WGC Cadillac	98.6	99.3	96.9	95.2[d]
Valspar	**96.6**	DNS	96.9	
Valero Texas	95.8	DNS	DNS	94.4[e]
Shell Houston	96.9	DNS	DNS	96.9[f]
Masters	**94.5**	100.5	99.4	
RBC Heritage	98.3	DNS	DNS	95.4[g]
Colonial	97.5	DNS	DNS	97.2[h]
Memorial	96.7	CUT	DNS	96.0[i]
U.S. Open	**96.0**	97.8	99.5	
John Deere	**96.0**	DNS	DNS	
British Open	97.0	97.0	100.2	96.7[j]
Bridgestone	97.2	97.6	96.9	94.8[k]
PGA	95.2	**94.1**	100.8	
BMW	98.2	**94.3**[l]	97.9	
Tour Championship	**96.3**	98.8	97.7	

Note: DNS = did not start. **a.** Brooks Koepka. Spieth was also beaten by Hideki Matsuyama, Bubba Watson, Ryan Palmer, Martin Laird, Jon Rahm, and Graham Delaet. **b.** Brandt Snedeker. Spieth was also beaten by Nick Watney, Charlie Beljan, Dustin Johnson, and Pat Perez. **c.** James Hahn. Spieth was also beaten by Paul Casey and Dustin Johnson. **d.** Dustin Johnson. Spieth was also beaten by J. B. Holmes, Bubba Watson, Adam Scott, Louis Oosthuizen, Bill Haas, Webb Simpson, Kevin Na, Rory McIlroy, Ryan Moore, Ryan Palmer, Danny Willett, Jim Furyk, Rickie Fowler, and Lee Westwood. **e.** Jimmy Walker. **f.** J. B. Holmes beat Spieth in a playoff. **g.** Jim Furyk. Spieth was also beaten by Kevin Kisner, Troy Merritt, Brendan Todd, Matt Kuchar, Sean O'Hair, Branden Grace, Louis Oosthuizen, Bo VanPelt, and Morgan Hoffman. **h.** Chris Kirk. **i.** David Lingmerth. Spieth was also beaten by Justin Rose. **j.** Zach Johnson. Spieth was also beaten by Louis Oosthuizen and Marc Leishman. **k.** Shane Lowry. Spieth was also beaten by Bubba Watson, Justin Rose, Jim Furyk, Robert Streb, Brooks Koepka, David Lingmerth, and Danny Lee. **l.** Spieth was also beaten by Daniel Berger, Scott Piercy, J. B. Holmes, Rory McIlroy, Rickie Fowler, Dustin Johnson, Hideki Matsuyama, Cameron Tringale, Kevin Na, and Bubba Watson

Spieth in 2015 simply wasn't as good as Woods was in 2007. Spieth's 68.94 stroke average of 2015 was a full stroke higher than Woods's 67.79 . . . and then some. In theory, that might be accounted for by tougher courses or conditions . . . except it's not. In 2007 the tour-wide stroke average was 70.94; in 2015 it was 70.95. It also undermines the oft-proposed theory that it's tough for Spieth—or anybody else—to win today because the competition is simply better and deeper. Nope, Woods was just that much better than everybody else. That's why he faced only 13 players in 2007 whose scores suggested a plausible chance of competing with him, while Spieth faced 147 such qualified challengers in 2015.

It also validates the idea that with the talent level so close and wide-spread, performance correlations are highly likely to come and go from week to week.

Finally, it establishes that Spieth and his contemporaries have a long way to go if they aspire to replicate Woods's brilliance of a decade ago.

Evidence buttressing this conclusion can be readily found in the early records of the two men. From the moment he joined the tour at the start of the 2013 season through 2015, Spieth played in eighty events. Woods's first eighty events as a pro began on September 1, 1996, in Milwaukee and continued through late March 2000. The two stars-to-be were roughly parallel in age, both in their early twenties. Side by side, here's how they stacked up:

	Woods, 9/1/96 to 3/27/00	Spieth, 2013–2015
Starts	80	80
Rounds	303	288
Wins	20	6
Top 5	40	23
Top 10	50	32
Cut	1	12
Stroke average	68.14	69.84
Field average	71.23	70.90
Dominance rating	95.7	98.5

With respect to dominance and chance, the current situation on the women's tour roughly parallels that on the men's tour. In 2015 the most dominant player on the women's tour was Lydia Ko, with a rating of 97.1. But, like Spieth, she was closely followed: by Inbee Park (97.3), Stacy Lewis (97.8), Shanshan Feng (98.0), Lexi Thompson (98.2), and a host of others. The upper limit of the second standard deviation of Ko's expected performance was 1.023, a level averaged or exceeded by eighty-nine pros on the LPGA Tour in 2015. Of thirty-one tournaments on the LPGA's Tour schedule in 2015, twenty-six were won by competitors with a season-long dominance rating below 99.8 and seventeen with a dominance rating below 98.6.

Again as with the PGA Tour, this remarkable competitive balance, while normal, is not necessarily required. As with Woods on the PGA Tour, one needs retreat only to 2007 to find dominance winning out. That year Lorena Ochoa had a dominance rating of 94.9. That means Ochoa was marginally even more dominant on the women's tour than Woods was on the men's tour. Her performance that season, which included eight victories—two of them majors—in twenty-five starts, translated to a first standard deviation scoring range between 93.7 and 97.3 percent of the field average, with a second standard deviation range between 91.1 and 98.7. Those numbers combined with her omnipresence—Ochoa played in twenty-four fields in 2007—suggest that more of her seventeen top-five finishes should have been wins.

As with Woods, few competitors actually had a legitimate chance to beat Ochoa unless they played near their absolute peak. She, after all, wasn't going to help them. (In her twenty-four 2007 starts, Ochoa never posted a four-round total that was higher than 99.2 percent of the field average, roughly the high end of her second standard deviation.) But for the record, here are the sixteen who tended to perform within two standard deviations of Ochoa's norm, listed in order of their own dominance scores:

97.1: Paula Creamer
97.6: Suzann Pettersen, Annika Sorenstam
97.9: Mi Hyung Kim
98.0: Stacy Prammanasudh, Morgan Pressel
98.1 Angela Park
98.3: Seon Hwa Lee, Jee Young Lee
98.5: Jeong Jang, Shi Hyun Ahn
98.6: Sophie Gustafson, Nicole Castrale, Laura Davies
98.7: Angela Stanford, Sherri Steinhauer

These sixteen averaged 98.2 percent of the field average score for the year, making that a good first benchmark. Aside from that lone 99.2 referenced above, Ochoa beat 98 percent of the field average every time out. As for Lorena's own average score of about 94.9, only Creamer had as much as a one-third prospect of equaling that. The average—and this is for Ochoa's sixteen closest pursuers—was about 10 percent.

And that was if she just shot her average game. If Lorena dialed her own performance up to the level she reached about one-third of the time, a score that was about 94.2 percent of the field average, plausible contenders began to fall away quickly. While there was better than a one-in-four chance that Ochoa would record a score that was 94 percent of the field average—and in fact she did so eight times in 2007—only Creamer, Pettersen, and Sorenstam could calculate as little as even a 10 percent chance of doing so.

In fact, Ochoa never lost in 2007 when she shot below 94 percent of the field average and lost only twice when she went below 94.8 percent of that target. Both defeats came in playoffs and both to likely suspects. At the Ginn Tribute, Castrale beat Ochoa in a playoff after both players shot 279 against a field average of 296.7. At the Long's Drug event, Ochoa and Pettersen tied at 277 against a field average of 294.5, Pettersen winning the playoff.

And as with the men's tour, none of this has anything to do with a deeper talent pool. In 2015 Ko's 69.44 stroke average was about 3 strokes better than the 72.37 average for all qualifying players. In 2007 Ochoa's 69.69 stroke average was 3.5 strokes better than the 73.34 average for all qualifiers. Relatively speaking, Ochoa in 2007 was a half-stroke better than Ko in 2015.

One can learn something about the microreasons winners of PGA Tour events succeed from week to week by dissecting the results of individual events. In doing so, it would be helpful if the actual event winners were, one might say, unexpected. After all, if Jordan Spieth wins, the most likely explanation is "Duh . . . he's Jordan Spieth!" This exploration focuses on four events from the 2015 PGA Tour season, each of them won by a player who ranked outside the top fifteen in stroke average during that season.

McGladrey Classic, October 23–26, 2014, Sea Island Golf Club, Sea Island, Georgia

Winner: Robert Streb, 266
Margin: Playoff over Brendon de Jonge and Will Mackenzie

The McGladrey is one of those off-season events that attracts a field consisting of second-tier pros largely there in order to make a buck. None of the top 15 in the final 2014–15 stroke-average list showed up; Streb, who would finish 18th, was highest ranked. De Jonge, statistically a cowinner, finished 48th; Mackenzie, who did not compete in enough events to develop a full statistical profile, finished 126th.

So the first explanation for Streb's victory was simply that he was the most talented player in a weak field. Nor do the particulars deliver much in the way of profound elaboration . . . either for Streb or for de Jonge. For the 71 players who completed four rounds, data publicly exist on 62 in four categories of analysis: driving accuracy, driving distance, greens hit in regulation, and putts per round. Here's what the data show:

DRIVING ACCURACY: Relatively speaking, Streb was a laser that week. He hit 73.21 percent of his fairways, exceeding his season-long 59.47 percent performance by 13.74 percent. Still, Streb—and de Jonge, for that matter—ranked in a 13-way tie for only 23rd in driving accuracy with, among others, Justin Leonard, who finished thirteen strokes behind them, and Martin Flores, fourteen back. First in driving accuracy, at 85.71 percent, was Chad Campbell, who finished nine strokes behind the leaders. Combine that with what has already been established about the general insignificance of driving accuracy, and it's impossible to make the case that Streb's heightened ability to find fairways led to his victory.

DRIVING DISTANCE: Streb's drives averaged 297 yards that week, almost precisely matching his 297.1 yard season average. (For the record, de Jonge was a fraction shorter than usual, averaging 282.8 yards off the tee, 2.5 yards below his average.) To the extent distance aided Streb's win, it had less to do with his performance than with the nature of the field. Although ranking only 36th on tour in driving distance for the season, Streb had the 5th-longest average among those in the McGladrey field, behind only Tony Finau (who finished in a tie for 14th), Jason Kokrak (tied for 66th), Justin Thomas (71st), Daniel Berger (tied for 22nd), and Hudson Swafford (tied for 12th). Since one knows that distance, like accuracy off the tee, is not a significant predicator of success on tour, the most one can say was that Streb's relative length benefited him against a weak field.

GREENS IN REGULATION: Chapter 1 established that the ability to approach the green well was a significant factor on tour. Streb hit 73.61 percent of his greens in regulation that week, a performance that was slightly but not profoundly better than his 69.14 percent season average. Yet it ranked only a very modest 40th among the four-round field. The leader, Stewart Cink at 86.11 percent, finished in a tie for 32nd. (De Jonge, at 83.33 percent, tied for 3rd in GIR that week.) It's safe to say that Streb's victory did not turn on his mastery of his fairway irons.

PUTTS PER ROUND: At 28.3 putts per round, Streb tied Fabian Gomez and Nicholas Thompson for number 1 in this category. One could, then, argue that this was the decisive element. To an extent, it's fair to say that Streb got warm, if not hot, on the greens at Sea Island; his seasonal average of 29.1 putting strokes—102nd tour-wide and 38th among those completing four rounds that week—was eight-tenths of a stroke higher than his field-leading performance that week. (De Jonge, for the record, averaged 30 putts per round that week, about one stroke worse than his 29.03 season-long average.) Obviously, that eight-tenths of a stroke advantage Streb had over his usual self could go a long way toward explaining a playoff win.

2015 Arnold Palmer Invitational, March 19–22, Bay Hill Course, Orlando

Winner: Matt Every, 269
Margin: 1 stroke over Henrik Stenson

Every finished 182nd on the season's stroke-average table, so his victory at Bay Hill can reasonably be described as one of the least likely on that season's tour. The Palmer field, while not a major-caliber one, contained names you're familiar with: Stenson, Hideki Matsuyama, Louis Oosthuizen, Jason Day, Zach Johnson, Rickie Fowler, and Adam Scott. Forty-one of the 64 players in that field who completed four rounds, and who competed enough to develop a full-season data profile, finished ahead of Every in the FedEx Cup rankings, and literally all of them finished with better season-long stroke averages than Every's 72.42. Yet Every won. How?

DRIVING ACCURACY: Every hit 73.21 percent of his fairways, good for a five-way tie for 30th among that week's full field, yet far better than his season-long 52.51 percent performance. In raw numbers, that translates to a dozen more fairways for the tournament, or three per round. However lightly one considers the ability to hit a fairway, hitting three more per round than usual can't be a bad thing.

DRIVING DISTANCE: Every coupled his accuracy with a 290.3-yard-average distance, about 3 yards better than his 286.6-yard season average and 31st best that week. But Scott, who tied for 35th, led the field at 308.4 yards, 18.1 yards longer than Every. In fact, 48 players finished 2015 with longer average driving distances than Every, while just 16 were shorter. So if the 3 yards Every picked up that week did anything, they at most kept him afloat. They certainly were not an explanation for victory.

GREENS IN REGULATION: If there was a key to Every's victory at Bay Hill, this plainly was it. He hit 80.56 percent of his greens in regulation, second best in the field (behind Francesco Molinari, 81.94 percent) and far better than his season-long standard. For the year Every would average just 58.1 percent of greens in regulation, ranking dead last among those finishing four rounds at Bay Hill. In raw numbers, his improvement amounted to sixteen greens for the tournament, or four per round. When you go from last to second in the field in the most significant skill, you have given yourself a chance.

PUTTS PER ROUND: Every required 28.3 putts per round at Bay Hill, tying him for 15th with three other players. The leader, Shawn Stefani at 26.5 putts per round, finished in a tie for 21st place, 11 strokes behind Every. Plainly this wasn't a putter's tournament. Every's performance on the greens was basically in keeping with his profile: he averaged 28.67 putts per round for the season.

2015 Crowne Plaza Invitational, May 21–24, Colonial Country Club, Fort Worth, Texas

Winner: Chris Kirk, 268
Margin: 1 stroke over Jordan Spieth,
Brandt Snedeker, and Jason Bohn

Sandwiched between the Players and the U.S. Open, the Colonial is one of those Texas tour events that the best players occasionally drop in on but don't consider an appointment stop. In 2015 the event drew four members of the eventual FedEx Cup top 10—Spieth, Zach Johnson, Danny Lee, and Charley Hoffman—and 3 of the 10 lowest season stroke averages, Spieth, Zach Johnson, and Paul Casey. Kirk, who would rank 93rd in stroke average, would hardly have stood out amid such company. Yet he built a 2-stroke lead on Spieth, number 1 in both FedEx Cup and stroke average, after three rounds and held him off on Sunday to win by 1. How does that happen?

DRIVING ACCURACY: Don't look here. Kirk hit just 50 percent of fairways, nearly 12 percentage points worse than his season-long average, seven fewer than Spieth, and only 59th best among the 69 players qualifying for this study.

DRIVING DISTANCE: Or here. Kirk averaged just 277.1 yards off the tee, about 9 yards less than his 2015 average and just 39th best in the field. For the record, Spieth was also off his average . . . but at 285.5 yards he could afford to be.

GREENS IN REGULATION: And certainly do not look here. Kirk hit just 63.89 percent of the greens in regulation that week, the 7th-worst performance in the field and fractionally worse than his standard 64.54 percent for the year. Which leaves only . . .

PUTTS PER ROUND: And here one arrives at Colonial's bottom line. Kirk required just 25.8 putts per round, the best performance in the field and nearly 3 strokes superior to his 28.6 putt per round season-long average. This was especially fortuitous against Spieth, the tour's number-1-ranked putter in 2015 at an average of 27.82 putts. At Colonial he needed 28.5, just far enough off his norm to cost Spieth at least a playoff berth. By the way, Kirk ranked 37th on tour in 2015 in putts per round. In essence he got and stayed blisteringly hot on the greens, and that more than offset all of his other flaws. So when announcers say putting is the decisive skill in golf, they're right . . . occasionally.

2015 Memorial Tournament, June 4–7, Muirfield Village, Dublin, Ohio

Winner: David Lingmerth, 273
Margin: Playoff win over Justin Rose

Featuring the Jack Nicklaus imprimatur, the Memorial is one of those midseason events that occupies the vast space just below the majors. As such it draws a representative field, including star-level talent. Spieth, Justin Rose, Dustin Johnson, and Phil Mickelson all played in 2015. Against such a field, Lingmerth, who would finish 75th in stroke average, would have hardly drawn any betting interest. Yet he held off Spieth by 2 strokes on Sunday and then defeated Rose in a playoff. From time to time, a relative outsider succeeds on tour simply because PGA fields are by their nature highly competitive. The outcome of the 2015 Memorial was decided less by what Lingmerth did remarkably well and more by the stars' failures to separate themselves from the pack.

DRIVING ACCURACY: With a 76.79 percent accuracy rate, Lingmerth easily outperformed his season-long 65.51 percent average. But fairway accuracy isn't a big deal on tour, and anyway Spieth, Johnson, and Rose all also outperformed their season-long measurements. In fact, the field averaged 70 percent of fairways, nicely above its 62.48 percent average for the season. So Muirfield's fairways were docile for everybody.

DRIVING DISTANCE: At a 289.5 yard average, Lingmerth was not one of the tour's longest hitters, and at Muirfield he failed to reach even that standard, averaging just 279.6 yards. Johnson led the field at 326.1, Rose also topped 300, and Spieth averaged 293.5 yards. In short, driving distance was not a determinative factor in the outcome. If it had been, Johnson, who eventually tied for 13th, would have breezed home.

GREENS IN REGULATION: Lingmerth hit 68 percent of his greens, modestly better than the 65 percent he usually hit that season. Rose, Spieth, and Johnson were all a couple of percentage points off their usual averages, but in none of those cases did the differences amount to more than a quarter of a green per round. To the extent this is a big deal, it's because for the season as a whole, Spieth, Rose, and Johnson all averaged between 3 percent and 6 percent more greens in regulation per tournament than Lingmerth. At the Memorial, Lingmerth led all three of those bigger names—just by a few points, but he did lead them.

PUTTS PER ROUND: Lingmerth averaged 26.5 putts per round, fractionally better than Rose and fractionally worse than Spieth or Johnson. Again, the key here is that Lingmerth stayed close, essentially giving fate a chance to tip the scales in his favor. For the season at large, he averaged 0.84 of a stroke more per round than Spieth. In the season-long averages, that 0.84 translates to the difference between being 1st in putting (Spieth) and being 40th (Lingmerth). At the Memorial, Spieth was 2nd in putting behind Patrick Reed, and Johnson was 5th . . . but Lingmerth, with only the 20th-best season-long average in the field, was 7th.

In the four tournaments studied, each was won by a player not generally ranked among the game's elites. One of those victors, Streb, won by dint of standing out as the best in a mediocre field. A second, Every, won by monotonously hitting fairways and greens. A third, Kirk, won by overcoming a series of shortcomings with his putter. A fourth, Lingmerth, won because none of his competitors did anything to distinguish themselves when he was enjoying a better than average week. Collectively, they suggest that there is no single key to winning in a given week . . . which is why picking winners in a golf tournament is a fool's errand. This will come as a terrible letdown to the wishes and hopes of Draft Kings types. But unless Tiger is in his prime, the competitive space between players is simply too narrow, and—at least on the PGA Tour—their performance is governed too much by artistry rather than mechanics.

Is it possible, however, to predict future stars? Is the ability to drive a ball long distances, or on an unerring path, or to hit a green in regulation, or to scramble from off the green for par, or to putt well, or any combination of those skills, useful in identifying who is likely to *become* a star?

On the 2016 PGA Tour were 21 players fitting a pair of criteria that would be useful in addressing the answer to that question. The first condition is that they were active on the Web.com Tour—the PGA's top minor-league tour—a reasonable number of seasons earlier . . . let's say five. The second condition is that since graduating to the PGA Tour, they were successful. For purposes of this discussion, "success" is defined as having at least $1 million in post-Web.com earnings. In descending order of post-2011 career earnings, the 21 players who fit both criteria are Russell Knox, Jonas Blixt, David Lingmerth, Danny Lee, James Hahn, Jason Kokrak, Roberto Castro, Brendon Todd, Brian Stuard, Ken Duke, Scott Brown, Billy Hurley III, Erik Compton, Greg Owen, Kyle Reifers, Will

Wilcox, Dicky Pride, Tyrone Van Aswegen, Luke List, Steve Wheatcroft, and Tim Wilkinson. Your initial reaction will be that this is not a collection of the tour's front-rank players. There's no Jordan Spieth, no Jason Day. It is, however, a solid representation of the tour's middle class. In combination, the 21 can claim 13 tour wins, 190 top 10s, and about $100 million in career winnings, the poorest among them, Wilkinson, still registering $1.8 million as of the end of 2016.

Let's take that group of 21 and ask a question: Looking at their 2011 performance on the Web.com Tour, did the group as a whole—or its individual members—stand out in any of the correlative skills measurements?

There were nearly 130 players sufficiently active on the Web.com Tour in 2011 to compile a statistical résumé, so the collection of 21 represents the roughly 15 percent who went on to greatest success. To ascertain whether that success might have been predicted based on 2011 Web.com data, one can begin by examining the ordinal placement of each of the 21 among the full field of nearly 130. If they bunch toward the top in any particular area, then that area will look suspiciously like a predictor.

Here's how the individuals, and the group as a unit, did in each of the five correlative skills.

DRIVING ACCURACY: Russell Knox was the 4th most accurate player on the Web.com Tour in 2011. Knox hit 73.57 percent of his fairways. This is interesting if only because he is Russell Knox, and Knox has already been established as the most successful 2011 graduate of the Web.com Tour. For the record, he has since won two tournaments and more than $10.1 million. Billy Hurley, however, is the only other of the 21 players who ranked higher than 15th in driving accuracy as a Web.com pro; Hurley's 72.41 percent of fairways was good for 8th place. The 65.36 percent accuracy average of the group was marginally better than the average for all Web.com pros that season, but it translated to only an average ordinal placement of 59.5, barely breaching the upper half. Nothing remarkable there.

DRIVING DISTANCE: At 318.6 yards, the longest driver on the Web.com Tour in 2011 was Jason Kokrak. The 5th longest, at 314 yards, was Luke List, and the 10th longest, at 308.9 yards, was Greg Owen. All 3, by the way, have lost a little muscle in the intervening years. Kokrak was down to 307.4 yards in 2016, List down to 306.9, and Owen down to 297.9. Those distances, it should be noted, were still good enough to rank 6th, 8th, and 39th on the big boys' tour.

Kokrak, List, and Owen were, however, the exceptions. The average 2011 driving distance of the 21 Web.com successes was 295.29 yards, the average ordinal placement a totally middle-of-the-road 65th. That's roughly where one would have likely wound up with any randomly selected group of 21 from the full field. At the other end of the scale from Kokrak, List, and Owen, Billy Hurley (273.8 yards) and Tim Wilkinson (282.6) both ranked among the bottom 10. Conclusion: driving distance is showy, but not indicative.

GREENS IN REGULATION: The data for GIR is not markedly different from the data for either driving distance or accuracy. Of the 21 eventually successful players, 2—Roberto Castro (4th) and Knox (8th)—ranked among the top 10. One, Brendon Todd (117th), ranked among the bottom 10. The group average of 69.36 percent of greens hit in regulation was slightly but not significantly better than the full-field average. The average ordinal rating was 57.19, about 2.25 places more favorable than driving accuracy but hardly a predictor of success.

SCRAMBLING ABILITY: If there is a predictor of future success, the data suggest this may be it. By converting 67 percent of his missed greens into pars or better, Tim Wilkinson ranked 1st on the Web.com Tour in 2011. Meanwhile, Dicky Pride, Billy Hurley III, Danny Lee, and David Lingmerth ranked 3rd, 4th, 7th, and 9th, respectively. That's 5 places among that season's top 10 occupied by current PGA Tour regulars. Among the second 20 were Erik Compton (11th), Knox (14th), and Kokrak (16th). Against those 7 in the top 16, only one (Wilkinson, 116th) ranked among the bottom 30. Tour-wide, the average Web.com player converted 58 percent of his scrambling opportunities in 2011; the select 21 converted 61.14 percent. That may not sound like much, but had the group been a person, they would have ranked among the top 35 on tour that season. Their average ordinal placement, 36.05, is 7 places higher than for any of the other measurements.

PUTTS PER ROUND: On the 2011 Web.com Tour, Blixt (2nd), Wheatcroft (3rd), Todd (5th), and Lingmerth (7th) all ranked among the top 5 for fewest putts per round. As with scrambling, there are few negative counterbalances; only Castro (102nd) ranked among the bottom 30. The average ordinal placement of the 21 was 43.6, noticeably less profound than the average ordinal placement for scrambling ability but also notably more substantive than for any of the other three categories.

All of that digression back to 2011 doesn't really prove anything beyond a shadow of a doubt about the long-term predictive abilities of the correlative data. But it does at least underscore the view that the surest way of escaping golf's minor-league system is by polishing that short game . . . something your pro has probably already told you. (Of course he charged you $100 or more for the advice.)

3   Tournament Rules

In athletic-related data analysis, there are two more or less overarching narratives. The first concerns the strength of relationship, if any, between particular measurable skills and performance. The first two chapters answered the basics of that question. The second question relates to the ability to comparatively assess golfers across generations. This is by far the more complex question, given the constantly evolving circumstances within which the game is played. But it is also by far the most intriguing, since a fair match between the great players of yesterday and today can occur only on paper.

If one hopes to make sense of the relative abilities of golfers who played in different times and conditions, one first needs some commonly understood and applied guidelines. One can think of these as the rules of an "all-time tournament." The guidelines will be designed to answer three broad questions: Who will be measured, what will be measured, and how will the measurements be done? The first two questions can offer leeway; the third cannot.

Who's in the Field, and Which Events Should Be Measured?

The essays that follow are based on examinations of the career records of about two hundred men and women from every era. Most of those whose stories are told herein would, most likely, be considered among a consensus ranking of the greatest players of all time, although a few who do not attain that status are included because their stories are worth telling.

Today's touring pros play between twenty and twenty-five events in a season. That's a generalization, of course. If you're Jason Day, you can make enough money for groceries and the mortgage in as few as fifteen events. Then there are workaholics who play forty-some tournaments a season because the tour only schedules that many. In confronting the question of which tournaments to rate, that issue of variable field quality is one excellent reason to exercise discretion. After all, should one view the Booz Allen Classic on a par with the Masters?

For cross-era comparison, far and away the most logical approach is to focus on performance in the major events. In addition to field quality— the best players almost always show up—there are several other good reasons for doing so.

1. They're familiar. Every 20-handicapper can name the men's majors: the Masters, U.S. Open, British Open, and PGA Championship.
2. The men's majors are stable and the women's events reasonably so. Whatever did happen to the Booz Allen, anyway? The Masters, the youngest of the men's majors, has been around for more than eight decades. Like the majors, the PGA Tour's FedEx Cup series also draws the best players . . . but that event has been played since only 2007. As a tool for ranking all but the current generation of players, it is useless.
3. They present a consistent and manageable amount of data.

Sadly for symmetry, the history of major women's tournament golf is less ordered than the history of major men's golf. To its credit, the LPGA long ago recognized the problem its occasionally checkered history had created. That checkered history began in 1930 when the Western Golf Association—which had been conducting a widely recognized tournament for men since the nineteenth century—anticipated gender equity and created the Women's Western Open. It was won by somebody named Mrs. Lee Mida, and that is virtually everything on record about Mrs. Lee Mida. Initially, the Women's Western did not draw many big names, probably because there weren't any. June Beebe won in 1931, and when she did it again in 1933 she became the first repeat champion. Opal Hill won back-to-back tournaments in 1935–36. The first winner there's actually an outside chance you've heard of was Betty Hicks, a longtime pro in the seminal days of the women's tour who took the 1937 championship and remained active for fifteen years thereafter.

Also in 1937 a group of women golf enthusiasts organized an event they called the "Titleholders Classic." There weren't many titles to hold if you were a woman in the late 1930s, but that didn't stop the game's best from journeying to Augusta, Georgia, each spring to compete at the most prestigious women's competition of its like at the time. It was held at the Augusta Country Club, where in addition to the golf the women could look at, but not touch, the all-male Augusta National situated directly through the azaleas. Patty Berg, then a nineteen-year-old phenom, won the Titleholders in 1937 and liked it so much she won again in 1938. She also took the third event in 1939, before Betty Hicks diversified the list of champions in 1940.

At the time, there was nothing "major" about those two events, either in prize money (which was negligible enough to go unreported) or in public attention. Occasionally, such as when Babe Zaharias won the Western in 1940 or when Louise Suggs took the Titleholders in 1946, the event would merit a few paragraphs in the *New York Times*, but that was about it. It was, after all, *women's* golf. The whole concept was so little a deal that the notion of a national championship for women didn't even coalesce until after World War II, when a loose entity of female professional golfers, styling themselves as the Women's PGA, pitched the notion to the Spokane Athletic Round Table, which offered facilities at the local country club for a match-play event. Berg won, defeating Betty Jameson 5 and 4 to claim the first prize: $5,600 in bonds. The entire purse was $19,000.

In 1947 a second Open, this one at medal play, was scheduled for Greensboro, North Carolina. But there was so little public interest in competitive women's golf that the purse won by Betty Jameson was 60 percent smaller. (It would be two decades before the Open purse again exceeded $19,000.)

In 1949 the Women's PGA collapsed, and a new entity, the Ladies Professional Golf Association, took charge of both the Open and tour play. The arrival of this entity, driven largely by Zaharias and Berg, marks the functional beginning of an ongoing oversight body. But the LPGA's interests lay as much in promoting the entire women's tour as in promoting the Open itself. So in 1953 it surrendered management of the Women's Open to the United States Golf Association, which had been running the men's U.S. Open since its creation in 1896. Two years later, the LPGA created its own branded event, the LPGA Championship (now known as the Women's PGA).

By the late 1950s, with Arnold Palmer's ascendancy driving interest in men's golf, the notion of four "men's majors" had locked into the public psyche. But that raised a question among those interested in the women's game: Were there also women's "majors"? To answer the question, the LPGA essentially decreed it so. The Open and LPGA, so closely paralleling men's majors, were obvious choices. The Titleholders, with a prestigious location that suggested status as the women's Masters and a prestigious list of winners dating to the 1930s, was the third. Since there was no obvious parallel to the British Open, the LPGA went to its oldest, retroactively designating the Women's Western Open as its fourth major.

That worked well enough until the late 1960s, when two of those majors hit the rocks. The Titleholders folded in 1967 (not counting a one-year comeback effort in 1972), the Women's Western in 1968. That left the women's tour with just three majors in 1967 and just two in 1968.

What it needed, the brains finally decided, was something with an international cachet that would counter the presence of the British Open in the men's schedule. The women's tour had just one regular international event at the time, the Peter Jackson Classic, which had been staged in Canada since 1973. Presto, in 1979 the Peter Jackson Classic became a major. Unlike the LPGA's handling of the Titleholders and Women's Western, though, previous winners were not elevated to major status retroactively. In 1983 du Maurier bought naming rights to the event, injecting cash into the pot that made it a "major" in that sense as well.

Also in 1983, the LPGA elevated the tournament previously known as the Colgate Dinah Shore—and rebranded over the previous winter by Nabisco as the Nabisco Dinah Shore—to major status. Shore, a golf enthusiast as well as a nationally known entertainer, had created the event in 1972. In all ways other than label, the Dinah Shore was widely considered a major well prior to 1983. It had star status, TV attention, and corporate sponsorship, factors that allowed Shore to offer a purse that was the envy of other tournaments. The inaugural event offered champion Jane Blalock a $20,500 first prize, nearly double the previous richest prize in golf history. The Open champion that year got $6,000.

Thus did the LPGA rota of majors enter a seventeen-year window of stability. But in the mid-1990s the European tour had begun pouring resources, including good sponsorship money, into the Women's

British Open. By 2001 the lure of an actual women's major played in Britain was too great to bypass, and the British Open bumped the du Maurier. Finally, in 2013 the LPGA decreed that the Evian Masters, a tournament played since 1994 in Évian-les-Bains, France, would be considered a fifth major.

Over time, then, eight different events have been recognized as women's majors for at least part of their experience, although just two—the U.S. Open and the LPGA—have constituted a reliable core. Two—the Titleholders and Women's Western—were majors for a time without knowing it. Two others, the Peter Jackson/du Maurier and the Shore/Nabisco/Kraft/ANA, weren't, then were (and, in the case of the du Maurier, then wasn't again). The last two, the British Open and the Evian, weren't, then were.

How do you handle all this coming and going? You declare that if it's good enough for the LPGA, it's good enough for us. You will find a year-by-year breakdown of the women's majors in the appendix.

One also needs to consider the odd cases that are the amateur championships. In the modern game, the U.S. Amateur is essentially a college tournament. But there was a time—think of the Bobby Jones era—when the Amateur was a huge-enough deal, attracting major media coverage, that its results should not be ignored. The same is true of its antecedent, the British Amateur, and of the U.S. Women's Amateur. At the same time, even in their most significant days, those events were weak by comparison with concurrent professional events. When Jones famously won the U.S. Amateur as part of his 1930 Grand Slam, there were only three other players in the thirty-two-person field who either had or eventually would make a national mark on golf. Those three were 1913 U.S. Open champion Francis Ouimet and future U.S. Open champions Johnny Goodman and Lawson Little. Ouimet was on the far fringes of his prime, Goodman and Little had not yet reached theirs, and as it happened Jones never faced any of them anyway. Instead, he defeated a fellow named Eugene Homans of Englewood, New Jersey, 8 and 7 in the finals. At that year's British Amateur, Jones won seven matches, none of them against an opponent even the most rabid golf researcher is likely to have heard of. For those reasons, included here are results from the various men's and women's Amateur tournaments with two conditions attached: Only players who were career amateurs, or who competed prior to World War II, the Amateur's precollege period, are considered. And because amateur-only fields were generally weaker than professional or mixed fields, results from amateur-only events are devalued by 50 percent.

Who Really Won at Oakmont?

In rating the competitors, one thing should be pretty clear: one can't just use scores from tournament leaderboards. Way too many variables would have to be overlooked to make such raw comparisons valid.

Consider that the U.S. Open has been played at the Oakmont Country Club outside Pittsburgh on nine occasions spanning nine decades. In 1927 Tommy Armour won with a four-round score of 301. Seven years later, the trophy went to Olin Dutra at 299. In 1953 Ben Hogan won by shooting 283, a score matched by Jack Nicklaus in 1962. In 1973 Johnny Miller won at 279, the same total as Ernie Els in 1994. Eleven years earlier, Larry Nelson had won with 280. In 2007 Angel Cabrera won by shooting 285. In 2016 Dustin Johnson won with a score of 276. Which of the nine was the superior accomplishment?

Certainly, 276 sounds better than 301. But Armour and Dutra used more primitive clubs than Hogan and Nicklaus, who in turn used less advanced clubs than Nelson or Els, whose equipment Johnson probably wouldn't touch. The rubber-core ball used by Armour and Dutra was out of fashion by Nicklaus's day and would be a museum piece today. Then there was the course itself. Els played a longer Oakmont than Armour, but Armour and Dutra had to contend with those famously furrowed Oakmont bunkers. The course was basically bare and windswept until the mid-1960s, when members undertook a tree-planting campaign. By the time Nelson won in 1983, parts of Oakmont looked like a forest course. By Els's 1994 victory, many of the trees had been removed; by Cabrera's 2007 win, they were all gone.

Same tournament, same course, but nine different setups, nine different sets of equipment, and nine vastly different outcomes. And one must not forget weather or agronomic advances. The task of any serious intergenerational rating system is to ascertain a fair basis on which to normalize all those variables.

There's actually a surprisingly comprehensive mathematical tool that can do what needs to be done. It's called standard deviation, and it's designed to ascertain how unusual a performance is compared to related performances. For a full explanation of standard deviation, see the appendix. For this book's immediate purpose, it's sufficient to understand that standard deviation automatically adjusts for all the variables that would otherwise confound us. The following paragraph, which is critical to everything that follows, explains why.

Although the equipment used by Tommy Armour to win the 1927 tournament was obviously inferior by today's standards, it was not inferior to the equipment used by his fellow competitors; in fact, like Armour, most were probably equipped with the state of the art. The weather, the course, and the ball would have changed markedly from year to year, but probably not very much each day. Because it measures Armour's performance strictly in relation to his peers who were competing under the same general conditions on the same course at the same time, standard deviation minimizes all the cross-era variables and reduces the generational comparison to a question of relative skill. It focuses on this pivotal question: In the conditions in force at that moment, how much better than their competitors were Armour, Els, Nicklaus, Hogan, Johnson, and all the rest?

If both the average and the standard deviation of a normally distributed set of data are known, it's a simple matter to calculate the number of standard deviations any individual bit of data is from the average. Mathematicians have an exotic term for that measurement of exceptionality, whose most familiar application today is probably in standardized testing. It's called a *Z score*, and in simplest terms it's an expression of the number of standard deviations an event lies outside the average. When the U.S. Open was played at Oakmont in 2016, Johnson's four-round total of 276 was three strokes better than his closest competitors and about 12 strokes below the field average for players completing four rounds. But more meaningfully for this book's purposes, it was 2.26 standard deviations better than that 288.30 field average. (One standard deviation that week amounted to 5.44 strokes.) Johnson, then, had a Z score of −2.26. Jason Day tied for eighth with a Z score of −1.16. Jordan Spieth tied for

37th with a Z score of +0.13. Spieth shot 289, marginally above the field average for playing completing four rounds.

Who actually had the best of it in the nine U.S. Opens played at Oakmont? The answer is Ben Hogan in 1953. When he shot 283, it was 19 shots below the field average of 302. Given a 6.38 standard deviation of the field performance that week, Hogan's 283 translates to a Z score of −2.98. Larry Nelson's 1983 total of 280—which produced a Z score of −2.69—was second best. Third best? That belonged not to any of the nine winners but to the man who finished runner-up to Nelson in 1983. Tom Watson shot 281, producing a −2.54 Z score that would have won any 1983 major except the one he happened to be playing in at the time. In fact, a month later Watson won the British Open with a −2.36 Z score.

Because standard deviation allows us to normalize all of the cross-time variables that would otherwise confound this process, it becomes the basis for the player rankings.

Peaks and Careers

Inevitable in the devising of any sort of rating system is the question of what one is trying to rate. Bill James laid this issue out so insightfully in his popular *Historical Baseball Abstract* that there is no need to do more than quote him. There will need to be one major adjustment to James's approach, which follows Bill's explanation of the basics: "When you ask who was a greater player than whom, do you want to know which was more valuable at some moment in his career, or do you want to know which was more valuable over the course of his career? . . . There is no standard or consensus answer to the question; some people mean one thing, some mean the other. The answer that it's some of one and some of the other won't do . . . because if you don't decide, you've got two correct answers to every question."

In baseball analysis, James frames the question by imagining a player's career path as a line graph. Those more interested in James's first posit—value at a particular point in a career—focus on the highest points of the line: what can be easily understood as a player's "peak value." Those interested in the second topic—essentially the player's "career value"—are effectively measuring the area below the line.

As James notes, you can do both, as long as you recognize that you are providing two separate and distinct answers. But in analyzing the performance of golfers, it seems to me that "peak value" is somewhat the truer, sexier number. Why? Keep in mind that unlike a peak Z score—which is an average of a player's best performances—career Z scores are cumulative. That is, you calculate a player's career Z score by the simple process of adding up all of his or her performances in the majors. That process begins when the player turns pro (except, obviously, in the case of career amateurs), and it ends only when the player retires or turns fifty.

When one applies statistical models that develop concepts such as relative winners and losers—as this book will—a player whose performance declines with age "gives back" career achievement he has previously banked. His career value, in other words, tends to retreat toward (and in some cases beyond) zero. In team sports, the issue of declining performance takes care of itself because at a certain point, the declining athlete loses his place on the team. Golf, however, is not a team sport; players can and often do continue to play in championship-tour events well into their forties and even in a few cases into their fifties. Not well, usually, but they play.

This means career-value calculations can confer an advantage on players who retire before their skills begin to recede. In the 1930s there was a fellow named Ralph Guldahl—good player, won a couple of U.S. Opens back to back. His record will be studied in greater detail in a couple of chapters. No one would assert he was as good a player as Tom Watson, who won eight majors and contested Jack Nicklaus for domination of the game between 1975 and 1985. But for a few years in the 1930s, Guldahl was considered the equal of Byron Nelson, which is saying something.

If—applying the methods to be outlined later in this chapter—you assess Guldahl and Watson strictly in terms of their career value, Guldahl rates higher. Given that everyone agrees Watson was the better player, how can this be? It can be because when Guldahl tired of competitive golf at age thirty-nine in 1950, he quit. His career Z score for the majors at that point was –31.24. When he was thirty-nine at the conclusion of the 1988 season, Watson's career Z score was –48.14, substantially better than Guldahl's. But Watson did not retire at age thirty-nine; he continued to play seriously for eleven years until qualifying for the senior tour. Along the way, he suffered recurring putting problems, his long game shortened, new challengers arose, and his scores climbed. Watson played forty-three majors after his thirty-ninth birthday, and his Z score in those forty-three was +31.66, eroding his career Z score to –16.48.

Determining both a player's "peak" and "career" begin with a couple of definitional adjustments.

As noted, golf is a game of lows, not highs, so when one expresses interest in a player's peak performance, graphically one is actually talking about who fashioned the deepest, widest trough, not the highest peak. Next question: How long should a peak be? Among the players constituting this field of study whose careers are complete or nearly so, the average career length was about 23.6 seasons. A half dozen played competitively for at least three decades. And of those with shorter careers—Willie Anderson and Tony Lema come to mind—the reason was generally an early death. In this study, a player's peak is defined as his or her period of five best consecutive seasons; that's about 22 percent of the average career for all the players under consideration. An exception is made for women players in the "five-major" era since 2013 to negate the statistical inequity created by selecting their ten best scores from among twenty-five. In the cases of post-2012 women, the standard will be four seasons, again encompassing twenty majors. There is a judgmental aspect to all of this. One could as easily make the case for an assessment period covering four consecutive years or six, fifteen scores, twenty, or more.

Match Play and Data Sufficiency

If one wants to evaluate historically important amateurs—and what's the point of an all-time evaluation that doesn't include Bobby Jones?—then one has to devise a method of handling match play, the dominant amateur form of competition. The problem is that in match play, there is no final "score" . . . at least not in the sense one is used to thinking about it. In match play, the length of a match varies, and a player's score is measured relative only to his or her opponent's rather than to par. That's consequential. In two matches, one player might "shoot" a round of 69 yet lose 3 and 2, while another might "shoot" a round of 75 yet win 3 and 2. Same final result, yet far different performance levels. In fact, neither competitor would have actually "shot" the projected number, since neither completed the requisite eighteen holes.

If one wants to incorporate match play, one has to accept the fact that one can only estimate, not precisely determine, Z scores.

Having laid out the problems, the lure of developing some means of at least estimating standard deviation into match play is still compelling because of the substantial difference it makes to many of the great players. Between 1916 and 1957, the PGA Championship was contested at match play. Those were also the years when many of the great career amateurs performed. The U.S. and British Amateurs were, for part of that time, viewed as "majors" on a par with the Opens, and the U.S. Women's Amateur was until 1930 the only meaningful tournament competition for American women. Ratings of players of the stripe of Bobby Jones, Walter Hagen, and Gene Sarazen are all materially affected by the inclusion or exclusion of match play. For women, the issue turns on the Amateur as well as the Women's Western Open from its inception in 1930 until 1954 and for the 1946 U.S. Open. The two women whose ratings are most impacted by the handling of match play are Patty Berg and Babe Zaharias.

The method employed to convert match-play results into a "score" involves looking at every possible match-play outcome and converting it to a stipulated stroke-play equivalent. For instance, in matches ending 1-up—that is, one player winning by one hole with none to play—a score of 71 is assigned to the winner and 72 to the loser. That step will be repeated for each possible outcome, the designated stroke margins increasing with the decisiveness of the match play result. These results are not necessarily representative of the actual stroke-play score at the time of the match, but the scores themselves are not important. In calculating standard deviation, what is important is the margin of the victory. If, given three matches decided by 1-up, one of those pairs of players shooting 65 and 66, a second pair shooting 71 and 72, and a third pair shooting 77 and 78, the critical element is that the winner was (approximately) 1 stroke superior to the loser.

Here are the assigned scores used:

Win	Result	Lose
72	extra holes	72
71	1-up	72
71	2-up	72
70	2 and 1	73
70	3 and 1	73
69	3 and 2	73
69	4 and 2	74
69	4 and 3	74
68	5 and 3	74
68	5 and 4	75
68	6 and 4	75
67	6 and 5	75
67	7 and 5	76
67	7 and 6	76
66	8 and 6	76
66	8 and 7	77
65	9 and 7	77
65	9 and 8	78
64	10 and 8	78
63	10 and 9	79

The second problem involves data sufficiency. Since 1958 on the men's tour, and for much of the women's tour, there have been four recognized major events played annually. That means in any five-year peak period, a player's record (unless he or she missed events) would be comprised of twenty major performances. But as previously noted, for much of the 1970s the LPGA got along with just three majors, and for a time there were just two. Today there are five. Go back far enough, and the same problem surfaces on the men's tour. True, as of the institution of the Masters in 1934 there were four "majors," but the British Open was separated by an ocean.

That means that prior to 1934, even a star-quality player could have competed in no more than fifteen presently recognized majors within a five-year period and then only if they made an ocean crossing. That was asking too much for many of the game's stars. True, Walter Hagen made it to ten British Opens over eighteen seasons and Gene Sarazen to eight (not counting his famous return to Troon as a septuagenarian in 1973). But Byron Nelson played in only two, and Bobby Jones, for all his emotional connection to St. Andrews and Scotland, completed just three British Opens his whole life. (Jones actually teed it up in four but withdrew during the 1921 event.) Willie Anderson, the greatest U.S.-based player of the first decade of the twentieth century, emigrated from Scotland but never returned to play there. The east-to-west crossings were even more rare; Harry Vardon played in just three U.S. Opens over two decades, J. H. Taylor in just two, and Ted Ray in three. Henry Cotton, the greatest British player between Vardon and Faldo, played in only four U.S.-based majors, none until he was in his forties. James Braid never made it to an American major.

If one uses five-year windows and considers only the recognized modern majors, the records of many of the men's game's greats prior to the mid-1930s become distressingly inadequate. But one can supplement this record. Into the second half of the century, the Western Open was widely viewed as major quality. (In fact, during the 1960s when the tour's World Series of Golf consisted only of the winners of the four major tournaments, the Western Open winner fleshed out the foursome if one man had won two of the others.) So prior to 1958, when the Atlantic Ocean ceased being a severe impediment to American participation in the British Open, the Western Open makes a perfectly valid supplement to the database.

Life also gets in the way of the assessment. Players of an earlier age simply competed in fewer events than pros do today. Travel, records availability, scheduling, and lack of financial incentive created too many obstacles. The following table shows the number of major tournaments played in by more than two hundred of the game's stars. It is based on the seasons they began their full careers and also their peaks during twenty-year increments beginning in 1900. The difference in major opportunities is clear.

Career began	Peak opportunities	Career opportunities
Pre-1900	9.62	19.23
1901–20	10.27	22.91

1921–40	14.15	45.67
1941–60	15.84	51.64
1961–80	15.67	61.87
1981–2000	18.19	70.61

There is an obvious inequity in attempting to compare Tiger Woods's performance over eighteen majors (for a peak rating) or seventy (for a career) to Harry Vardon's performance over ten or nineteen. Golf has its own way of dealing with this; it's called the handicapping system, and those of you with an official handicap already know how it works. But for the others, here's a brief course. Take your most recent twenty scores, throw out the ten worst, and average the ten best. With a couple of minor adjustments, the difference between your average and par is your handicap. With an exception noted below, the rule will be that only a player's ten best scores among the twenty within his or her peak window are averaged to produce a peak rating.

Special Exemptions

A few of the game's early greats—notably the nineteenth-century British pros whose only available major was the Open championship—never competed in as many as ten recognized majors during a five-year period. Under a rigid interpretation of the tournament rules used here, these players could not be included because of the impossibility of developing a peak performance rating.

For such players, the five-year rule will be extended to enable those players to put together the requisite ten stroke-play majors. And in the cases of Young Tom Morris and John McDermott, whose entire careers consisted of fewer than ten major tournaments, they'll be graded based on the number of tournaments they did play.

Outliers, Gaps, and Other Adjustments

From time to time throughout the history of major tournament golf, there have been participants who—to be blunt—should not have been allowed in the championship without a ticket. This was especially true in the early days of tournaments (pre–World War I for the men and pre-1973 for the women.)

In 1967 Kathy Whitworth won the Women's Western Open with a score of 289, 11 strokes under par on the 6,505-yard par-75 Pekin, Illinois, Country Club course. There were forty-two contestants in the event, among them a woman named Mona Erickson. Two years earlier, Mrs. Erickson had teed it up in the Women's Western Open—the first professional event of her life—and shot rounds of 87, 86, 93, and 88 for a four-round total of 354, 62 strokes above par and 64 behind the winner. In 1967, having sharpened her game not very much, Mrs. Erickson recorded scores of 88, 87, 95, and 92 for a four-round total of 362. That, as you might guess, was good for dead last in the field, 73 strokes behind Whitworth and 11 behind her nearest competitor.

Based solely on her golf skills, Mrs. Erickson did not belong in the field for either the 1965 or the 1967 event. But for reasons known only to history (a need to flesh out the field, a desire to include host club members), even big tournaments have from time to time accepted entries from relative duffers . . . players who produce scores plainly out of step with the skills of the better players of the period in question. Such players can be considered *outliers*, a term that derives from the fact that their data (scores) lie outside the normal range of expected performance. In major tournament golf, outliers haven't been a problem for decades. The last true outlier was the grand old lady Patty Berg, who at age sixty-one completed four rounds in the 1979 Dinah Shore in 343 strokes—an average of just under 86 per round—because Dinah didn't have the heart to cut a legend.

For this book's purposes, the problem with outliers is that while they were technically part of the field, the inclusion of their results distorts the full-field data and thus any data-based conclusions. If I were ruled eligible to compete in the U.S. Open, I might shoot 450, a performance that all by itself would raise the overall field average a couple of strokes and also increase the standard deviation of that week's performance. Statistically, in other words, my presence would be meddlesome and effectively misleading. It's the same principle that would apply if a musician of little skill played second violin in the philharmonic. The negative effect would accrue to an assessment of the whole performance, even though the real problem lay with one performer.

Back to golf. By her mere presence in the 1967 Western Open, Mrs. Erickson and a handful of fellow outliers raised the tournament average 2 strokes, from 313.4 to 315.4 and raised the standard deviation from 10.32 to 13.69. These changes are consequential for the Z score of every player in the field. Accepting such scores as legitimate, Ms. Whitworth's winning 289 translates to a Z score of –1.93. Discounting such outlier showings, the reduced field average and standard deviation make Ms. Whitworth's Z score –2.36.

Because they exist chiefly as mischief makers, the solution for us—as it would be for the symphony—is pretty straightforward: boot the outliers. Hence, for this book's purposes, the various Mona Ericksons of major tournament golf, male and female, do not exist.

Outliers are a modest problem, but players who miss the cut are a more serious one. For most of professional tournament history, the practice has been to lop from the field those who fall far behind the front-runners after a certain point, usually halfway. These days that usually reduces the number of weekend competitors to the top seventy and ties. Obviously, if a player fails to make the cut, he does not have a four-round score for the tournament. This isn't much of a concern as one tries to calculate a peak-performance rating. If in twenty majors a player doesn't have at least ten scores better than "missed cut," there's little need to rate his playing "peak." But career ratings are cumulative. One way to deal with this problem would be to base the calculations on per-round scores rather than four-round scores. But that would muddy the calculations since some conditions—weather and hole locations being the most obvious—could have changed in the interim, and the validity of the calculations hinges on environmental neutrality. Since there is no way to calculate what a player would have shot if he or she had not missed the cut, one will declare a rule for doing so. Such a player will be assigned a "four-round score" that is three strokes higher than the highest four-round score recorded in that tournament, and his or her Z score will be calculated accordingly.

One must also confront what can be thought of as the Lee Trevino provision. Trevino, whose predominant shot was a left-to-right fade, was noted for his aversion to the Masters, a strong right-to-left ball-flight course. Four times in the 1970s he did not even accept his invitation to compete, and when he did he rarely contended. Only once in eighteen Masters appearances did Trevino reach the top ten, and that finish—a tie for tenth—came in 1985, on the forty-six-year-old's fourteenth attempt.

Golfers worthy of consideration as the best of all time cannot have too many jinx courses by tour standards. Accordingly, every major tournament in which a player competes during his or her five-year peak period must be represented at least once among the scores used to calculate his peak rating. If none of a player's ten best scores come from a major in which he or she participated, then better scores must be struck until all majors the player participated in during that peak period are represented at least once. This rule does *not* penalize players who never played in a particular major during their peak. For example, an American player during the 1930s who never competed in the British Open would accrue no penalty. But if that same player made one appearance during his five-year peak in the Brit, his Z score from that one appearance must be among the ten factored into the peak score.

For the record, Trevino's peak rating includes his nineteenth-place finish at the 1969 Masters in which he registered a Z score of –0.18. That replaces his tenth-place showing and –0.68 Z score at the 1973 British Open. (It also changes Trevino's average Z score for the period from –1.70 to –1.63.)

Converting Standard Deviation to Stroke Average

In this book, excellence is measured by standard deviation. In golf, however, excellence is measured by a stroke average. That makes it desirable to convert the former to the latter.

As a rule of thumb, 1 stroke in a major professional golf tournament is equal to between 0.16 and 0.17 of a standard deviation in performance. Armed with this information, and assuming that 0.0 standard deviations equals a score slightly less than 288 on a par 72 course, one can assign an estimated stroke value to every increment of standard deviation. A tabular breakdown of all the major intervals is in the appendix.

There is, however, a catch: converting standard deviation to an estimated stroke value works well only in determining peak ratings. That's because a peak rating is a representation of performance at a particular point in time. Career ratings, however, are volume measures. That's why a player's career rating is not translated to an estimated stroke average.

4 Pioneers

The sport of golf lacks a creation moment. But documentary evidence traces the game back to 1457, when Scotland's King James II banned it out of fear that its play interfered with archery practice. The ban held for close to a half century, until James's grandson James IV rescinded it . . . and ordered a set of clubs for himself.

We do, however, have at least a notion of the identity of the first "professional" golfer. That distinction is generally accorded to Allan Robertson, his age's foremost maker of clubs and "feathery" golf balls. Robertson grew up in and around St. Andrews in the first half of the nineteenth century and supplemented his business income by playing matches against challengers—or teams of them—for money.

Robertson was, by all accounts, good at his skill, occasionally earning as much on the course as he did from the sale of featheries. He took on an apprentice—a St. Andrews lad named Tom Morris, teaching him the ball maker's art and—on the side—the game of golf as well. Within a few years, Robertson and Morris became a team, excelling at "foursomes" play—we call it alternate shot—whereby pairs of twosomes challenge one another, the members of each team taking turns at striking the same ball. Before long the duo of Robertson and Morris garnered a nickname: they were "the Invincibles."

They were also leading figures in one of those intercity rivalries that occasionally propels a sport beyond the bounds envisioned for it. In Scotland at the time, there were two golf-mad communities—St. Andrews and Musselburgh—and they lay on opposite shores of the Firth of Forth. Inevitably where town pride and sporting cash resided, a match was arranged: Robertson and Tom Morris against Musselburgh's best, twins Willie and Jamie Dunn. Amazingly to the St. Andrews faithful, the Dunns won, their backers walking away with hundreds of dollars and the Dunns themselves with an unknown number of side bets. A rematch was demanded and accepted. This time Robertson and Morris won, hundreds of dollars more changing hands among the backers, along with additional side bets to the players. Both matches got a lot of attention in regional publications. The playing of golf had become a business.

But the team of Robertson and Morris did not stay in business for long. The story goes that Allan Robertson wandered onto the St. Andrews links one afternoon to see the unthinkable: his aide and partner, Tom Morris, using a newfangled gutta-percha ball. The so-called gutties were made of hard rubber, far cheaper to make, and longer flying than Robertson's featheries, for all of which reasons they threatened Robertson's ball-making business. Robertson fired Morris for disloyalty on the spot, a gesture whose power was diluted when the Prestwick Club hired Morris as its greenskeeper . . . and when Robertson began selling gutties.

In another year or two, the Invincibles were reunited, defeating Willie Dunn and a new Musselburgh partner in another widely followed foursomes match. For much of the 1850s, they swept aside wishful challengers from the region's golf-playing communities, Prestwick, Edinburgh, Musselburgh, Muirfield . . . and, of course, from St. Andrews. Their only true rivals were each other . . . and to the extent a record exists, it shows them having played each other only once. Tom Morris won. Word was the defeat wised up Allan Robertson to the risks to his own reputation involved in playing Tom Morris. So Robertson never again accepted a one-on-one match. Instead, Tom occupied himself playing another Musselburgh product, Willie Park. It was said that they played nearly two dozen times over five seasons, usually for stakes of 100 pounds sterling or more, eventually establishing that they were evenly matched. Both obviously hoped to win a "championship" match against Robertson, but the outcomes never forced the acknowledged king to give either man a try. Then the issue became moot. Robertson died suddenly in 1859, leaving the Scottish golf world without a "champion."

The gentlemen of the Prestwick club, Tom Morris's own, seized the opportunity, extending an opportunity to the eight players they perceived to be the best in Scotland and England to meet in October 1860 for a competition—thirty-six holes played in one day—settling the issue of "champion golfer." Willie Park, who dropped a thirty-foot putt on the final hole, emerged the winner, defeating Tom Morris by two strokes, the remainder of the field well behind.

The idea of a "major" national championship had begun. In 1894 the "Open" test was extended to seventy-two holes, an occurrence that coincided with the arrival of the three great stars—Harry Vardon, John Taylor, and James Braid—who as a group would come to be known as "the Triumvirate." One year later, the changing of the game's original guard was set in stone: Old Tom Morris, well into his seventies, made his thirty-first and final competitive tournament appearance. It came, of course, at St. Andrews.

Old Tom Morris

What modern golf fans know about Old Tom Morris is largely drawn from commercials for GolfNow, the online tee-time booking site. The presentation of him as a golf-mad geezer with a flowing white beard is inspired by images from late in his life.

One of the interesting things to speculate about Old Tom is how many British Opens he might have won if given a lifelong chance. Old Tom was born in 1821, making him a robust thirty-nine years old at the time of the inaugural tournament. In other words, his best years had probably been wasted in matches against locals.

Old Tom made up for his failure to beat Park in 1860 by winning in 1861. In 1862 he spread-eagled a field of eight by 13 strokes. That's still the record margin of victory. He finished second to Park again in 1863 but won his third title in 1864 and his fourth in 1867. Until the sixth Open was played in 1865, Tom Morris never finished behind anybody other than Willie Park. They were to each other as Arnold Palmer and Jack Nicklaus would be a century later, worthy, reliable adversaries at the top of their games whose greatness would also underscore the other's greatness.

Two things stopped Old Tom's domination in 1868. One was his age: he was forty-seven, and his putting touch was ever so marginally beginning to show it. The second was his seventeen-year-old son, Young Tom Morris, by then a rising star on the Scottish professional golf circuit. For several years, Old Tom and Young Tom formed a virtually impregnable team in foursomes. Of the first twenty-one Opens that were played, Old Tom started twenty, missing only the 1875 event for reasons that will shortly be elaborated upon. He finished among the Open's top ten as late as 1883, when he was sixty-two years old. At St. Andrews in 1895, the seventy-three-year-old Morris completed all four championship rounds, shooting 107-92-96-97 to post a 392. It was good for only forty-seventh place, 70 strokes behind the champion, but it counted. He entered the 1896 event at Muirfield but picked up after three rounds, never having broken 100. Old Tom lived on as the game's elder statesman for more than a decade, dying in St. Andrews in 1908 . . . at the golf course.

This is an appropriate time to acknowledge that no system of comparative assessment—whether based on statistics or more subjective criteria—is perfect. The flaw inherent in standard deviation is its tendency to minimize exceptionality in relatively small sets of numbers; for instance, the fields of five or ten from the juvenile years of the British Open. This particularly hurts Old Tom and Young Tom Morris, who dominated those seasons. As noted above, Old Tom won the 1862 Open by a record 13 strokes. In fact, the second- and third-largest margins of victory in Open history were by Young Tom by 12 strokes in a field of eleven in 1870 and by 11 strokes in a field of six in 1869. For those routs he received Z scores of –2.07 and –1.82, respectively. Old Tom's 13-stroke 1862 victory, in a field of eight, translates to a –1.61 Z score. For comparison purposes, Zach Johnson emerged from a field of eighty to win the 2015 Open in a three-way playoff and received a –2.45 Z score. It is not mathematically possible to adjust the impact of field sizes on data to represent something that did not actually occur . . . not legitimately, anyway. But doing it informally is possible, and this is the result: Had Old Tom and Young Tom received Z scores comparable to those of players of later generations who excelled by similar margins, Old Tom's –0.81 peak rating would become –1.96, and he would rank among the twenty-five greatest golfers of all time for peak performance. In the same fashion, Young Tom's –1.09 Z score would become –2.17, and he would rank on a level with Tom Watson, among the top-ten golfers of all time.

On that basis, if you want to make the argument that the laws of mathematics unfairly penalize the Morrises for beating up on smaller fields, feel free to do so.

Tables such as the ones that follow itemize the ratings of each of the players discussed. The first table notes the components of each player's peak rating: the tournament and his or her position, score, and Z score. The second table breaks down the career rating by major tournament. The concluding line graph illustrates the components of the career rating on a season-by-season basis.

Old Tom Morris in the Clubhouse

Tournament	Finish	Score	Z score
1860 British Open	2nd	176	–1.10
1861 British Open	**1st**	**163**	**–1.74**
1862 British Open	**1st**	**163**	**–1.61**
1863 British Open	2nd	170	–1.15
1864 British Open	**1st**	**167**	**–1.33**
1865 British Open	5th	174	+0.95
1866 British Open	4th	178	–0.40
1867 British Open	**1st**	**170**	**–1.53**
1868 British Open	2nd	157	–1.09
1869 British Open	6th	176	+0.91

Note: Average Z score: –0.81. Effective stroke average: 70.78.

OLD TOM MORRIS'S CAREER RECORD (1860–70)

British Open: 11 starts, 4 wins (1861, 1862, 1864, 1867), –8.83
Total (11 starts): –8.83

Tom Morris Sr.

1860	–1.10
1861	–1.74
1862	–1.61
1863	–1.15
1864	–1.33
1865	0.95
1866	–0.40
1867	–1.53
1868	–1.09
1869	0.91
1870	–0.74

Young Tom Morris

Professional sports has few iterations of true prodigies: child stars who spring fully formed to the head of their game's competition. That was Young Tom Morris.

He was recognized as a serious competitor around the links at St. Andrews by 1864—he was thirteen at the time. The teen had plenty of competition, frequently teaming with—or against—future Open champion Jamie Anderson as well as Davie Strath, a future three-time runner-up. He tried the 1865 Open, but in a gesture presaging Bobby Jones's impetuous debut more than a half century later, Young Tom picked up his ball in frustration after falling far behind and walked off the course. A distant ninth to Willie Park in 1866, he returned for a third try in 1867. A few weeks before that, Young Tom had joined his dad as part of the field in a professional event held at Carnoustie, emerging in a deadlock for the title with Willie Park and Bob Andrews. Young Tom won the playoff by 4 strokes, after which an embarrassed Park challenged the teen to a match, each side putting up five pounds. Tommy won that contest 8 and 7.

That victory provided a backdrop to the Open, where the teen stood as the most serious challenger to his dad's hope for a fourth championship. Perhaps it was a blow to his pride, but Young Tom finished fourth, 5 strokes behind his dad and 3 behind Park.

By then, the signs of change were unmistakable. At the 1868 Open, Young Tom and Old Tom headed a field of twelve, played like the previous iterations in three rounds during a single day on Prestwick's twelve-hole course. There may have been ten other competitors, but there was little doubt that a Morris would win. Young Tom broke with a first-round 51, 3 strokes ahead of Old Tom and 7 better than Willie Park. Old Tom retaliated with a midday 50 to take a 1-shot lead on his son, who carded a 54. Nobody else was within 3 shots of either as the final round began. Old Tom closed with a 53 for a total of 157, but Young Tom posted the tournament's low round, 49, to claim the championship belt by 3 strokes at 154.

At age seventeen, Young Tom had clearly superseded his dad as the game's star. In the 1869 tournament, again at Prestwick, Young Tom opened with a 50, 3 better than anyone else and 6-up on Old Tom.

The highlight was his iron to the 166-yard eighth hole over a series of mounds collectively known as the Alps and then over a half-acre bunker to which locals had given the name Sahara. His ball landed on the front of the green, charted a curving course toward the hole, and fell in for the first hole in one of which we have any record. He followed with rounds of 55 and 52 to win by 11 strokes, only two other rounds of 55 or better being shot by anybody. In 1870 Young Tom, still just twenty, dominated again. His first-round 47 set a new Open record and gave him a 5-stroke lead over the field. Consecutive rounds of 51 put him in at 149, a dozen strokes better than the runner-up.

There was a rule at the time providing that the winner of three consecutive Open titles would take permanent possession of the championship belt. Supposedly, the Prestwick Golf Club had put the rule in place to encourage participation, assuming nobody could ever actually win three straight. After all, the best Old Tom had ever done was win two straight. But Young Tom's 1870 victory, his third in succession, foiled those assumptions. His walking off with the belt so flummoxed the Prestwick bigwigs that the 1871 tournament was canceled, nobody having figured out what to use for a trophy. Happily for the history of golf, somebody eventually discovered a claret jug laying around, and in 1872 the Open resumed. Young Tom trailed by 5 strokes entering the final round but shot 53, while his old buddy Davie Strath, the third-round leader staggered home in 61, giving Young Tom a fourth straight title.

At that moment, there was every reason to assume that Young Tom would dominate the game, and especially the Open, for years to come. He was, after all, still in his early twenties. Yet fate had other plans. In 1873 the tournament moved to St. Andrews, to be contested over two rounds on the eighteen-hole course. It poured rain in the days leading up to the tourney, a severe complication given a local rule assessing a 1-stroke penalty for lifting from casual water. Hit with several such penalties, Young Tom shot 94-89. While that was decent given the conditions, it only counted for a tie for third, 4 strokes in back of Tom Kidd, a St. Andrews caddie who made the best of his local knowledge. At Musselburgh in 1874, Young Tom opened with an uncharacteristic 83, good for second but 8 strokes behind Mungo Park, the younger brother of Willie Park. He rallied during the final round and came to the seventeenth hole with a chance to win. But a missed short putt there, followed by a drive through the green at the last hole, cost 2 shots. It was exactly the margin by which Mungo Park won, 159 to Young Tom's 161.

That 1874 runner-up finish was also Young Tom's last Open appearance. He had been scheduled to play in the 1875 event, to be held back at Prestwick in September, around the time his wife was to go into labor with their first child. Young Tom and his dad were two holes from the finish of a match against the Park brothers the previous weekend at North Berwick when Young Tom received a telegram summoning him home. His wife's labor had begun early, and it was difficult. The Morrises finished the match—beating the Park brothers, the record notes—and then hurried home. Their haste was for naught. Mother and child died before they arrived.

It goes without saying that Young Tom was crushed. But nobody knew how crushed. He and Old Tom both canceled their participation in the 1875 Open and returned home to mourn. Tom did little of consequence the remainder of the year, and then, on Christmas Day, his father found him dead in his bed. The cause was heart failure. He was still four months short of his twenty-fifth birthday. Is this a Hollywood script or what? The answer is yes. A dramatization of the Morrises' lives and relationships, titled *Tommy's Honour* and based on a 2007 book of the same name, was released in the United States in 2017.

Young Tom Morris in the Clubhouse

Tournament	Finish	Score	Z score
1866 British Open	9th	187	+0.89
1867 British Open	4th	175	0.00
1868 British Open	**1st**	**154**	**−1.53**
1869 British Open	**1st**	**157**	**−1.82**
1870 British Open	**1st**	**149**	**−2.07**
1872 British Open	**1st**	**166**	**−1.28**
1873 British Open	T-3	183	−0.97
1874 British Open	2nd	161	−1.46

Note: Average Z score: −1.03. Effective stroke average: 70.45.

YOUNG TOM MORRIS'S CAREER RECORD (1866-74)

British Open: 8 starts, 4 wins (1868, 1869, 1870, 1872), −8.24

Total (8 starts): −8.24

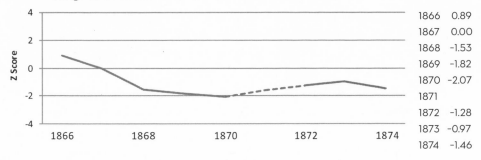

Young Tom Morris

Year	Z Score
1866	0.89
1867	0.00
1868	−1.53
1869	−1.82
1870	−2.07
1871	
1872	−1.28
1873	−0.97
1874	−1.46

Harry Vardon

Number 14 Peak, Number 20 Career

A product of the Channel Islands between England and France, Vardon came from a family of nine, his interest in golf growing out of a course constructed in his hometown when he was a child. It was said that he never had a lesson. Indeed, his interest was casual at best—he seemed more comfortable pursuing the gardening trade—until his older brother Tom's successes as a professional inspired him. At just five-foot-nine and 155 pounds, Vardon did not look like a golfer. But he was reported to have unusually large hands, and he understood their relationship with the club.

Beyond that, Vardon had a perfect golfer's temperament: virtually imperturbable. In short order his natural talent came to the fore. "I do not think anyone who saw him play in his prime will disagree as to this, that a greater genius is inconceivable," remarked Bernard Darwin, the most famous golf writer of the era.[1] He described Vardon's swing as "so wonderfully smooth and rhythmic that it was . . . almost impossible to detect him making an extra effort."[2]

Vardon's mustache was conservative; his golf was another matter. Vardon was known as an innovator, popularizing the overlapping grip that is standard today (and bears his name). He also refined the standard swing, which until his arrival had been characterized by a wide stance and a long, flat arc. Vardon took a narrower, more vertical approach that yielded a higher ball flight that in turn translated to greater distance.

He arrived at the Open in 1894 and quickly established a position at or near the top of the leaderboard. Vardon won in 1896, again in 1898, and a third time in 1899; finished second annually from 1900 through 1902; and then won a fourth championship in 1903. Between 1894 and 1908—a string of fifteen tournaments—Harry Vardon never finished outside the Open's top ten.

By the summer of 1900, golf had grown in popularity in the United States, prompting Vardon to undertake a tour—in company with J. H. Taylor—designed primarily to market his new line of golf equipment to a growing audience. The whole thing culminated in their participation in the U.S. Open, held at the Chicago Golf Club. The event, by the way, was pushed back two months from its usual schedule just so Vardon could play; that's drawing power.

Jointly, Vardon and Taylor delivered a persuasive illustration of the ground the U.S. game had to make up in order to be on a level with the best Brits. Vardon won by 2 strokes over Taylor, with the third-place competitor another 5 shots behind. Taylor shot the tournament's low round, a 76, on the first day, only to see Vardon match it in the third round. Of nine tournament rounds below 80, Vardon or Taylor provided six.

The only gap in Vardon's résumé is a decline in the middle of the first decade of the twentieth century. He was stricken by tuberculosis following the 1903 Open, and the illness handicapped his performance for several seasons. Given that TB was the leading cause of death in most of the civilized world at the time, he was probably fortunate his golf career was merely slowed. In some sense, the illness underscored his greatness. Despite it he managed to finish fifth in 1904, eighth in 1905, third (behind Braid and Taylor) in 1906, seventh in 1907, and fifth (behind Braid again) in 1908. His worst performance, and first finish out of the top twenty-five, came in 1909.

But the 1911 Open proved that the game's first internationally recognized figure had not been permanently laid low. He carded a four-round total of 303 to tie Arnaud Massy, the 1907 champion, for first and then so thoroughly dispatched the Frenchman in the scheduled thirty-six-hole playoff that Massy walked off the course on the thirty-fifth hole. After Taylor added a fifth championship in 1913, equaling Braid and Vardon, Harry broke the championship tie with a 3-stroke victory over Taylor at Prestwick in 1914, the final British Open contested prior to the outbreak of World War I. In the interim, Vardon—accompanied by second-generation golfing great Ted Ray—steamed to the United States in the late summer of 1913 to reprise his 1900 promotional tour and try the Open once again. That was the famous tournament in which the two British stalwarts were defeated by unknown twenty-year-old American amateur Francis Ouimet at the Country Club in Brookline, Mass.

Plainly, Vardon was at his best before the disease. In 1903 he won the British Open by taking just 92.5 percent of the average number of strokes required of the field, a margin that was 2.71 standard deviations below the norm. That brought the five-year rolling average of his standard deviation in the majors to –2.29—his and the Triumvirate's apex—for the 1899–1903 period.

Vardon's 1920 season, the year he turned fifty, merits additional comment. At the British Open, he managed a tie for fourteenth with a total of 318 that was 7 strokes below the field average. His third appearance at the U.S. Open, at Inverness, nearly brought forth the ghosts of his youth. But leading by 4 shots as he stood on the twelfth tee of the final round, Vardon fell victim to a storm that sabotaged his increasingly shaky short game. Vardon basically bogeyed in and lost the title by a single shot to Ray. "I could do better by kicking the ball around those last few holes with my boot," he was said to have remarked in frustration that evening.[3]

It was the effective end for the greatest golfer to that time. Like Taylor and Braid, Vardon continued playing, making his last British Open appearance at age fifty-nine in 1929. Unlike Taylor, he was a shell of his former golfing self after 1920, a fact probably attributable to the lingering effects of his TB as well as his age. He died in 1937.

Vardon in the Clubhouse

Tournament	Finish	Score	Z score
1896 British Open	1st	316	–1.54
1897 British Open	6th	320	–1.45

1898 British Open	1st	307	**−2.26**
1899 British Open	1st	310	**−2.33**
1900 U.S. Open	1st	313	**−2.14**
1900 British Open	2nd	317	−1.93
1901 British Open	2nd	312	−2.23
1902 British Open	2nd	308	−1.86
1903 British Open	1st	300	**−2.95**
1904 British Open	5th	302	−1.63

Note: Average Z score: −2.03. Effective stroke average: 68.98.

VARDON'S CAREER RECORD (1894–1914)

U.S. Open: 2 starts, 1 win (1900), −3.92

British Open: 22 starts, 6 wins (1896, 1898, 1899, 1903, 1911, 1914), −33.96

Total (24 starts): −37.88

1893	0.61
1894	−1.08
1895	−0.29
1896	−1.76
1897	−1.29
1898	−2.13
1899	−2.51
1900	−2.21
1901	−2.13
1902	−1.87
1903	−2.70
1904	−1.63
1905	−0.79
1906	−1.91
1907	−1.42
1908	−1.12
1909	−0.91
1910	−0.55
1911	−1.85
1912	−2.06
1913	−1.70
1914	−2.44

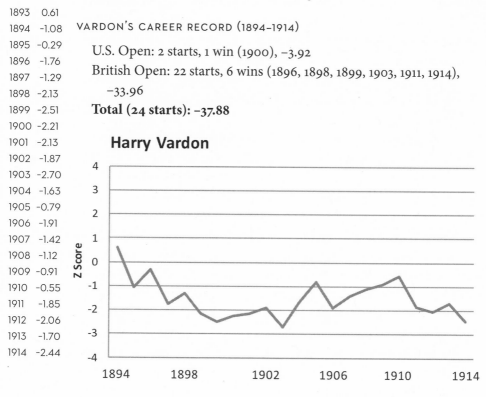

Harry Vardon

John H. Taylor

Number 18 Career

Among the Great Triumvirate, Taylor was the one within whom the competitive fires burned most deeply. "He must be boiling and bubbling all the time," Bernard Darwin said of him, adding that "if there is one thing that rouses his ire it is a young golfer who professes not to enjoy the fight."[4] Taylor freely admitted to this trait. "Lightheartedness of endeavour is a sure sign of eventual failure," he wrote.

The 1894 Open was Taylor's second and the first held outside Scotland. He came to it brimming with confidence out of proportion both to the expectations of the day and to his own résumé.

At that Open, which was typical of the era, directional posts were erected in the middle of numerous "blind shot" holes on the Royal St. George's course to indicate to golfers the preferred but hidden paths. The confident Taylor ordered the directional posts removed before he hit, fearful, he told onlookers, that if he aimed toward them, his drives would ricochet off them. He won by 5 shots. He repeated in 1895, only one competitor coming within 9 shots of his 322 total.

The 1896 Open championship at Muirfield was a showdown between Taylor and Vardon. Taylor launched his bid for a third straight championship with rounds of 77-78, taking a 1-stroke lead into the final day's thirty-six holes. A morning 81 left him two strokes ahead of Vardon but one behind leader Sandy Herd. Taylor posted a final-round 80 for 316, a score that looked like it might hold up when Herd turned in an 85. But Vardon came to the final hole with a chance to par in for 76 and a winning 315. Instead, he made bogey, under the rules setting up a thirty-six-hole playoff two days later, which Vardon won.

With Braid, Taylor, and Vardon had already that June contested an Open that would cement the image of the Triumvirate in golf lore. They finished 1-2-3. In reality, the competition belonged to Taylor.

The Open then was played over two days, with thirty-six holes contested each day. Taylor and Vardon opened with matching morning 79s, Taylor building a 4-stroke advantage by day's end with a 77 to Vardon's 81. A third-round 78 extended Taylor's advantage to 6 strokes, a margin he padded by 2 more that afternoon. With rounds of 79-77-78-75, Taylor became the first player to post four rounds in the 70s. He needed just 91.3 percent of the field-average number of strokes, a dominance even Tiger Woods never equaled.

Taylor nearly won again at Hoylake in 1907. He led Massy by 1 stroke entering the final round, but hit into the rough on the third hole, carded a 7, and lost by 2 strokes. His 1909 performance, at Deal, was a reprise of his 1900 victory. Rounds of 74-74-73-74 provided Taylor's fourth win by a comfortable 6-stroke margin over Braid and Tom Ball.

Taylor's career was marked by a unique and defining tendency. When he won, he did it big. His five Open titles came by margins of 5 strokes in 1894, 4 in 1895, 8 in 1900, 6 in 1901, and 8 in 1913. Only fourteen times in Open history has a player won by 6 strokes or more; on three of those occasions, Taylor was that player. Yet his record in Opens in which he finished within 4 strokes of his closest competitor was a less than impressive 1-7, the sole victory coming in 1895. He lost the playoff to Vardon in 1896 and lost by 1 stroke to Jack White in 1904 and by 2 to Massy in 1907 and Vardon in 1911.

On those winning occasions, Taylor's hallmark was his consistency, which as it did in 1900 and 1909 simply eroded all the competition. Until he was into his fifties, Taylor never experienced a British Open in which he shot higher than the field average. His fifth title, again at Hoylake in 1913, provided a final illustration. At 148, he was 1 stroke behind Ray after two rounds, but he pulled away during the final thirty-six holes. The clincher came on the final round's fourteenth hole when Taylor holed out a fifty-yard pitch from the rough for a birdie three.

Until World War I halted his opportunities, a five-year rolling average of Taylor's standard deviation from the Open field never fell below −1.20. And even when he resumed playing after the war at age forty-nine in 1920, the five-year rolling-average standard deviation between Taylor's performance and the field continued negative (which is to say a good) for another nine years. In other words, he was an effective, if not contending, golfer in the game's premier championship until age fifty-eight.

Taylor became a club maker, course designer, and author late in life, his best-known work being *Golf, My Life's Work*. Taylor lived until 1963, just short of his ninety-second birthday.

Taylor in the Clubhouse

Tournament	Finish	Score	Z score
1900 U.S. Open	2nd	315	−2.02
1900 British Open	**1st**	**309**	**−2.67**
1901 British Open	3rd	313	−2.13
1902 British Open	T-6	314	−1.24

1903 British Open	T-9	316	-0.88
1904 British Open	2nd	297	-2.08
1905 British Open	T-2	323	-1.50
1906 British Open	2nd	304	-2.19
1907 British Open	2nd	314	-1.94
1908 British Open	7th	307	-1.08

Note: Average Z score: -1.77. Effective stroke average: 69.37.

TAYLOR'S CAREER RECORD (1893–1920)

U.S. Open: 2 starts, 0 wins, -1.67
British Open: 22 starts, 5 wins (1894, 1895, 1900, 1909, 1913), -37.02
Total (24 starts): -38.69

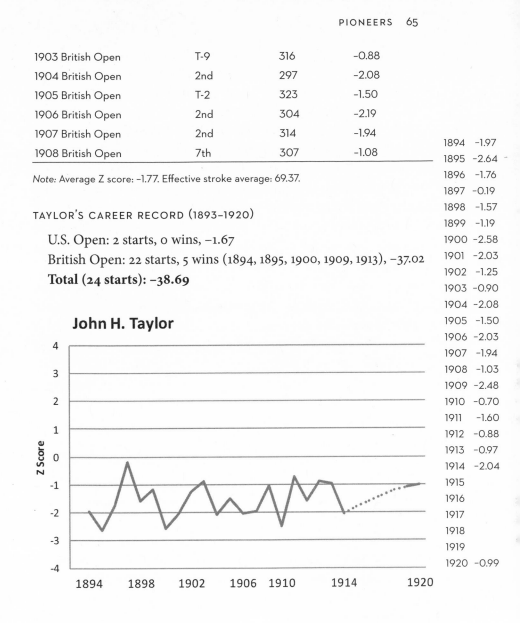

1894	-1.97
1895	-2.64
1896	-1.76
1897	-0.19
1898	-1.57
1899	-1.19
1900	-2.58
1901	-2.03
1902	-1.25
1903	-0.90
1904	-2.08
1905	-1.50
1906	-2.03
1907	-1.94
1908	-1.03
1909	-2.48
1910	-0.70
1911	-1.60
1912	-0.88
1913	-0.97
1914	-2.04
1915	
1916	
1917	
1918	
1919	
1920	-0.99

James Braid

Number 7 Peak

Braid—the eldest of the Triumvirate by three months—was the only Scot among them. The 1894 Open was his first, and his tenth-place finish marked the first time the Triumvirate made a unanimous showing among the top ten. Although not a headline-grabbing debut, Braid established his own identity with a second-place finish (to Harold Hilton) in 1897. He was fifth in 1899 and third in 1900, leading to his breakout victory by three strokes over Vardon at Muirfield in 1901.

Given that three of his Open titles overlapped Vardon's recovery from tuberculosis, it's possible that Braid's ascendancy was aided by Vardon's misfortune. Even so, between 1904 and 1908, Braid's three Open championships translated to dominance ratings consistently below 95.0, dipping to a low of 93.8 in his 1908 championship. At Prestwick that year, Braid so dominated the field that he shrugged off an 8 made during the third round to still win by 8 strokes. The standard deviation of his score that week was −2.66. Had he recorded a 5 instead of that lone 8, it would have been −2.92, and that would have stood as the record for dominance in a major championship more than a quarter century into the future.

Relative to the field, the most dominant stretch of his career really was only just starting. In 1912 the five-year rolling average of his standard deviation from the field peaked at a low of −2.05, meaning that between 1908 and 1912 he consistently played more than 2 standard deviations below the field average. In 1908 his victory at Prestwick came by eight shots, his 291 total breaking the record by 9 strokes. Yet probably even more impressive was his fifth and final British Open victory in 1910, a 4-shot win at St. Andrews in which Braid separated himself from the field average by 2.72 standard deviations. The record shows that between 1899 and 1912—that's fourteen tournaments—Braid never finished worse than fifth.

Surviving film footage shows a lithe, calm, fluid player whose most unique trait was an open putting style. Old-time Britishers used to say that "nobody could be as wise as James Braid looked." Braid's most recognized trait was his imperturbability, two episodes providing legendary evidence.

The first occurred in 1906. Braid arrived early the morning of the opening round at Muirfield, expecting to play two full rounds that day, as had been the practice. As the defending champion, he knew the established routine. What Braid forgot was that in anticipation of a large starting field, tournament officials that year had extended the competition to three days, meaning only a single round would be played the first two days. As luck would have it, Braid drew a late starting time, opening with a 77 he felt had been influenced by sitting around. To alleviate that, prior to his second day's afternoon round he played a full morning eighteen holes on a nearby course, returning to Muirfield and posting . . . another 77. He still beat Taylor by 4.

The other incident occurred during the 1910 tournament. Under calm skies, Braid opened well, but conditions soon changed, and a heavy thunderstorm rolled through the Old Course. Water rose, in some places washing across greens and—it was said—occasionally prompting putts to literally float over holes.

So harsh were the conditions that tournament organizers did the unthinkable, declaring the entire opening round null and void and retroactively pushing play back a day. At least it was unthinkable to Braid, who was playing the thirteenth hole when the stoppage was declared. Refusing to believe that proper Britishers could have done such a thing, he insisted on finishing the round in the heavy weather. He turned in a 76 that matched the best score by anyone competing before the storm hit. "A magnificent piece of golf in the conditions; one of the great rounds of golf that do not count," Bernard Darwin said of Braid's showing.[5]

The 1910 victory was Braid's last, but it hardly marked the end of his golfing career. A club maker at Walton Heath since 1904, Braid continued that specialty for four decades until his death in 1950. He also became a noted golf course architect, involved in the construction of an estimated 250 courses, most in Scotland. His best known are probably the King's Course at Gleneagles and a new layout at Royal Musselburgh. "They're all full of good fun," five-time British Open champion Peter Thomson said of Braid's designs.

Braid in the Clubhouse

Tournament	Finish	Score	Z score
1901 British Open	1st	309	−2.55
1902 British Open	T-2	309	−1.86
1903 British Open	5th	310	−1.66
1904 British Open	T-2	297	−2.08

1905 British Open	1st	318	-2.08
1906 British Open	1st	300	-2.73
1907 British Open	T-5	318	-1.53
1908 British Open	1st	291	-2.66
1909 British Open	T-2	301	-1.89
1910 British Open	1st	299	-2.72

Note: Average Z score: –2.18. Effective stroke average: 68.76.

BRAID'S CAREER RECORD (1894–1914)

British Open: 20 starts, 5 wins (1901, 1905, 1906, 1908, 1910), –33.63

Total (20 starts): –33.63

1894	-0.30
1895	
1896	-0.89
1897	-1.83
1898	-0.55
1899	-0.94
1900	-1.45
1901	-2.42
1902	-1.77
1903	-1.58
1904	-2.08
1905	-2.08
1906	-2.52
1907	-1.53
1908	-2.48
1909	-1.80
1910	-2.66
1911	-1.60
1912	-1.70
1913	-0.50
1914	-1.13

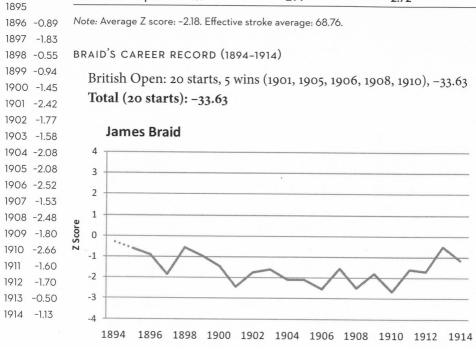

James Braid

THE TOP-TEN GOLFERS OF ALL TIME FOR PEAK RATING AS OF THE END OF THE 1900 SEASON.

Rank	Player	Seasons	Z score	Effective stroke average
1.	Willie Park Jr.	1883–92	-1.14	70.29
2.	Bob Ferguson	1868–86	-1.11	70.34
3.	Willie Fernie	1882–91	-1.07	70.40
	Sandy Herd	1891–1900	-1.07	70.40
5.	Young Tom Morris	1866–74	-1.03	70.45
6.	Bob Martin	1874–88	-0.959	70.56
	Jamie Anderson	1869–82	-0.955	70.56

8.	Harold Hilton	1887–94	–0.89	70.66
9.	John Ball	1890–94	–0.813	70.78
	Old Tom Morris	1860–69	–0.809	70.78
	John Laidlay	1888–93	–0.806	70.78

THE TOP-TEN GOLFERS OF ALL TIME FOR CAREER
RATING AS OF THE END OF THE 1900 SEASON.

Rank	Player	Seasons	Z score
1.	Bob Ferguson	1868–89	–21.12
2.	Harold Hilton	1887–1900	–16.18
3.	J. H. Taylor	1893–1900	–15.86
4.	Willie Fernie	1873–1900	–13.99
5.	Harry Vardon	1893–1900	–13.84
6.	John Laidlay	1885–1900	–13.53
7.	Willie Park Jr.	1880–1900	–12.72
8.	Willie Park Sr.	1860–82	–11.58
9.	Sandy Herd	1888–1900	–10.00
10.	Bob Martin	1873–91	–9.68

5 Coming to America

In the summer of 1895, Horace Rawlins, a twenty-one-year-old émigré from England, won the inaugural U.S. Open golf championship. The tournament was played at Newport, Rhode Island, Country Club, where Rawlins had only recently accepted a position as an assistant pro.

Dominance of stateside tournaments by English- or Scottish-born players was by no means surprising; in short order it would become a common occurrence. James Foulis, a St. Andrews native and acquaintance of Old Tom Morris who had recently emigrated to become the pro at the Chicago Golf Club, won the following year. He was succeeded in 1897 by England's Joe Lloyd, who spent his summers teaching golf in Massachusetts—and in 1898 by Fred Herd, another émigré from Scotland. In fact, all of the first sixteen U.S. Open champions were either British émigrés (like Willie Anderson) or citizens (like Harry Vardon). Not until Philadelphia's nineteen-year-old John McDermott won a three-way playoff in 1911—beating fellow American Mike Brady and Scottish émigré George Simpson—did an American-born and American-trained player emerge with the trophy. In fact, not until 1939 could the U.S. Open boast more American-born than foreign-born winners.

The same circumstance held true in the U.S. Amateur and Western Open, the two other U.S.-based tournaments that drew a major-level of competition in those early days. The inaugural Western in 1899 was won by Willie Smith, a Scottish émigré who had also won that year's U.S. Open. Again it took McDermott, in 1913, to break the foreign-born or foreign-trained stranglehold on the event. As for the Amateur, seven of its first nine champions were foreign born.

Such were the growing pains American golf went through prior to the second decade of the twentieth century, a period when born-and-bred North Americans were only still learning the game, generally from English or Scotch instructors. In fact, the story of major tournament golf in the years surrounding World War I is the gradual transition from a British-dominated to an American-dominated sport.

Willie Anderson

Anderson's name periodically circulates around the playing of the U.S. Open because he was the first to win four of them. Anderson triumphed in a playoff at Myopia Hunt Club in 1901, won again at Baltusrol in another playoff two years later, repeated at Glen View in 1904, and took his fourth (and third straight) back at Myopia in 1905.

Contemporaries described Anderson as "sturdy," although surviving images suggest one would view him as unremarkable, even for his day. A Scottish native who came to the United States to take advantage of his golfing skills in a more forgiving competitive environment, Anderson used an unusually full swing, giving him extra distance. The trade-off logically should have been decreased accuracy, but Anderson was blessed with abnormally large hands, which he used to maximize club control.

A U.S. Open competitor since the tournament's earliest days, Anderson had followed a second-place finish in 1897 with third and fifth places. He dropped to eleventh in 1900, the year of the Vardon-Taylor sweep, but broke through in 1901, defeating Alex Smith by a stroke in a playoff.

The Golf Hall of Fame notes that was also the year Anderson chose to stage a personal protest over the second-class conditions put up with by touring pros, who were looked on at the time as members of the tradesman class. As was the custom of the day, Myopia's members had passed a rule prohibiting professionals from entering the clubhouse, the sole exception being for meals, which they were required to take in the kitchen. Anderson's Hall of Fame citation describes his reaction to that bit of news as follows: "Nae, nae, we're nae goin' t' eat in the kitchen." He said that while swinging his club and taking a divot out of the club's lawn. Myopia agreed to erect a tent for the pros, a compromise seen at the time as a victory for the players.

For two years Anderson held the record for both highest and lowest winning scores. He had followed his laborious 1901 victory at Myopia by placing fifth in 1902, then winning in 307 strokes at his home Baltusrol course. In 1904 he shot 303 to break the record he and Laurie

Auchterlonie had shared. Back at Myopia in 1905, he managed only a 314, although that was good enough to best Smith by 2 shots. Anderson finished fifth, 12 back, in 1906.

Aside from the U.S. Open, there were few other opportunities for professionals of Anderson's stripe to prove themselves. The "tour" existed only in a rudimentary fashion—an occasional tournament here or there. The most prestigious of those was the Western, which Anderson won in 1902, again in 1904, again in 1908, and a fourth time in 1909. Though Scotch, he never found his way back to compete in the British Open, meaning that he never competed in more than one major (plus the Western) per year. Otherwise, Anderson made his living as did all golf pros of the day, by giving lessons and winning exhibitions.

Privately—such things were always kept private—Anderson was known as the kind of fellow who didn't let his game interfere with his pursuit of the good life. Whatever those pursuits consisted of, they were catching up with him. After 1905, despite being just twenty-five years old, his play went into decline . . . at least by Anderson's standards. In 1907 the great champion, not yet twenty-eight, finished 14 strokes out of the running in the U.S. Open. He recovered somewhat to place fifth and sixth in 1908 and 1909, still 8 and 9 shots behind winners Fred McLeod and George Sargent, both of them contemporaries who had not previously been considered in Anderson's class. In 1910 Anderson's best effort placed him fourteenth, a stroke behind his brother, Tom.

And that was the end . . . literally. Within a few months, Anderson was dead, of a cause that has been a matter of dispute. Some attributed it to arteriosclerosis, a malady commonly known as hardening of the arteries that is far more readily associated with older people. Others cited an epileptic fit. Anderson was barely thirty.

Anderson's unusual success at Myopia—he won two of the four Opens played there—make this an apropos time for a digression into the matter of the course itself. Statistically, it's the most difficult golf course in the history of the U.S. Open. Competitors had so much trouble with Myopia that the USGA hasn't come back in more than a century. Yet even now one suspects that if the game's most important tournament ever did return to the course outside Boston, Myopia would defeat the pros again.

The numbers for the U.S. Open's first four iterations at Myopia are simply daunting. In sixteen championship rounds between 1898 and 1908, not a single competitor—representing the nation's best golfers—broke 75. (There were a half dozen in the 1907 U.S. Open alone, plus four more in that year's Western Open, both largely featuring the same cast.) In 1898 the average four-round score of the twenty-five top finishers was 351. Alex Herd won in 1898 by shooting 328, the highest winning score until the Open returned to Myopia in 1901.

That's when the fun really began. Anderson won the first of his four U.S. Open titles that year by shooting 331, the highest winning score in the tournament's history. Anderson never broke 80 that weekend and never needed to, because only one man—Alex Smith—bettered his final-round 81. Smith shot 80 to force a playoff, which he lost the next day, shooting 86 to Anderson's 85. The tournament returned to Myopia in 1905 (Anderson shot 313 to win) and for a final time in 1908. The victor that year was Fred McLeod, whose 77 won a playoff by 6 shots from Willie Smith.

Was all this high scoring merely a sign of the times? Not entirely. The top twenty-five that year averaged 338, 23 strokes worse than at Philadelphia Cricket Club in 1907 and 35 strokes worse than at Englewood in 1909. In other words, the difficulty *was* Myopia. McLeod's winning four-round total of 322 gives Myopia the distinction it retains today of having hosted the three highest championship scores in the Open's history. The fourth highest is 315, a full 7 strokes better.

Myopia's secret was not length. The course only played to 6,335 yards at the time, making it a normal championship track for the period and just a couple hundred yards shorter than it is today. But Myopia was (and is) spectacularly penal. Although bunkers came and went, players at times reported finding as many as two hundred of them strewn around the rolling landscape. Reportedly, club designer H. C. Leeds loved nothing better than laying obstacles in the path of skillful competitors. If one of his playing partners hit a stray shot, Leeds marked the spot and then dug a trap.

Leeds not only liked his bunkers but liked them deep and difficult. A 40-yard-long, 4-yard-wide cross-bunker still forces the carry to the

339-yard eleventh hole. Fronting the tenth green is an 8-foot-deep bunker named after former President William Howard Taft, ostensibly for his frequent visits. The local legend is that each Taft visit would prompt Leeds to dig the bunker deeper, until caddies literally stood by with a rope to extricate the three-hundred-pound golfer from what had become a sandy pit.

Complicating life at Myopia were greens the size of bulletin boards. The one at the seemingly innocent 240-yard first became notorious because it featured a shaved left fringe feeding down to a steep bunker. Miss left by any margin, and the bunker was a sure resting place. From there an explosion played too timidly to the small green stood every chance of rolling right back into the sand, and so on and so on indefinitely.

Players also swore (and continue to do so) over the thirteenth, a 350-yard par four to a green that sits seventy feet above the fairway. Such a sharp elevation change for an approach would be unthinkable to modern designers.

Enough of the Myopia torture chamber; back to Anderson. If his U.S. Open record alone were considered to be a sufficient basis for assessment, Anderson would rank among the all-time greats. When he won at Myopia in 1901, he required just 92.9 percent of the average number of shots taken by the field. His 1903 victory at Baltusrol was even more efficient, Anderson needing just 91 percent of the field average. At Glen View in 1904, he was nearly as dominant, taking just 91.9 percent of the average.

That meant that at his peak—the period between 1901 and 1906 when he won four Opens, Anderson averaged just 92.7 percent of the field stroke average. Vardon's best five-year average was 93.3, Braid's 93.8, and Taylor's 94.3. As can be said of Vardon vis-à-vis the United States, had Anderson tested himself more regularly in Britain, we might consider him today as the sport's nonpareil.

Anderson in the Clubhouse

Tournament	Finish	Score	Z score
1901 U.S. Open	1st	331	–1.76
1902 U.S. Open	T-5	318	–1.40

1902 Western Open	1st	299	–1.84
1903 U.S. Open	1st	307	–1.96
1903 Western Open	5th	323	–0.93
1904 U.S. Open	1st	303	–2.23
1904 Western Open	1st	304	–2.08
1905 U.S. Open	1st	314	–2.01
1906 U.S. Open	5th	307	–1.58
1906 Western Open	T-3	311	–1.35

Note: Average Z score: –1.71. Effective stroke average: 69.46.

ANDERSON'S CAREER RECORD (1897–1910)

U.S. Open: 14 starts, 4 wins (1901, 1903, 1904, 1905), –20.87
Western Open: 7 starts, 4 wins (1902, 1904, 1908, 1909), –11.42
Total (21 starts): –32.29

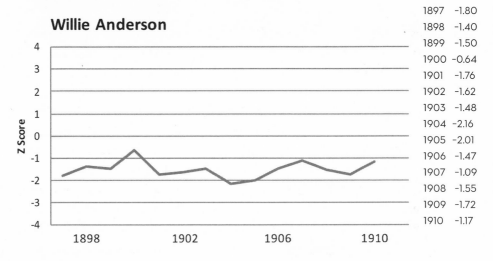

Year	Z
1897	–1.80
1898	–1.40
1899	–1.50
1900	–0.64
1901	–1.76
1902	–1.62
1903	–1.48
1904	–2.16
1905	–2.01
1906	–1.47
1907	–1.09
1908	–1.55
1909	–1.72
1910	–1.17

Laurie Auchterlonie

He is perhaps the least known of all the noteworthy male American golf-ers. Of course, calling Lawrence "Laurie" Auchterlonie an American may itself be a stretch. He was born in 1867 and raised in St. Andrews, Scot-land. In 1948 he also died and was buried there. His brother, Willie, won the 1893 Open—the British one. But Laurie Auchterlonie's professional career was contested entirely in the United States. He was part of the migration of what can only be described as second-tier British players who—staring at Vardon, Taylor, and Braid—chose instead to take their chances with the fledgling U.S. game. Auchterlonie arrived in the late 1890s, landing a pro shop job at the Glen View Club, just outside Chicago.

His championship résumé at that time was wafer thin, consisting of three appearances as an amateur in the British Open, His best finish was a tie for thirteenth in 1895, 18 strokes behind Taylor and 2 behind Vardon. Already thirty-two, he quickly set about to remedy the thin portfolio, entering the 1899 U.S. Open—only the fifth ever held—in Baltimore. Although never in title contention, he managed four rounds in 333 strokes, good for a tie for ninth place in the fifty-player field. The Western Open debuted that year, happily for Auchterlonie at Glen View. U.S. Open champion Willie Smith beat him again, but this time it took an eighteen-hole playoff. For his effort, Smith won $50; Auchterlonie settled for $40.

One year later at Chicago Golf Club in nearby Wheaton, Auchterlonie ran into a pair of old nemeses, Vardon and Taylor. The Britishers dominated. Vardon finished two strokes ahead of Taylor, who in turn was seven ahead of the lead American, David Bell. Auchterlonie placed fourth.

However disappointing the performance was, it was good enough to win Auchterlonie a promotion to head pro at Glen View, a position he maintained for a decade. As head pro, Western Open champion, and a two-time top-ten finisher in the U.S. Open, he was among the favorites for the 1901 event at the Myopia Hunt Club. There, however, Auchterlonie would run afoul of two new presences that would frustrate him for much of the next half decade. Those two were Myopia itself and Anderson. He shot 335, good enough for a tie for fifth. Auchterlonie salved his wounds better than most. At that year's Western Open a few weeks later, he shot an opening 79 for a 2-stroke lead and made that stand up to defeat Bell. The champ walked away with $125.

From the Myopia hellhole, the nation's best retreated to the Garden City Country Club outside New York for the 1902 championship. For its time, the field was loaded, featuring Anderson, inaugural champion Horace Rawlins, former champions James Foulis, Fred Herd and Willie Smith, future champion Alex Smith, Walter Travis—a three-time U.S.

Amateur champion and the codesigner of Garden City—plus Hall of Fame course designers to be Donald Ross and C. B. Macdonald. Auchterlonie immediately put his stamp on the field, opening with a 78 that was 1 better than Anderson. Entering the final round, his uncannily steady play—posting rounds of 78, 78, and 74—had him 5 ahead of a comparative unknown, Stewart Gardner, and 7-up on Anderson. Travis was 9 back on his own course, while both Smiths faced double-digit deficits.

Auchterlonie showed no mercy in that final round. His 77 not only wrapped up the trophy and $200 first-place check by 6 shots over Stewart but also made him the first player in U.S. Open history to post four rounds in the 70s.

From that point on, Auchterlonie was destined to play in Anderson's shadow. At that summer's Western Open in Cleveland, Anderson posted a 299, while Auchterlonie languished in fifth with a 316. In his defense of his Open title at Baltusrol in 1903, Auchterlonie shot 321—good for seventh—but Anderson won the first of three straight. Auchterlonie was runner-up to Alex Smith at the 1903 Western, but in 1904 his best efforts were a tie for fourth (11 behind Anderson) at the U.S. Open and third (11 behind Anderson) at the Western.

By then Auchterlonie was forty-one and past his prime. When Anderson returned to Myopia for his fourth Open title (and third straight) in 1905, Auchterlonie finished twenty-fourth, his 332 barely above the field average. He managed a fourth place at the Western, but that was 16 strokes behind the champion, Arthur Smith. He made a last-hurrah sort of showing at the 1906 U.S. Open championship at Onwentsia outside Chicago, but never really contended in finishing third, 10 strokes behind Alex Smith.

Considering that he played brilliantly for five years in the only two U.S.-based events worthy of "major" recognition, Auchterlonie's record is impressive. It includes two championships, nine other finishes among the top five, and two more in the top ten between 1899 and 1904. His U.S. Open or Western Open losses, although not always close, were to some of the era's greats: they included six to Willie Anderson, two to Willie Smith, and two to Alex Smith.

One can debate whether the name of Laurie Auchterlonie ought to be ranked among the game's immortals. But there is no debate that he was a pivotal figure during the game's first full decade of development in the United States.

Auchterlonie in the Clubhouse

Tournament	Finish	Score	Z score
1899 U.S. Open	T-9	333	-1.09
1899 Western Open	2nd	156	-1.60
1900 U.S. Open	4th	327	-1.33
1901 U.S. Open	T-5	335	-1.38
1901 Western Open	**1st**	**160**	**-2.05**
1902 U.S. Open	**1st**	**307**	**-2.24**
1902 Western Open	5th	316	-1.07
1903 Western Open	2nd	320	-1.17
1904 U.S. Open	T-4	314	-1.29
1904 Western Open	3rd	315	-1.34

Note: Average peak Z score: -1.46. Effective stroke average: 69.82.

AUCHTERLONIE'S CAREER RECORD (1899–1909)

U.S. Open: 11 starts, 1 win (1902), -11.40

Western Open: 9 starts, 1 wins (1901), -11.07

Total (20 starts): -22.47

1899	-1.35
1900	-1.33
1901	-1.72
1902	-1.76
1903	-1.12
1904	-1.32
1905	-0.65
1906	-1.36
1907	-0.67
1908	-0.68
1909	-0.15

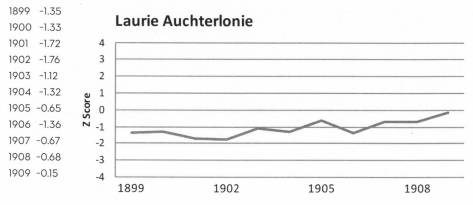

Laurie Auchterlonie

Ted Ray

Never part of the Vardon-Taylor-Braid Triumvirate, Ray nevertheless was of the same era. He is perhaps best known today as the third man in the Ouimet-Vardon 1913 U.S. Open showdown and might be more highly regarded had he been a more reliable presence in America. He was an engaging figure, heavy set, approachable, and gregarious in a way that Vardon never could be.

Ray made three trips to the United States, winning the 1920 U.S. Open. (The third trip, in 1927, came at the end of his career; Ray was fifty at the time and finished in a tie for twenty-seventh.) But it was in the British Open that Ray made his name. He entered annually beginning in 1899 and continuing into the 1930s, winning in 1912 and placing second in 1913 and again in 1925.

Surviving footage of Ray's swing shows a fluid, wristy approach common of the early twentieth century, with more hip sway than would be acceptable today. His left heel can be seen flying high off the ground, and his front foot even slides slightly forward on impact, something that would send modern teaching pros into conniptions. In an era of primitive equipment, it was all Ray's way of throwing his large and ample body fully behind the strike. He believed in power. A fan once asked Ray how to hit the ball as far as he did. "Hit it a bloody sight harder," Ray replied.[1]

Those same images also show the curved pipe that was a veritable fixture anywhere Ray played. "When I have tried to play with a pipe in my mouth I have always been afraid of hitting it with my arm, and with grave danger to my teeth, in the act of following through," famed golf writer Bernard Darwin once wrote in marvel of Ray. "However," Darwin added, "there was certainly no lack of rude vigor" in Ray's follow-through.[2]

That length was never more on display than at Muirfield, site of the 1912 British Open. Organizers had lengthened the course to more than sixty-four hundred yards, equivalent to about seventy-five hundred yards today, given equipment changes. Yet Ray drove the green on both the thirteenth and fifteenth holes, blows in excess of three hundred yards. Ray opened with 71-73 to sleep on a 3-shot advantage over Vardon. His third-round 76 on the championship's deciding day created a 5-shot edge over Braid, Vardon faltering, and removed all drama from the afternoon play. Ray closed with 75 to beat Vardon by 4 strokes.

Ray had a chance for back-to-back titles at Hoylake in 1913. He led Taylor by 1 stroke after thirty-six holes, only to awaken to gale-force winds the next morning. That was a distinct disadvantage to Ray's game, higher and more power oriented than Taylor's, which favored a lower, more controlled ball flight. The result was a third-round 81, leaving Ray 3 shots behind the four-time champion. Needing to gamble his way back into contention, Ray took an 8 on the afternoon's third hole, essentially finishing his championship hopes. His four-round total of 312, although still one better than third-place finishers Vardon and Michael Moran, was 8 strokes worse than Taylor's 304.

In golf terms, Ray was one of the principal victims of the Great War. The British Open was canceled between 1915 and 1919, when Ray was in his performance prime. The U.S. Open was held in 1915 and 1916, but, wartime ocean travel being perilous, he did not risk the crossing. To the extent they have value, a projection estimates that Ray could have averaged between 2 and 3 standard deviations better than the field had British Opens been held in those five years. How would that have fared? In the five Opens held between 1910 and 1914, there were only five Z scores above −2.00, the best being James Braid's −2.72 in 1910. Ray, in other words, would have been positioned to dominate the period. As it is, we are left to judge what we have.

Ray in the Clubhouse

Tournament	Finish	Score	Z score
1908 British Open	3rd	301	−1.67
1909 British Open	6th	304	−1.46
1910 British Open	T-5	308	−1.31
1911 British Open	T-5	305	−1.63
1912 British Open	**1st**	**295**	**−2.42**
1913 U.S. Open	T-2	304	−1.78
1913 British Open	T-2	312	−1.46
1914 British Open	T-10	316	−1.13
1920 U.S. Open	**1st**	**295**	**−1.78**
1920 British Open	3rd	306	−2.06

Note: Average Z score: −1.67. Effective stroke average: 69.51.

RAY'S CAREER RECORD (1899–1926)

U.S. Open: 2 starts, 1 win (1920), –3.56
British Open: 23 starts, 1 win (1912), –22.04
Total (25 starts): –25.60

Ted Ray

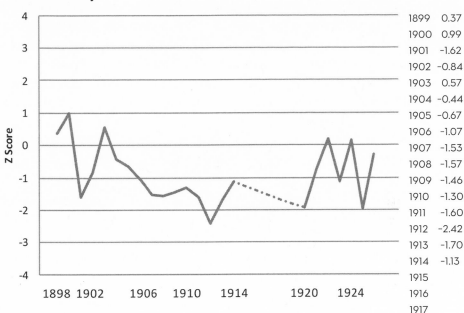

Year	Z Score
1899	0.37
1900	0.99
1901	-1.62
1902	-0.84
1903	0.57
1904	-0.44
1905	-0.67
1906	-1.07
1907	-1.53
1908	-1.57
1909	-1.46
1910	-1.30
1911	-1.60
1912	-2.42
1913	-1.70
1914	-1.13
1915	
1916	
1917	
1918	
1919	
1920	-1.92
1921	-0.77
1922	0.20
1923	-1.13
1924	0.17
1925	-1.96
1926	-0.29

John McDermott

The first man to break the British hegemony in American professional golf was barely a man at all. John McDermott was a lad of nineteen when he survived a playoff with Mike Brady and George Simpson to win the 1911 championship at the Chicago Golf Club. Although not yet able to vote, it was McDermott's second consecutive U.S. Open playoff, the teen having been defeated by Alex Smith in 1910.

But then McDermott was always a precocious—maybe impetuous—fellow. Although reputed to be a strong student, he had caddied as a youth and found the game more to his liking than books, so he abruptly dropped out and took a job in a pro shop not far from his Philadelphia-area home. Having already relocated to Atlantic City to take a second club job, he made his Open debut in 1909 at age seventeen, finishing well off the pace.

His age, the exigencies of ocean travel, the absence of an organized tour, and his professional standing all conspired to limit McDermott's competitive options, which fundamentally boiled down to the U.S. Open, the Western Open, and a handful of regional events of markedly lesser stature. Fortunately for McDermott, the 1910 Open was being contested at the Philadelphia Cricket Club, a short distance from his home. Back-to-back 74s left him 2 strokes behind Smith, and when the 1906 champion shot a third-round 79, McDermott's 75 bolted him into a 2-stroke lead. McDermott closed with another 75, but Smith's 73 and brother Macdonald Smith's 71 created a three-way playoff, which Alex Smith won.

Having come so close, McDermott staked himself to a return effort the following year in far-off Chicago. This time he took a 4-stroke lead into the final eighteen holes, then staggered through a rainstorm with a 79 to find himself in the Brady-Simpson playoff. He shot 80 in that extra competition, while Brady shot 82 and Simpson 86.

The defending champion, McDermott came to the Country Club of Buffalo for the 1912 Open as something of a celebrity. Trailing Brady by 2 strokes after the first two rounds, McDermott drove out-of-bounds on the opening hole and then did it again, surviving with a double bogey because the rules in force at the time penalized only for distance, not stroke and distance, as is the case today. Reprieved, McDermott closed with 74-71 to overtake Brady and hold off fast-closing Tom McNamara, the runner-up, by 2 shots. Later that season at the Western Open outside Chicago, McDermott finished third, 4 shots behind Macdonald Smith. He was eighth at the famous Ouimet-Vardon-Ray Open of 1913, one month later winning the Western at Memphis by 7 shots over Brady. That fall he became the first American native to challenge the world's best at the British Open, which was being contested in Liverpool. He finished fifth, 11 strokes behind John Taylor but only 3 behind Ted Ray and 2 behind Harry Vardon.

Following a top-ten finish in the 1914 U.S. Open, McDermott made plans for a return appearance at the Open championship, but fate conspired against him. His ship failed to arrive in England on time. Then fate doubled down, his return voyage interrupted by a harrowing at-sea collision. McDermott's weakness was always his mercurial emotional nature, and there are those who believe the close ocean escape unhinged him. That's speculation. This isn't: collapsing shortly after returning to his Atlantic City country club pro shop, the young golf champion never played again. He spent the final half century of his life in mental institutions or under the care of family members. In 1971, a few weeks before his death at age seventy-nine, McDermott left his long seclusion to watch Lee Trevino beat Jack Nicklaus in their memorable playoff at the U.S. Open at Merion outside Philadelphia.

The sad conclusion leaves us to wonder how golf history might have been different had McDermott's career not ended so abruptly.

McDermott in the Clubhouse

Tournament	Finish	Score	Z score
1909 U.S. Open	T-49	322	+0.91
1910 U.S. Open	T-2	298	-1.56
1911 U.S. Open	**1st**	**307**	**-1.70**
1912 U.S. Open	**1st**	**294**	**-2.47**
1912 Western Open	3rd	303	-1.82
1913 U.S. Open	8th	308	-1.33
1913 British Open	5th	315	-1.14
1913 Western Open	**1st**	**295**	**-2.22**
1914 U.S. Open	T-9	300	-0.91

Note: Average Z score: -1.36. Effective stroke average: 69.98.

MCDERMOTT'S CAREER RECORD (1909-14)

U.S. Open: 6 starts, 2 wins (1911–12), -7.06

British Open: 1 start, 0 wins, -1.14

Western Open, 2 starts, 1 win (1913), -4.04

Total (9 starts): -12.24

John McDermott

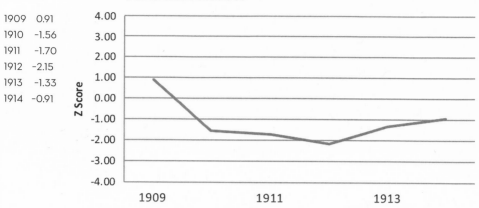

1909	0.91
1910	-1.56
1911	-1.70
1912	-2.15
1913	-1.33
1914	-0.91

Charles E. "Chick" Evans Jr.

The first great American amateur golfer, anticipating Bobby Jones by a decade, was a baby-faced kid out of the Chicago caddie shacks good enough to beat the pros at their own game.

Those pros couldn't have taken Chick Evans very seriously when he showed up on the first tee of the Beverly Country Club in late August 1910. He was a twenty-year-old college dropout, his only reputation having been attained at Evanston Academy, where he had dominated interscholastic tournaments two years earlier. But in a field of seventy that included the top pros and amateurs of the era—veterans of the stripe of Jock Hutchison, Jim Barnes, Laurie Auchterlonie, former Western Open champion Robert Simpson, and former U.S. Open champion James Foulis—Evans was an anonymity on the entry sheet.

He was, anyway, until qualifying began for the tournament, which was being conducted that year at match play. Evans breezed through the preliminary round, posting an astonishing 71 on a day when the field average was 79.8, and nobody else broke 74. Following a nerve-wracking opening match in which he needed twenty holes to dispatch James Donaldson, an area pro, Evans beat Lee Nelson and fellow amateur Ned Sawyer to advance to the thirty-six-hole final, where George Simpson, a former Scottish Amateur champion who had since turned pro, awaited.

It was no contest. Evans took the lead for good on the third hole, completed the morning round 2-up, and birdied the seventh and ninth holes to build his lead to 4. Birdies at the thirtieth and thirty-first holes closed out the headline-grabbing 6 and 5 victory. As an amateur, Evans, of course, could not claim the prize money, which went to Simpson . . . all $100 of it.

Aside from a trip the following spring to Britain to play in the Open and Amateur, the twenty-year-old did absolutely nothing to trade on his newfound fame. He did not even enter the Western again for five years and largely contented himself with regional events until entering the 1914 U.S. Open, again being played at the conveniently situated Midlothian Country Club outside Chicago. Mustering only a thirty-six-hole total of 150 that put him 8 strokes behind leader and eventual champion Walter Hagen, Evans rallied and came to the seventy-second hole—a 277-yard par 4—needing an eagle to force a playoff. He boomed his drive to the fringe, only to slightly pull the potential tying putt, which stopped 10 inches squarely to the left of the cup.

There were no such near misses in 1916, when Evans put together probably the greatest season to that date by an American-born player, amateur or professional. It began at the U.S. Open at Minikahda Country Club in Minneapolis, where Evans defeated Hutchison by 2 strokes and Barnes by 4 in June. The margin was more comfortable than that, Evans carrying a 7-stroke lead into the final thirty-six holes. Whatever doubts lingered following a morning 74 on Saturday were dispatched on the twelfth hole of the afternoon round, when Evans's two-wood second shot finished 18 feet from the cup on the 535-yard par 5.

The two most important tournaments in the United States at that time were the Open and the Amateur, the latter being held that September at Merion, and no man had ever won both in the same year. Evans qualified fourth in the thirty-two-person match-play field but quickly emerged as the favorite when the three men seeded ahead of him all lost in the opening two rounds. He won his third round match 10 and 9, breezed through the quarterfinal 9 and 8, took his semifinal 3 and 2, and beat Charles Gardner, a fellow Chicago-area product from Hinsdale, 4 and 3, to win the trophy.

The war interrupted Evans's fame for two seasons, canceling both the Open and the Amateur in 1917 and '18. At the 1919 Amateur event, the defending champion qualified well and breezed through his opening match 7 and 6 before being eliminated on the final hole by Ouimet. He would get revenge one year later at the 1920 Amateur, held at Roslyn, New York. There Evans rolled through the preliminary rounds, running up wins by scores of 8 and 7, 7 and 6, and 10 and 8. His only close call came during a third-round match against Reginald Lewis, which Evans won on the fifth extra hole. That set up a championship-round rematch with Ouimet, who had eliminated Bobby Jones 6 and 5 in the semifinals, and Evans breezed to a 7 and 6 victory. Of his five matches, four had ended with five or more holes remaining.

It was Evans's final major victory, but not his final brush with glory. He returned to the Amateur as defending champion in 1921 and reached the semifinals before being eliminated by the eventual champion, Jesse Guilford. At the 1924 Western Open, he placed third, and three years later he tied for seventh at the same event. Evans was well into his thirties by then, ancient for a lifelong amateur, and although he would continue to make sporadic appearances at the U.S. Open and Western, his championship career was essentially over. The one event he always made room for on his calendar was the Amateur, teeing it up there a record fifty consecutive times, a string that stretched from 1907 to 1962. In 1975 he was elected to the World Golf Hall of Fame.

Trained as a caddie, Evans never forgot his roots. A college dropout for financial reasons whose business success was influenced by his golfing achievements, Evans in 1928 established the Evans Scholars program to underwrite scholarships for caddies. Two years later, the first two Evans Scholars enrolled at Northwestern University, the school Evans had been forced to abandon twenty years earlier due to costs. Authorities say that more than 10,600 former caddies have since taken advantage of the scholarship's opportunities.

Evans was no saint. He was said to have developed an intense jealousy for Ouimet and also for 1915 Open champion Jerome Travers because those two contemporary amateurs had beaten him to the Open title. The same jealousy was reported regarding Jones, whose fame soon eclipsed Evans's own. In his later years, though, Evans reconciled with his contemporaries. He died in 1979, one of the most admired men in golf history.

Evans in the Clubhouse

Tournament	Finish	Score	Z score
1914 U.S. Open	2nd	291	–1.94
1914 British Amateur	4th round	match play	–0.02
1915 U.S. Open	18th	307	–0.59
1915 Western Open	T-22	324	–0.42
1916 U.S. Open	**1st**	**286**	**–2.50**
1916 U.S. Amateur	**1st**	match play	**–0.97**
1919 U.S. Amateur	2nd round	match play	–0.64
1919 U.S. Open	T-9	313	–0.95
1920 U.S. Open	T-6	298	–1.46
1920 U.S. Amateur	**1st**	**match play**	**–1.06**

Note: Average Z score: –1.06. Effective stroke average: 70.41.

EVANS'S CAREER RECORD (1907–37)

Western Open: 14 starts, 1 win (1910), –1.04
U.S. Open: 13 starts, 1 win (1916), –5.74
U.S. Amateur: 22 starts, 2 wins (1916, 1920), –6.08
British Open: 1 start, 0 wins, +0.65
British Amateur: 4 starts, 0 wins, –0.35
Total (54 starts): –12.56

Chick Evans

1907	–0.19
1908	
1909	–0.75
1910	–1.69
1911	–0.23
1912	–0.75
1913	–0.43
1914	–0.62
1915	–0.17
1916	–1.74
1917	
1918	
1919	–0.80
1920	–1.26
1921	–0.76
1922	–0.69
1923	–0.16
1924	–0.58
1925	
1926	–0.40
1927	0.48
1928	1.57
1929	
1930	0.78
1931	1.00
1932	0.50
1933	0.20
1934	2.55
1935	1.01
1936	–0.25
1937	–0.61

Jim Barnes

Number 12 Career

He was known as "Long Jim," not just due to his distance off the tee but in recognition of his size. At a time when the average American male stood a shade under five-foot-nine, Barnes was an imposing six-foot-four, an attribute he used to leverage tee shots that sailed beyond the hopes of most of his competitors.

A native of England, Barnes emigrated at the age of twenty in 1906 and turned professional, supporting himself for the next decade by giving lessons at various clubs in the western United States and Canada. He was twenty-seven when he debuted at the memorable 1913 U.S. Open won by amateur Francis Ouimet; Barnes tied Walter Hagen for fourth, three strokes out of the playoff.

The experience fueled Barnes's passion for the game's competitive side. He returned for the next three Opens, finishing thirteenth, fourth, and third, and adding victories in the 1914 and 1917 Western Opens and 1916 inaugural PGA Championship along the way. Like most golf tournaments, the PGA was canceled in deference to the Great War in 1917 and 1918; when it returned in 1919, Barnes won again, dispatching Fred McLeod 6 and 5 in the final.

Although approaching thirty, Barnes was only then coming into his prime. He added the Western Open in 1919, finished a shot behind Hutchison in 1920, and in 1921 routed the field to claim the U.S. Open title at Columbia Country Club in Chevy Chase, Maryland. Posting an opening-round 69 for a 4-stroke lead through thirty-six holes, he drove into the rough on the 309-yard par-4 second hole. Barnes lofted a nine-iron over a tree and watched the ball roll down a slope of the green into the hole for an eagle 2. So relaxed was the final round that the Marine Corps band accompanied Barnes down the final fairway, playing a victory march. His final 9-stroke victory margin remained the all-time Open record for nearly eight decades, until Tiger Woods won by 15 in 2000.

Like Ray, it is interesting to speculate about the effect of the Great War on Barnes's reputation. Between 1917 and 1919, he missed five major events due to that conflict, events in which projections estimate that he might have been able to average a –2.20 Z score . . . That's an 11-point bump to his career record. As it is, Barnes ranks twelfth on that career list; give him those 11 points, and he jumps ahead of Ben Hogan—who has his own missed-tournament issues—into the top ten.

A British native, Barnes was the first American to make the British Open an annual event, playing with just one exception from 1920 through 1930. At the 1925 Open at Prestwick, he trailed Macdonald Smith by 5 shots through fifty-four holes. Posting a seventy-two-hole score of 300, Barnes retired to the clubhouse before Smith had even teed off, in the slim hope that the leader, who needed only a 78 to win, might falter. He did. Pressured by a gathering throng, Smith surrendered 3 early strokes to par, shot a front nine of 42, and came home with an undistinguished 82, making Barnes the champion.

Barnes's victory completed what amounted to the early game's "grand slam," since he had already won the U.S. and Western Opens and the PGA. On the nascent PGA Tour, he won twenty-one times through 1937. He was an inaugural inductee into the PGA Hall of Fame in 1940 and joined the World Golf Hall of Fame in 1989. Barnes died in 1966 at age eighty.

Barnes in the Clubhouse

Tournament	Finish	Score	Z score
1919 Western Open	1st	283	–2.13
1919 PGA	1st	match play	–1.75
1920 U.S. Open	T-6	298	–1.46
1920 British Open	6th	309	–1.74
1920 Western Open	T-2	297	–1.69
1921 U.S. Open	1st	289	–2.65
1921 British Open	T-6	302	–1.26
1921 PGA	2nd	match play	–2.04
1922 British Open	T-2	301	–1.86
1923 PGA	quarterfinals	match play	–1.51

Note: Average Z score: –1.81. Effective stroke average: 69.31.

BARNES'S CAREER RECORD (1913–32)

1913	-1.44
1914	-1.12
1915	-1.11
1916	-1.64
1917	-2.30
1918	
1919	-1.55
1920	-1.27
1921	-1.68
1922	-0.99
1923	-1.21
1924	-1.42
1925	-1.14
1926	0.39
1927	-0.36
1928	-0.50
1929	-0.82
1930	-1.49
1931	
1932	0.74

U.S. Open: 13 starts, 1 win (1921), –11.54

Western Open: 7 starts, 1 win (1919), –11.21

PGA: 9 starts, 2 wins (1916, 1919), –8.82

British Open: 10 starts, 0 wins, –13.01

Total (39 starts): –44.58

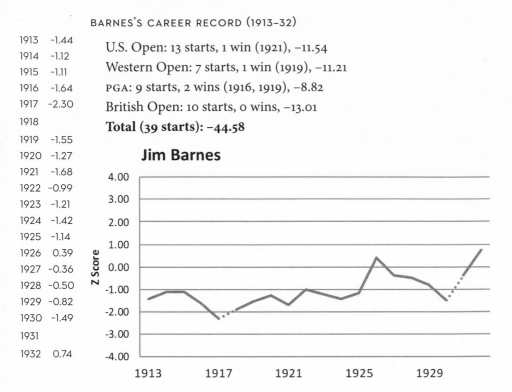

The Women Amateurs: Margaret Curtis, Alexa Stirling (Fraser), and Glenna Collett (Vare)

In the United States, women's golf arrived almost simultaneously with men's golf. The first women's tournament of significance, the Women's Amateur, was held in November 1895, only a little more than a month after the inaugural men's Amateur. But from that start, there equally quickly emerged one vital distinction, the absolute absence of women professionals. Literally, the only outlet for the best women players was the amateur game.

Until the early 1930s, that game was dominated by three names who came along pretty much in succession. Among them, Margaret Curtis, Alexa Stirling (Fraser), and Glenna Collett (Vare) won twelve U.S. Women's Amateur titles and added seven runner-up finishes between 1900 and 1935, roughly one every other season. Sadly for those interested in rivalry, they met head-on only twice, Stirling and Collett splitting those contests in the mid-1920s.

Curtis emerged first, showing up at the 1897 Amateur—only the third ever held—as a precocious thirteen-year-old. Equipped with four clubs, she recorded a score of 122 in the eighteen-hole qualifying test—good for fourth-best—before bowing out 8 and 6 to the defending, and soon-to-be repeat, champion, fellow teenager Beatrix Hoyt.

As an arguably more mature sixteen-year-old, Miss Curtis returned in 1900 to challenge Hoyt, by then a three-time champion. Qualifying with a 94 that earned medalist honors, she sailed through her first two matches, then eliminated Hoyt 1-up over twenty holes in the semifinals. She was, however, unable to sustain that level of play into the finals, losing 6 and 5 to Frances Griscom.

In company with her older sister, Harriott, Margaret soon made the Curtis name a dominant one in women's golf. She reached the semifinals in 1902 and the finals three years later. That same year the sisters traveled with a picked team of American females to play an arranged match against a select group of British women. That informal competition eventually became the inspiration for creation of the Curtis Cup, the equivalent for amateur women of the Ryder, Solheim, and Walker Cups. The Curtis sisters donated the trophy, which was named for them.

In 1906 health issues prevented Margaret from competing, but Harriott burnished the family name, winning the championship. Margaret returned in 1907, and the sisters jointly rolled through eight matches without once seeing the eighteenth hole. In the final, Margaret took Harriott out 7 and 6. Her victory set the stage for a unique double in American sports history. Less than a year later, Margaret took time out from her golf pursuits to show her tennis skills, teaming with reigning singles champion Evelyn Sears to win the United States Tennis Association's women's doubles championship. The victory made Margaret Curtis the only woman to simultaneously hold recognized national championships in two different sports.

Competitive tennis did not, however, maintain its sway over Curtis. She added a second title in 1911—again without ever seeing the eighteenth hole—and repeated in 1912 after medaling with an 88. With the coming of World War I, Curtis—then in her thirties—gave up competitive play, although continuing to be involved in an administrative sense. Her final U.S. Amateur match was a first-round defeat in the 1914 event, one that saw the debut of another teen prodigy, Alexa Stirling.

Alexa, two months old when Margaret Curtis debuted at the 1897 Amateur, was just a week past seventeen when she shot 93 to qualify for the 1914 tournament and then lost in the first round to the medalist. She came with a certain golf pedigree. Stirling learned the game at the Atlanta Athletic Club, where her fellow pupils included Bobby Jones. In 1909 the twelve-year-old Stirling had been pitted against the seven-year-old Jones in a club championship. "I'd love to go over that round . . . because I'll always believe that Alexa won that Cup," Jones confessed in his mid-1920s autobiography.[3] But the tournament officials, who probably couldn't stomach the thought of a girl beating a boy, awarded the cup to Jones.

From that point on, Alexa didn't lose many cups. A semifinalist as an eighteen-year-old in 1915, she prevailed a year later. The Amateur was not contested in 1917 or 1918, so Stirling joined prominent male stars—including Jones—in a series of fund-raising matches for the benefit of the Red Cross.[4] With the war's end in 1919, Stirling successfully defended her 1916 title, adding a third straight title in 1920. That ran her string of match victories to fifteen, stretching back to her 1915 semifinal defeat, and it grew to nineteen straight before Marion Hollins surprised the field with a 5 and 4 win in the 1921 finals.

Glenna Collett, whom Herbert Warren Wind would eventually describe as "the female Bobby Jones,"[5] was by then on hand, having qualified with an 85 to win medalist honors in that 1921 field. It was Collett's second Amateur appearance, but she surprisingly bowed out in the opening match. There were no such upsets following Collett's medal-winning 81 in 1922; her five victories came by margins of 2-up or better, taking out England's Mrs. William Gavin—who had eliminated Stirling 5 and 4 in the quarterfinals—to win the title.

Stirling was twenty-eight and married the previous spring to a Canadian named Fraser, Collett just twenty-two, when their paths collided in the 1925 final. The meeting was essentially foreordained, Stirling having medaled with 77, 1 stroke better than Collett and 3 better than anybody else. Reporters billed it as determining the best women player, but Collett settled the outcome early. She led by three when both players' drives sliced into a fairway trap and then laid out on the thirteenth hole of the morning eighteen. Nearly 180 yards out, Collett struck a three-wood that plopped four feet from the cup, finishing the first eighteen holes 4 ahead and eventually winning 9 and 8. It was the largest rout in the history of the tournament's championship round to that point.

Fraser gained some measure of revenge when she ousted Collett 2 and 1 in the second round of the 1927 championship. But Collett added a third title in 1928, this time by an even more dominating 13 and 12 over Virginia Van Wie. Her fourth crown came in 1929—the year of Stirling's retirement—and her fifth in 1930, running her own streak of match victories to fifteen since the loss to Fraser. That streak ended at nineteen in the finals of the 1931 tournament when Helen Hicks edged Collett, by then married and known as Glenna Collett Vare, 2 and 1. She was thirty-two by her sixth and final championship, over a field of sixty-four in 1935. She beat a Minneapolis teen named Patty Berg 3 and 2 in the final.

As Stirling's star receded, Collett found a new rival overseas. She toured Europe, drawing headlines when she battled two-time British women's Amateur champion Joyce Wethered in the third round of the 1925 event at Troon. Wethered, enjoying a ten-hole stretch she played in 6 under par, won and went on to capture her third title. Collett returned to the British Amateur in 1929 and 1930, losing again to Wethered in 1929.

Vare continued to compete until World War II halted the tournament. When the World Golf Hall of Fame was established in the mid-1970s, she was among the inaugural inductees. When the LPGA tour created an award to be given to the player with the lowest stroke average, they named it the Vare Trophy.

Curtis in the Clubhouse

Tournament	Finish	Score	Z score
1900 U.S. Amateur	2nd	match play	−0.37
1902 U.S. Amateur	semifinals	match play	−0.72
1904 U.S. Amateur	3rd round	match play	−0.78

1905 U.S. Amateur	2nd	match play	–0.86
1907 U.S. Amateur	**1st**	**match play**	**–1.30**
1908 U.S. Amateur	quarterfinals	match play	–0.22
1909 U.S. Amateur	1st round	match play	+0.24
1911 U.S. Amateur	**1st**	**match play**	**–0.86**
1912 U.S. Amateur	**1st**	**match play**	**–0.74**
1913 U.S. Amateur	quarterfinals	match play	–0.04

Note: Average Z score: –0.57. Effective stroke average: 71.13.

CURTIS'S CAREER RECORD (1897–1914)

U.S. Women's Amateur: 12 starts, 3 wins (1907, 1911, 1912): –4.47
Total (12 starts): –4.47

1897	1.24
1898	
1899	
1900	-0.75
1901	
1902	-0.72
1903	
1904	-0.78
1905	-0.86
1906	
1907	-1.30
1908	-0.22
1909	0.24
1910	
1911	-0.86
1912	-0.74
1913	-0.04
1914	

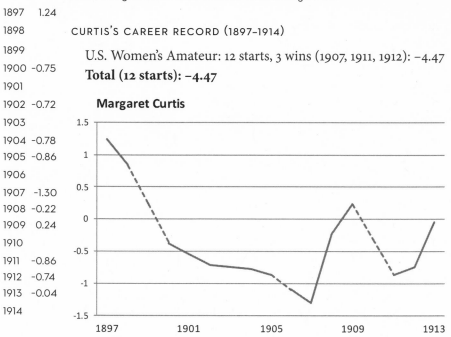

Margaret Curtis

Stirling (Fraser) in the Clubhouse

Tournament	Finish	Score	Z score
1914 U.S. Amateur	1st round	match play	+0.48
1915 U.S. Amateur	semifinals	match play	–0.62
1916 U.S. Amateur	**1st**	**match play**	**–0.65**
1919 U.S. Amateur	**1st**	**match play**	**–0.68**
1920 U.S. Amateur	**1st**	**match play**	**–0.80**
1921 U.S. Amateur	2nd	match play	–0.43
1922 U.S. Amateur	quarterfinals	match play	–0.85

1923 U.S. Amateur	2nd	match play	−0.67
1925 U.S. Amateur	2nd	match play	−0.08
1927 U.S. Amateur	semifinals	match play	−0.83

Note: Average Z score: −0.62. Effective stroke average: 71.06.

STIRLING'S CAREER RECORD (1914–29)

U.S. Women's Amateur: 11 starts, 3 wins (916, 1919, 1920): −5.17

Total (11 starts): −5.17

Alexa Stirling (Fraser)

1914	0.48
1915	−0.62
1916	−0.65
1917	
1918	
1919	−0.68
1920	−0.80
1921	−0.43
1922	−0.85
1923	−0.67
1924	
1925	−0.08
1926	
1927	−0.83
1928	
1929	−0.04

Collett (Vare) in the Clubhouse

Tournament	Finish	Score	Z score
1922 U.S. Amateur	1st	match play	**−0.95**
1923 U.S. Amateur	quarterfinals	match play	−0.86
1924 U.S. Amateur	semifinals	match play	−0.73
1925 U.S. Amateur	1st	match play	**−0.96**
1926 U.S. Amateur	quarterfinals	match play	−0.74
1927 U.S. Amateur	2nd round	match play	−0.05
1928 U.S. Amateur	1st	match play	**−1.10**
1929 U.S. Amateur	1st	match play	**−1.02**
1930 U.S. Amateur	1st	match play	**−1.05**
1931 U.S. Amateur	2nd	match play	−0.79

Note: Average Z score: −0.83. Effective stroke average: 70.75.

COLLETT'S CAREER RECORD (1919–31)

1919	-0.17
1920	0.31
1921	0.28
1922	-0.95
1923	-0.86
1924	-0.73
1925	-0.96
1926	-0.74
1927	-0.05
1928	-1.10
1929	-1.02
1930	-1.05
1931	-0.79
1932	-0.57
1933	
1934	-0.82
1935	-0.88
1936	
1937	-0.23
1938	-0.06
1939	-0.06
1940	
1941	-0.47

U.S. Women's Amateur: 20 starts, 6 wins (1922, 1925, 1928, 1929, 1930, 1935): –10.39

Total (20 starts): –10.39

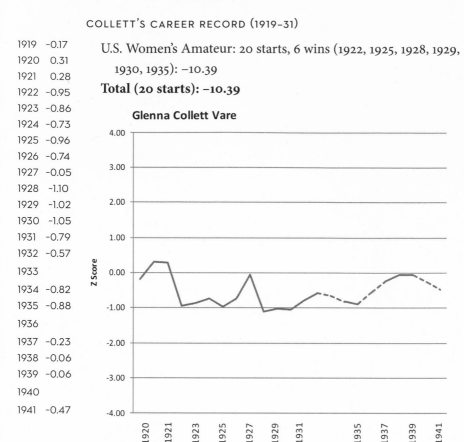

Jock Hutchison

When Jock Hutchison won the 1921 British Open in a thirty-six-hole playoff, the golf world took notice for two reasons, one sentimental, the other mechanical.

Although a U.S. citizen and a familiar figure on what passed for the American golf "tour" in those days—Hutchison had won the 1920 PGA Championship—he was a native of St. Andrews, site of the 1921 Open, and thus was welcomed home as a sort of long-lost family member.

He was, anyway, until the locals caught sight of his bag. It contained clubs that disdained the "dimpled" faces popular at the time in favor of the "grooves" we have long since come to view as standard. That was not the prevailing view in 1921, the Royal and Ancient (R&A) having already passed a rule prohibiting grooved faces on irons. Indeed, famed golfer J. H. Taylor likened playing with grooved clubs to "buying a shot out of a shop." But the R&A rule change would not take effect until July 1; the Open, fortuitously for Hutchison, was scheduled for the final week in June.

Hutchison took full advantage of the serendipitous timing. His opening-round 72—highlighted by an ace at the eighth hole—gave him a two-stroke lead. In fact, Hutchison narrowly missed consecutive aces in that round: his tee shot at the 278-yard par 4 ninth lipped the cup but stayed out, and he had to settle for a 2. Then a closing 70—at the time the lowest round ever recorded in British Open play at St. Andrews—cemented a tie with respected British amateur Roger Wethered. The thirty-six-hole playoff was no contest, Hutchison besting Wethered by 3 strokes during the morning eighteen and winning by 9. He became the first North American to take the Claret Jug across the ocean.

Hutchison's golf genes surfaced early. After arriving in America, he caddied as a youth, debuted in the U.S. Open in 1908—he tied for eighth—and in 1911 finished fifth, 2 strokes behind John McDermott. The 1916 season was both one of Hutchison's best and one of his most frustrating, with runner-up finishes in all three of America's biggest professional events. At that summer's 1916 U.S. Open he battled Evans, eventually losing by 2 strokes. In August he lost the Western Open title to Walter Hagen by 1. Then in October, Hutchison plowed through the PGA match-play field, defeating a pair of opponents by scores of 11 and 9 in thirty-six-hole matches and gaining revenge on Hagen, taking him out 2-up in the semifinals. In the championship match, however, Hutchison lost 1-up to Jim Barnes when Barnes took two of the final three holes.

Barnes, who repeated in 1919, was favored to win for a third time in 1921, but his second-round upset at the hands of Clarence Hackney cleared the way for Hutchison. As in 1916, he rolled through the preliminary matches and this time held on to his early lead in the title match against Douglas Edgar, winning 1-up.

In an era still fresh with the memories of legendary British figures Vardon, Taylor, and Braid, Hutchison's frequent showdowns with Hagen and Barnes soon earned them a collective nickname: "the American Triumvirate." Although not in a class with Hagen or Barnes in terms of championships won, Hutchison did bag a dozen other tour victories in addition to his two majors between 1918 and 1928, among them the 1920 and 1923 Western Opens. Surviving footage shows him as a carefree figure—Herbert Warren Wind called him "a contagious chuckler—befitting his nickname "Jovial Jock." With a club in hand, however, his personality changed. He became, again quoting Wind, "as nervous as a mosquito," sweating profusely and habitually twiddling his thumbs.[6]

To the extent Hutchison is lightly recalled today, that is more a reflection on one's fleeting memories than on his game. At his peak, he was a dominant player. Consider that between 1919 and 1923, Jock Hutchison entered the world's most prestigious professional golf tournaments—the U.S. and British Opens, the PGA Championship, and the Western Open—thirteen times. In those thirteen attempts, he finished third or better ten times, emerging with four championship trophies.

Hutchison in the Clubhouse

Tournament	Finish	Score	Z score
1919 U.S. Open	T-3	306	–1.63
1919 Western Open	3rd	287	–1.78
1920 U.S. Open	T-2	296	–1.68
1920 Western Open	1st	296	–1.77
1920 PGA	1st	match play	–2.11
1921 Western Open	2nd	292	–2.05
1921 British Open	1st	296	–1.90
1922 Western Open	T-2	301	–1.85
1923 U.S. Open	3rd	302	–1.44
1923 Western Open	1st	281	–2.06

Note: Average Z score: –1.83. Effective stroke average: 69.28.

HUTCHISON'S CAREER RECORD (1908–33)

U.S. Open: 19 starts, 0 wins, –7.06
Western Open: 17 starts, 2 wins (1920, 1923), –18.77
PGA: 5 starts, 1 win (1920), –6.70
British Open: 1 start, 1 win (1921), –1.90
Total (42 starts): –34.43

Jock Hutchison

1908	-0.76
1909	-0.15
1910	-0.85
1911	-1.48
1912	-0.39
1913	-0.21
1914	
1915	-1.03
1916	-1.88
1917	-1.99
1918	
1919	-1.54
1920	-1.85
1921	-1.44
1922	-1.85
1923	-1.75
1924	-0.60
1925	-0.32
1926	0.04
1927	0.09
1928	-0.28
1929	0.69
1930	2.43
1931	
1932	0.35
1933	-0.41

THE TOP-TEN GOLFERS OF ALL TIME FOR PEAK RATING AS OF THE END OF THE 1910 SEASON.

Rank	Player	Seasons	Z score	Effective stroke average
1.	James Braid	1901–10	–2.18	68.76
2.	Harry Vardon	1896–1904	–2.03	68.98
3.	J. H. Taylor	1900–1908	–1.77	69.37
4.	Willie Anderson	1901–6	–1.71	69.46
5.	L. Auchterlonie	1899–1904	–1.46	69.82
6.	Alex Smith	1904–10	–1.36	69.97
7.	Sandy Herd	1901–10	–1.20	70.21
8.	Willie Park Jr.	1883–92	–1.14	70.29
9.	Bob Ferguson	1868–86	–1.11	70.34
10.	Willie Fernie	1882–91	–1.07	70.49

THE TOP-TEN GOLFERS OF ALL TIME FOR CAREER RATING AS OF THE END OF THE 1910 SEASON.

Rank	Player	Seasons	Z score
1.	Willie Anderson	1897–1910	–32.29
2.	J. H. Taylor	1893–1910	–32.22

3.	James Braid	1894–1910	–28.66
4.	Harry Vardon	1893–1910	–28.49
5.	Alex Smith	1898–1910	–22.67
6.	Laurie Auchterlonie	1899–1909	–22.47
7.	Sandy Herd	1888–1910	–22.02
8.	Bob Ferguson	1868–89	–21.12
9.	Harold Hilton	1887–1910	–21.03
10.	John Laidlay	1885–1910	–15.32

THE TOP-TEN GOLFERS OF ALL TIME FOR PEAK
RATING AS OF THE END OF THE 1920 SEASON.

Rank	Player	Seasons	Z score	Effective stroke average
1.	James Braid	1901–10	–2.18	68.76
2.	Harry Vardon	1896–1904	–2.03	68.98
3.	Jock Hutchison	1916–20	–1.78	69.35
4.	J. H. Taylor	1900–1908	–1.77	69.37
5.	Willie Anderson	1901–6	–1.71	69.46
6.	Jim Barnes	1916–20	–1.67	69.51
7.	Ted Ray	1908–20	–1.67	69.51
8.	Laurie Auchterlonie	1899–1904	–1.46	69.82
9.	Walter Hagen	1913–19	–1.42	69.88
10.	Alex Smith	1904–10	–1.36	69.97
	John McDermott	1909–14	–1.36	69.97

THE TOP-TEN GOLFERS OF ALL TIME FOR CAREER
RATING AS OF THE END OF THE 1920 SEASON.

Rank	Player	Seasons	Z score
1.	J. H. Taylor	1893–1920	–38.70
2.	Harry Vardon	1893–1914	–37.88
3.	James Braid	1894–1914	–33.63
4.	Willie Anderson	1897–1910	–32.29
5.	Harold Hilton	1887–1914	–26.12

6.	Jock Hutchison	1908–20	–24.94
7.	Alex Smith	1898–1920	–24.38
8.	Jim Barnes	1913–20	–22.82
9.	Laurie Auchterlonie	1899–1909	–22.47
10.	Ted Ray	1899–1920	–22.11

6 Interwarriors

Although golf did not come of age during the period between the great wars, it took large strides toward maturity. The progress is measurable in several ways. Bobby Jones, the game's greatest star, initiated a new "major" tournament, the Masters, in 1934. American golfers led the increasingly international aspect of the game with more frequent ocean treks to play in the British Open. They not only played; they won. Beginning with Walter Hagen in 1924 and continuing through Denny Shute in 1933, Americans won every British Open title, all ten of them. In the eight-plus intervening decades, no country—not the United States and not Britain itself—has approached that successive number of victories.

The game also changed mechanically. Prior to the turn of the century, golf had been largely a ground game. Wooden-shafted clubs and gutta-percha balls in use at the time dictated that players use a flatter arc and more body sway to achieve distance. You can see this in surviving footage of the swing of James Braid and other great players of that era. The by-product was a relatively low trajectory that emphasized roll. Introduction of the rubber-core ball, and especially the steel shaft, enabled players to play a higher trajectory with greater carry. This also reduced the luck factor that was inevitable anytime a ball started rolling.

But the real driving force in the game's popularity was the growth of its first American star class, with Jones the best known. He had plenty of competition for headlines, notably Walter Hagen, Gene Sarazen, Ralph Guldahl, and Byron Nelson.

Collectively, they represent white American male laboring archetypes of the period. The qualifiers are important. Few women and no minorities were welcome, of course. The game was certainly played by the rich and educated but generally not seriously, Jones being the primary exception. That left the professional opportunities to hard-bitten raconteurs of the Hagen stripe, immigrant opportunists such as Sarazen, steady and serious day laborers like Guldahl who fashioned glory from their own sweat and failure, and sons of the rural South, exemplified by Nelson, who made success seem so effortless. All were sufficiently well-to-do to be afforded the opportunity, yet not so burdened by wealth as to have that opportunity proscribed as déclassé.

Walter Hagen

Number 11 Peak, Number 2 Career

Like Ted Ray and Jim Barnes, Hagen's résumé may have been clipped by World War I. Certainly, he was a budding star of the game when the guns fired, having won the 1914 U.S. Open at the age of twenty-one. An assertive personality who anticipated the larger-than-life sports era of Ruth and Dempsey—and who won the first U.S. Open after the war's conclusion in 1919—Hagen doubtless would have endorsed the claim that he was, in a sense, a war victim, although the evidence is not fully supportive. In fact, U.S. Opens were played in 1915 and 1916, prior to American involvement in the conflict, and Hagen did only so-so in both of them, trailing the champion by ten and nine strokes, respectively.

Whatever else they consider him, many consider Hagen to be one of the game's great showmen. "He impresses one beyond everything else as really enjoying the fight," Bernard Darwin wrote.[1] A hustler at heart who gained renown for intimidating his opponents—a reputation that made him especially talented at match play—Hagen really was the world's first full-time tournament professional. Prior to him, pros made their living by offering lessons, relying on tournament winnings merely as supplements. So charismatic was Hagen that he created interest in the professional game, making the tour itself viable.

Hagen was a man without pretense. The story is often and fondly told of the round he played during the mid-1930s with the future King Edward VIII of England. Preparing to putt, Hagen is said to have casually addressed his royal partner thusly: "Eddie, hold the flag, will you?" There are those who say the exchange never happened—at least not at that familiar a level. Yet even if apocryphal, it illustrates the very public ease with which he moved, an ease that helped to break down social barriers. At a dinner honoring Hagen, Arnold Palmer saluted him with the suggestion, "If not for you, this dinner tonight would be downstairs in the pro shop, not in the ballroom."[2]

Hagen enjoyed profound success at match play; he won the PGA Championship five times in the 1920s, including four in succession. That encompassed a stretch of twenty-two straight thirty-six-hole match victories in the PGA. Between 1921 and 1927, he won five of the six tournaments he entered (Hagen skipped the 1922 event due to "exhibition commitments") and lost the 1923 championship match 1-up in thirty-eight holes to Sarazen. Aside from that finals loss, Hagen won thirty consecutive matches, sixteen by margins of 5 and 3 or better, including a 12 and 11 slaughter of George McLean in the 1922 semifinals. Only five of those thirty wins went to the final hole.

The key to Hagen's success was his easygoing inventiveness, a talent that gave his more precise opponents fits. "I expect to make at least seven mistakes a round," he once said. "Therefore, when I make a bad shot, it's just one of the seven."[3] Even the unflappable Bob Jones fell victim to Hagen's self-assurance, venting following his defeat by Hagen in a 1926 challenge match that "when a man misses his drive, and then misses his second shot, and then wins the hole with a birdie, it gets my goat."

It was all a natural extension of his overall philosophy of life. Born in Rochester, New York, on December 21, 1892, the son of a blacksmith, Hagen came from modest beginnings and entered golf as a caddie, but his zest for life demanded that he exceed the expectations normally coming with his background. "I never wanted to be a millionaire," he said. "I just wanted to live like one." Although an imposing six feet tall with slick black hair and favoring the finest fabrics, Hagen nonetheless had a kindly face and a twinkle that invited rather than repelled the common man. His gestures were grand but wonderfully human.

Hagen's professional debut nearly overshadowed what is today considered the seminal moment in American competitive golf. It came at the 1913 U.S. Open at Brookline, the one featuring amateur Francis Ouimet's stunning upset of British champions Vardon and Ray. Among four men just three strokes back and tied for fourth was Hagen, who had ridden over from Rochester on the money he could scrape together from supporters. So obscure was he to the golfing press that the *New York Times* report referred to him as "Willie Hagins of Rochester." His backers could have had no expectations for the kid who at that point had never been to a serious outside competition, but

Hagen did. Asked on his return how he did, he is supposed to have replied tartly, "I lost."

A serious athlete who considered himself as much a baseball player as a golfer, Hagen journeyed to Florida that winter, where he met Phillies manager Pat Moran and star pitcher Grover Cleveland Alexander on the links. An invitation to work out with the team led to some exhibition appearances, which in turn led to an offer to return to the following spring's camp as a player. Hagen, determined to take the offer, advised friends and backers that he was putting his golf career on hold, to the extent of not playing in the 1914 Open.

It was a rash decision, and cooler heads—among them Ernest Willard, sports editor of the local newspaper, told Hagen so. Willard did more than that; he volunteered to front Hagen's expenses to the Open at Midlothian Country Club outside Chicago. That investment proved one of the most prescient in the game's history when Hagen won by a shot over Chick Evans. He never went back to baseball.

But it was with the war's end and the arrival of something that resembled a professional golf "tour" that Hagen blossomed. His 1919 U.S. Open victory over Mike Brady in a playoff at Brae Burn probably did more than any event to burnish Hagen's reputation as a psychological killer. The previous day, standing over an eight-foot putt on the final hole to beat Brady, who had already finished, Hagen supposedly summoned his challenger from the clubhouse to witness his own defeat . . . only to miss the putt. At a too late soiree that evening, a friend urged Hagen to retire, asserting that Brady by then doubtless had been asleep for hours. "He may be in bed, but he ain't asleep," Hagen replied.[4] In his autobiography, Hagen reported telling Brady on the playoff's second hole to roll down his sleeves "so the gallery won't see your arms shaking."[5] Hagen took a one-shot lead to the final hole but topped his drive little more than a hundred yards, barely clearing a creek in front of the tee. He followed that with a fairway wood close to the green, chipped on, and saved his clinching par four. The following year he tied for second behind Jim Barnes.

Hagen's penchant for the British Open made him America's first international star and coincided nicely with his own heyday. These trips did not always go smoothly. At his debut at Deal in 1920, he showed up with a wardrobe of a dozen splendid golf outfits and a chauffeur-driven Austin-Daimler limo. He entered the locker room only to be advised that professionals were unwelcome in those facilities. Furious, Hagen retreated to his limo and changed outside the club's front door. That's the same place where he took a champagne lunch, a practice he repeated for several years to follow.

That ostentatiousness got Hagen loads of attention from the British press. His game in Britain, however, did not initially justify the glamour. The 1919 U.S. Open champion shot 329, tying for fifty-second place, 26 shots behind champion Ted Ray and 13 shots behind J. H. Taylor, who was then nearing fifty. He improved to sixth place in 1921 and the following summer edged out George Duncan and Jim Barnes by a shot at Royal St. George's.

By that time Hagen was the defending PGA titleholder as well as a two-time U.S. Open champion. He failed by 1 shot to repeat his British Open title in 1923 and then in 1924 succeeded by 1 shot. He was the obvious choice to captain the U.S. team in the inaugural Ryder Cup match in 1927, and in 1928 he won his third British Open title. Between 1921 and 1934, Hagen played in twenty-two stroke-play "majors"—a string that began with his 1921 loss to Barnes and continued through the first Masters—without once turning in a card that was above the field average.

Hagen in the Clubhouse

Tournament	Finish	Score	Z score
1923 British Open	2nd	296	-2.00
1923 PGA	2nd	match play	-2.13
1924 British Open	**1st**	**301**	**-2.10**
1924 PGA	**1st**	match play	**-2.39**
1925 U.S. Open	T-5	293	-1.64
1925 Western Open	T-2	287	-1.60
1926 British Open	T-3	295	-1.89
1926 Western Open	**1st**	**279**	**-2.62**
1926 PGA	**1st**	match play	**-2.18**
1927 Western Open	**1st**	**281**	**-2.47**

Note: Average Z score: -2.10. Effective stroke average: 68.88.

Masters: 4 starts, 0 wins, +0.16

U.S. Open: 22 starts, 2 wins (1914, 1919), −23.75

British Open: 10 starts, 4 wins (1922, 1924, 1928, 1929), −13.97

PGA Championship: 13 starts, 5 wins (1921, 1924, 1925, 1926, 1927), −13.50

Western Open: 14 starts, 5 wins (1916, 1921, 1926, 1927, 1932), −22.88

Total (63 starts): −73.94

Walter Hagen

Year	Z Score
1913	-1.44
1914	-2.06
1915	-0.79
1916	-1.19
1917	-2.10
1919	-1.73
1920	-0.37
1921	-2.00
1922	-1.85
1923	-1.47
1924	-1.97
1925	-1.43
1926	-2.04
1927	-1.68
1928	-1.54
1929	-1.21
1930	-0.74
1931	-1.22
1932	-1.11
1933	-0.91
1934	1.05
1935	-1.15
1936	-0.45
1937	0.47
1938	
1939	0.41
1940	-0.52

Bobby Jones

Number 10 Peak, Number 17 Career

By the early 1920s, the focus of the golfing world had shifted from Britain to the United States. With the war's end, Americans took to imposing themselves upon the British Open field, achieving dramatic results. Three of those titles went to Jones, often acclaimed as the greatest of them all.

A native of Atlanta, Jones set his life's course early, winning the Georgia Amateur in 1916 for the first of three straight times. He was just fourteen. Bernard Darwin, who saw Jones at the dawn of his career, declared that he possessed "a drowsy beauty." There was an art to Jones's dominance, a gentlemanly, cultivated perfection, Darwin implied, that even his victims might appreciate. He was, said Darwin, "the highwayman who was forced to take his victim's purse, but took it with the courtliest of bows."[6]

Others, however, saw a different, more fiery side of him. Grantland Rice wrote that the young Jones "had the temper of a timber wolf." Jones did not disavow the characterization. "To me, golf was just a game to beat someone," he would say of those years, adding, "I didn't know that someone was me."[7]

Barely eighteen, he debuted at the 1920 U.S. Open at Inverness in Ohio and tied for eighth, just four strokes behind Ray—and two ahead of Hagen. He moved up to fifth in 1921, second to Gene Sarazen in 1922, and in 1923 he completed his steady climb up the standings ladder with a playoff victory over Bobby Cruickshank at Inwood.

The story—probably true but indicative even if apocryphal—is told in golf circles of Jones's steely resolve and calm nerve over the final holes of that playoff, which had become necessary only when he played the final three regulation holes in four over par. "I finished like a yellow dog," Jones said.[8] He and Cruickshank were tied as they stood in the eighteenth fairway of the playoff, facing the prospect of another eighteen holes since the USGA did not at the time recognize sudden death under any circumstances. Equally daunting was the shot that faced Jones, a long iron over water on the 425-yard par four.

Cruickshank, after driving into the rough, had already laid up. Jones's caddie assumed he would do the same, but Jones was having none of it. "One way or another, I'm ending it right here," he is said to have declared, thereupon skipping the two-iron across the pond and within six feet of the cup. Jones himself never owned up to that assertive comment . . . or any other thought prior to the shot. Indeed, he claimed to have no memory of what he was thinking as he prepared to hit the ball. We do know this, though: Jones made a par and beat Cruickshank; it was his first major victory.

In an era when giants strode the athletic earth—think of Babe Ruth, Red Grange, and Bill Tilden—Jones was widely viewed as their equal. Some declared him the greatest golfer of all time, and a few ventured so far as to knight him the greatest athlete. Between the playoff win over

Cruickshank and his completion of the 1930 Grand Slam, Jones entered twenty events at the time considered to be majors and won thirteen of them. Those titles included four U.S. Opens as well as three British Open titles in as many tries—1926, 1927 (by six strokes), and 1930. None was more dramatic than his victory in the 1929 U.S. Open at Winged Foot. Jones held a six-stroke lead with six holes to play, but a triple bogey jeopardized that once-sure win, and he came to the eighteenth needing a twelve-foot putt to merely tie Al Espinosa. Jones made the putt and in the next day's thirty-six-hole playoff beat Espinosa by thirteen strokes.

Although thin in comparison with modern stars, Jones's résumé is a stunning and persuasive one. From 1920 through what amounted to his retirement following the 1930 Grand Slam, Jones never took more than 96 percent of the field average of shots in any major tournament season, and that occurred in his debut year. Between 1922 and 1926, he averaged 94 percent of the field's strokes. His very worst performance occurred in the 1927 U.S. Open at Oakmont, when he missed the top ten by a stroke. Then there were those Amateurs: five American titles (1924, 1925, 1927, 1928, 1930) plus the 1930 British Amateur. In 1928 Jones defeated John Beck 14 and 13 in the quarterfinals, dispatched Phillips Finlay 13 and 12 in the semifinals, and claimed the trophy 10 and 9 over Thomas Perkins. During his Grand Slam season, Jones won his final three U.S. Amateur matches by scores of 6 and 5, 9 and 8, and 8 and 7.

His performance in that concluding event of the Grand Slam season conveys a false impression that Jones sailed through those victories without serious challenge. Nothing could be further from the truth. At the first, the British Amateur, Jones won three of his eight matches 1-up—one of them in nineteen holes—and enjoyed only two routs. At the British Open, fellow American Leo Diegel missed a short putt at the seventy-second hole that would have tied Jones, who eventually won by 2. At the U.S. Open, he shot a final-round 75 capped by a forty-foot birdie putt on the last hole to hold off Macdonald Smith, again by 2.

There was always a little bit of the Jeffersonian Renaissance man in Jones. He walked away from his playing career after the 1930 season, declaring those other interests. He had received a degree in mechanical engineering at Georgia Tech, studied English literature at Harvard, and passed his bar exam after studying law at Emory. Unlike most great athletes, his sport never held Jones in its thrall. Yet so masterful was his self-discipline that he could simultaneously manage all of these competing interests.

After his "retirement," he helped found and lay out the Augusta National Golf Club, organizing and hosting that club's annual invitational tournament—an event Jones's presence made special. Within a few years, it would be formally rechristened by the name it had borne informally almost from the start—the Masters. Jones came out of retirement to play in 1934, tying with Hagen for thirteenth place. But his return to competition only underscored the sagaciousness Jones had shown by retiring in the first place. He continued as a host-competitor through 1948 without once contending. There is no intimation in this that Jones subsumed his competitive instincts to his role as host.

He left golf in 1948, after developing syringomyelia, a fluid-filled cavity in his spinal cord causing first pain and then paralysis. Jones was eventually restricted to a wheelchair until his death on December 18, 1971.

Jones in the Clubhouse

Tournament	Finish	Score	Z score
1926 U.S. Open	1st	293	–2.10
1926 British Open	1st	291	–2.40
1927 British Open	1st	285	–2.89
1928 U.S. Open	2nd	294	–1.95
1928 U.S. Amateur	1st	match play	–1.87
1929 U.S. Open	1st	294	–2.20
1930 British Amateur	1st	match play	–1.04
1930 British Open	1st	291	–2.28
1930 U.S. Open	1st	287	–2.57
1930 U.S. Amateur	1st	match play	–1.84

Note: Average Z score: –2.11. Effective stroke average: 68.87.

JONES'S CAREER RECORD (1916–30)

Western Open: 1 start, 0 wins, –1.73
U.S. Open: 11 starts, 4 wins (1923, 1926, 1929, 1930), –20.06
U.S. Amateur: 13 starts, 5 wins (1924, 1925, 1927, 1928, 1930), –10.26

British Open: 3 starts, 3 wins (1926, 1927, 1930), −7.57
British Amateur: 3 starts, 1 win (1930), −2.16
Total (31 starts): −39.62
Note: Total does not include 1921 British Open, when Jones withdrew
during the event.

Bobby Jones

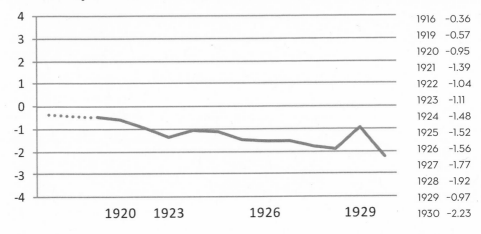

1916	−0.36
1919	−0.57
1920	−0.95
1921	−1.39
1922	−1.04
1923	−1.11
1924	−1.48
1925	−1.52
1926	−1.56
1927	−1.77
1928	−1.92
1929	−0.97
1930	−2.23

Gene Sarazen

Number 23 Peak, Number 9 Career

Gene Sarazen was the undersize immigrant trying to crash the neighborhood game . . . then starring in it. Born Eugenio Saraceni, the son of a Sicilian carpenter, on February 27, 1902, in Harrison, New York, he quit school in sixth grade to make his living. Yet the precise route delivering this natural to golf has been related so variously over the years—including by Sarazen himself—that the truth may never be certain. Some say he started as a caddie at ten, attracted by the swells at a local club. Others say he apprenticed to his dad's carpentry trade, only to find himself allergic to sawdust, and sought solace in outdoor activity. Still others say the allergy was a ruse to get him away to the golf course.

Whatever the facts, by fourteen Sarazen was a runt caddie, picking up enough tips along the way to fashion a fair self-taught game. Although topping out at five-foot-five and a wispy 145 pounds, Sarazen never let his lack of size get in the way of his ambition. Rather, he compensated by emphasizing technique, over time acquiring a reputation as a stylist. Naysayers dismissed him as merely fortunate, but he paid them no mind. "The more I practice, the luckier I get," he is said to have retorted. He turned pro at nineteen, changing his name to Sarazen because, he once said, "It sounded like a golfer."

Sarazen's other natural gift was his competitive heart. An unknown twenty-year-old, he arrived at Skokie Country Club for the 1922 U.S. Open, his first, playing in a bow tie. He trailed Hagen, the prohibitive favorite, by four shots after the first round and remained four back of surprise leader Jones entering the final eighteen holes. But Sarazen, brimming with confidence at being so close to contention so early in his career, fashioned a brilliant fourth round over the 6,563-yard par-70 layout. Coming to the final hole, a short par 5, 1 under par and level with Jones and John Black, Sarazen laid a drive in the center of the fairway and then used the same club to stop his second shot fifteen feet from the hole. Two putts allowed him to post a final 68 for a score of 288. When neither Jones nor Black could muster the par-par finish they needed, Sarazen's fans hoisted him to their shoulders and carried him off in surprising glory. As if to demonstrate that his victory had been no fluke, Sarazen followed up by winning the PGA Championship that same summer at Oakmont. It made him the first player to hold both titles simultaneously. Again, Sarazen demonstrated the rare self-confidence to dismiss his critics. "I don't care what you call me, just spell my name right," he admonished them. Over time, the phrase became his calling card.

Initially, Sarazen rarely joined Hagen and a growing band of American tourists for the British Open championship. His first attempt came in 1923, and he failed the thirty-six-hole qualifying attempt. Returning in 1924 following a mediocre performance at the U.S. Open, where he tied for seventeenth, Sarazen made the ocean trip as part of an American delegation that also included Hagen and Barnes. He was never a factor, his 323 barely making the top forty, two dozen strokes behind Hagen. Sarazen did not return for four years, during which he placed fifth, third, and third at the U.S. Open. When he finally did in 1928, he lost to Hagen, although this time finishing second, just 2 shots off his illustrious companion's pace at Royal St. George's. The difference lay in Sarazen's loss of composure at the famous "Suez Canal" fourteenth hole. Driving into the rough, he eschewed the safe play—an iron short of the Canal—for a wood, which he misfired and then misfired again. The result: a double bogey 7.

What developed through the late 1920s was a running Hagen-Sarazen rivalry. It was stark with contrasts, and they didn't just involve size. Both were brash, but Hagen more engagingly so, Sarazen more forcefully. "He had no affectation, no trifling," Darwin once wrote of him.[9] Where Hagen appeared at times to play by instinct, Sarazen was much more the technician. The two men met head-on in major tournament match play only once, in the final of the 1923 PGA Championship. Sarazen was 3-up after entering the final nine holes, but Hagen birdied to win the twenty-ninth hole, then evened the match by claiming the thirty-fourth and thirty-fifth holes. Play continued even until the thirty-eighth hole, when a Sarazen drive into deep rough near an out-of-bounds marker appeared to give Hagen the edge. "I'll put this one so close to the hole that it will break Walter's heart," Sarazen was said to have told the gallery members. He did, his iron winding up two feet from the hole for an easy birdie. Hagen put his own second into a bunker, and when his explosion barely missed falling, Sarazen claimed the match.

Later Sarazen challenged Hagen to a seventy-two-hole exhibition for the "world championship," and Sarazen won again. "When Sarazen saw a chance at the bacon hanging over the last green," wrote Jones, "he could put as much fire and fury into a finishing round as Jack Dempsey could put into a fight."

With maturity came some of Sarazen's best performances. In fact, his most consistent stretch of play began in 1927, when he was already an established star. Third again in the Open in 1929, he dominated the 1930 tour, winning the Miami, Agua Caliente, Florida West Coast, Concord Country Club, United States Pro Invitational, Western, Lannin Memorial, and Middle Atlantic events. In majors, of course, he joined the rest of the golfing world in deference to Jones. He played on the first six Ryder Cup teams between 1927 and 1937.

Sarazen was fourth at the U.S. Open and third in the British Open in 1931, giving him seven top-ten placings in majors (but no victories) since 1923. That changed abruptly in 1932, when Sarazen dominated the British Open field at Sandwich, winning by five shots over Macdonald Smith. His play was aided by his own new invention, an extra flange of metal soldered onto the bottom of his wedge to ease his escape from sand traps. The shot baffled even veteran pros, but Sarazen's new design—he called it a sand wedge—gave him a significant edge. Following the tournament, Sarazen donated the original to the club at Sandwich, where it remains a treasured artifact today.

Sarazen wasn't through. Carrying a new sand wedge at the U.S. Open field at Fresh Meadow a few weeks later, he won by three shots. Sarazen took just one hundred strokes—eight fewer than par—over the final twenty-eight holes, a sensational stretch of sustained golf at the time. He added the 1933 PGA Championship, winning all of his matches by 4 and 3 or better, and beating Willie Goggin 5 and 4 in the final.

In 1935, Sarazen became the first player to win the modern Grand Slam when he captured the Masters. He did it by authoring a shot that would be iconic today if anyone had been around with a camera to record it. Standing in the middle of the fifteenth fairway, 235 yards from the flag on the 500-yard par-five hole, Sarazen trailed leader Craig Wood by three strokes. Since all chance at victory hinged on making as low a score as possible on this last of the par fives, Sarazen's caddie handed him a four wood with instructions to gamble. The ball carried the pond in front of the green. "Well, you've got one of them back," Sarazen later quoted his caddie as observing. The ball slowly and certainly traced a path toward the flag. "You've got two of them," the caddie remarked, alluding now to the likelihood of an eagle three. The ball nestled softly into the bottom of the cup for a double eagle two. "Hell," said the stunned caddie, "you've got all three!"

In retrospect, the surprising part is that Sarazen, with three holes remaining, didn't make one more birdie to win outright or one bogey to lose. He finished with three pars and then defeated Wood in the eighteen-hole Monday playoff.

Viewed initially by the British as something between a hot dog and a hothead, Sarazen's personality grew on the game's experts as he aged.

Wrote Darwin in 1932, "He was a fine, sensible manly player who did what he could . . . but that was more than anyone else could even affect to do."

A regular at Augusta for decades, Sarazen in time joined Jones as the game's elder statesman. That honorific was only enhanced by his paternal host role on Shell's *Wonderful World of Golf* television series in the 1960s. In 1973, on the fiftieth anniversary of his first appearance in the British Open, the seventy-one-year-old Sarazen made a hole in one with a punched five-iron at the short par-three eighth hole, known as the Postage Stamp, at Troon. After 1935, he never won another major, although he came close, losing in a playoff to Lawson Little for the U.S. Open title in 1940. Altogether, Sarazen won seven major championships among his more than fifty victories around the world.

Sarazen in the Clubhouse

Tournament	Finish	Score	Z score
1929 U.S. Open	T-3	296	-1.90
1929 Western Open	4th	284	-1.40
1930 Western Open	**1st**	**278**	**-2.65**
1931 U.S. Open	T-4	296	-1.30
1931 British Open	T-3	298	-1.64
1931 Western Open	T-3	287	-1.75
1932 U.S. Open	**1st**	**286**	**-2.72**
1932 British Open	**1st**	**283**	**-2.84**
1933 British Open	T-3	293	-1.47
1933 PGA	**1st**	**match play**	**-2.08**

Note: Average Z score: -1.98. Effective stroke average: 69.06.

SARAZEN'S CAREER RECORD (1920–51)

Masters: 13 starts, 1 win (1935), -6.67
U.S. Open: 28 starts, 2 wins (1922, 1932), -15.25
British Open: 8 starts, 1 win (1932), -11.02
PGA Championship: 25 starts, 3 wins (1922, 1923, 1933), -15.60
Western Open: 7 starts, 1 win (1930), -9.55
Total (81 starts): -58.09

Gene Sarazen

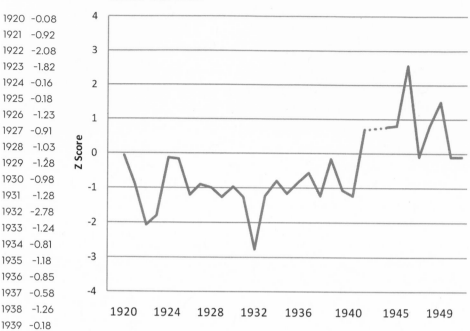

1920	-0.08
1921	-0.92
1922	-2.08
1923	-1.82
1924	-0.16
1925	-0.18
1926	-1.23
1927	-0.91
1928	-1.03
1929	-1.28
1930	-0.98
1931	-1.28
1932	-2.78
1933	-1.24
1934	-0.81
1935	-1.18
1936	-0.85
1937	-0.58
1938	-1.26
1939	-0.18
1940	-1.08
1941	-1.24
1942	0.67
1943	
1944	
1945	0.77
1946	2.55
1947	-0.10
1948	0.74
1949	1.48
1950	-0.11
1951	-0.12

Craig Wood

It's interesting to contemplate how great a player Craig Wood might be considered today:

- If only Gene Sarazen hadn't made that famous double eagle on the fifteenth hole of the 1935 Masters, Wood would have won the tournament. Instead, he lost to Sarazen in a playoff.
- If only Wood had recorded a final round score better than 75 in the 1933 British Open. Had he done so, he would have won. Instead, he tied Denny Shute, and Shute won that playoff.
- If only Horton Smith hadn't holed a twenty-foot birdie putt on the seventy-first hole at the inaugural 1934 Masters. Had Smith missed, Wood would have tied him for the championship. Instead, Smith won by a stroke.
- If only Wood had been able to hold his one-hole lead against Paul Runyan over the final seven holes of their thirty-six-hole playoff for the 1934 PGA Championship. Had he done so, Wood would have won that tournament as well. Instead, Harmon and Wood

tied at the end of the regulation thirty-six holes, and Harmon won
on the playoff's thirty-eighth hole.

- If only Byron Nelson hadn't holed out on a 384-yard par-four
third hole in the third round of the 1939 U.S. Open, Wood might
have won that championship in a playoff with Denny Shute. As it
was, Nelson joined that playoff and won it by three strokes ahead
of Wood, Shute finishing third.

But for those few strokes spread across six seasons, Wood's record
would show seven major championships. As it is, he stands with Greg
Norman as the only player to have lost all four majors in playoffs.

Born in Lake Placid, New York, late in 1901, Wood joined the tour in
the mid-1920s. But he was a late bloomer, finishing among the U.S. Open's
top ten only once and winning only a handful of minor tour stops until
1933. His victory in that year's Los Angeles Open marked him as a contender, a status he ratified with a third-place finish in the Open behind
Johnny Goodman and Ralph Guldahl. Those playoff losses in the 1933
British Open, 1934 and 1935 Masters, and 1934 PGA followed in quick
succession. Wood still wasn't a winner, but he was a perennial contender.

Still the victories remained rare: two in 1934, none in 1935, one in 1936,
none in 1937, and one in 1938. Wood was thirty-seven by then, beyond
the physical prime of most athletes, but only entering his. It proved to
be a brief and spectacular one. A sixth-place finish in the Masters preceded his playoff loss to Nelson in the Open. In 1940 he tied for seventh
at Augusta and finished fourth in both the U.S. and Western Opens.

The experience acquired during all those near misses finally paid
off in 1941. At the Masters, Wood assumed a 5-shot lead after the first
round and breezed home 3 ahead of Nelson. The victory was so seam-
less, the champion already holding such a high reputation that it seemed
impossible to understand he had just won his first major. His second
didn't take long; at the summer's U.S. Open, Wood took command with
a third-round 70 and beat his old rival, Shute, by 3 shots.

Although it seemed inconceivable at the time, Wood was essentially
through as a competitive golfer. With the onset of World War II, only
that year's Masters was played, and Wood shot an uninspired 302, 22
strokes behind Nelson. He was in his midforties when major stroke-play
competition resumed with the 1946 Masters. He died in 1968.

Wood in the Clubhouse

Tournament	Finish	Score	Z score
1939 Masters	6th	284	–1.35
1939 U.S. Open	2nd	284	–1.93
1940 Masters	T-7	288	–1.07
1940 U.S. Open	4th	289	–1.47
1940 PGA	round of 32	match play	–1.58
1940 Western Open	4th	296	–1.22
1941 Masters	**1st**	**280**	**–2.10**
1941 U.S. Open	**1st**	**284**	**–2.26**
1941 PGA	2nd round	match play	+0.92
1942 PGA	quarterfinals	match play	–0.77

Note: Average Z score: –1.28. Effective stroke translation: 70.09.

WOOD'S CAREER RECORD (1925–51)

Masters: 11 starts, 1 win (1941), –4.55

U.S. Open: 17 starts, 1 win (1941), +12.37

British Open: 1 start, 0 wins, –1.62

PGA Championship: 10 starts, 0 wins, –3.27

Western Open: 7 starts, 0 wins, –3.14

Total (46 starts): –0.21

1925	–0.18
1926	–1.15
1927	0.69
1928	0.62
1929	–0.38
1930	–0.88
1931	
1932	–0.27
1933	–1.70
1934	–0.06
1935	0.52
1936	0.03
1937	0.39
1938	1.19
1939	–1.64
1940	–1.34
1941	–0.78
1942	–0.17
1943	
1944	–0.86
1945	
1946	2.25
1947	1.59
1948	1.44
1949	0.29
1950	3.60
1951	1.10

Craig Wood

Ralph Guldahl

(Tie) Number 15 Peak

Compared with athletes in many sports, top-level golfers tend to enjoy comparatively lengthy careers. All three members of the Triumvirate remained in the game's front ranks for two decades after their primes. The same was true of Sarazen, Hogan, Snead, Nicklaus, and Player. Ralph Guldahl was the exception. Guldahl rose meteorically from golf obscurity, enjoyed a small window of dramatic success, and then retreated. Winner of the 1931 Santa Monica Open as an amateur, he was the game's preeminent player by late that same decade yet used up by the start of World War II

Born in 1911 in Dallas, the precocious Guldahl first tried his hand competitively at the 1930 U.S. Open at Interlachen, outside Minneapolis. At least it put him on the scene of history, as Bob Jones closed in on his Grand Slam. The nineteen-year-old amateur recorded a tie for nineteenth with an unremarkable score of 308. His Santa Monica victory prompted Guldahl to try the professional game in 1932, and he won the Arizona Open. But on the big stage he backslid, tying for twenty-fourth at the U.S. Open in 1931 and for fifty-eighth in 1932. Coming to North Shore for the 1933 U.S. Open as the rankest of outsiders, Guldahl recovered from an opening 76 with three consecutive rounds below par 72. That surge lifted him to a position where he stood on the seventy-second tee needing a par to tie amateur Johnny Goodman for the championship. Bunkering his approach, Guldahl lipped the four-foot par try that followed, packed his bags, and went home to Dallas, where he balanced occasional spasms on tour with what became his principal income, selling used cars.

This fit of self-abnegation lasted off and on for two years, during which he still managed to place eighth at the 1934 Open; in 1935, however, he staggered home fortieth.

One is left to guess what took hold of Guldahl following that 1935 Open embarrassment. But he resumed a serious practice schedule, showing up on tour in 1936 with a new focus that some found off-putting. He played slowly and devoid of emotion, pausing only occasionally to comb his thick black hair. "If Guldahl gave someone a blood transfusion, the patient would freeze to death," opined Sam Snead.

Perhaps, but the chilly technique worked for Guldahl. He surprised the field by finishing eighth at that year's U.S. Open and then surprised the tour again by winning the Western Open—for the first of three straight times. It was one of three tour victories for the man who had never previously shown a winner's heart. Suddenly a star, he came to Augusta for the 1937 Masters and battled fellow Texas Byron Nelson memorably through the stretch that would come to be known as Amen Corner. The Guldahl-Nelson fight lifted the holes to legendary status. Leading by 4 shots with 7 to play, Guldahl lost two balls in Rae's Creek on holes 12 and 13, scoring 5-6 as Nelson played the same holes in 2-3 and fashioned his eventual 2-shot margin of victory. Still, with the U.S. Open coming to Oakland Hills that summer, Guldahl was counted with Snead among the favorites.

The two began the final round tied with each other and a shot behind Ed Dudley, who quickly succumbed to a case of leader's nerves. Snead finished well before and 1 stroke ahead of Guldahl, who responded by playing the next two holes eagle-birdie to take a 2-shot lead. But he still had a full nine holes to play. Recalling his failures at Augusta and during the 1933 Open, Guldahl berated himself. "If I can't shoot 37 on the back nine, I'm a bum and don't deserve to win," he said.[10] He promptly bogeyed ten and eleven to give away the lead, but this time birdied twelve and thirteen to reclaim it and finished without further incident. His 69 gave him a score of 281 that stood as the record until 1948.

Guldahl finished second (this time to Henry Picard) in the Masters again in 1938 but repeated his Open championship at Cherry Hills in Denver. He looked like a poor bet after three rounds, trailing Dick Metz by 4 strokes. But Metz blew up to a 79, putative runner-up Jimmy Hines staggered home at 83, and Guldahl posted 69 for what turned out to be a comfortable 6-stroke margin.

Finally, in 1939, Guldahl got his green jacket. With Snead in the clubhouse, having posted a record score of 280, Guldahl fired a 33 on Augusta National's back nine, highlighted by a three-wood second to the par-5 thirteenth that finished six feet from the hole and led to an eagle. That scoring record stood until Ben Hogan shattered it in 1953. His bid for a third straight U.S. Open crown, a feat accomplished only by Willie Anderson, died when he placed seventh, 4 strokes behind Nelson. But

Guldahl added the Greater Greensboro Open, Dapper Dan Open, and Miami Biltmore Four-Ball and then in 1940 won the Milwaukee Open and Inverness Invitational Four-Ball. He was only fourteenth at the Masters but fifth at the U.S. Open. He performed credibly at the 1941 majors, although contending for the title in neither.

Then as suddenly as Guldahl's game had arrived, it left him. They played the Masters despite the war in 1942, and Guldahl scraped together a twenty-first-place finish in the reduced field. Somebody offered him the chance to write an instructional book, and one theory goes that the effort got him to thinking about swing mechanics, something he had not previously done.

Others questioned his continued fire, an easy topic to raise given his deliberately stoic demeanor. "He went about his golf most of the time in a solemn, sluggish way that was utterly lacking in showmanship," famed American golf writer Herbert Warren Wind said of him.[11] Guldahl dismissed that theory. "Behind my so called poker face, I'm burning up," he said. Others suggested back problems. This much is known: possibly the best golfer of the last half of the 1930s—better than contemporaries Nelson, Snead or Hogan—Ralph Guldahl left the tour in 1942, not yet thirty years old, returning only for the majors and those only until 1950.

Guldahl in the Clubhouse

Tournament	Finish	Score	Z score
1936 Western Open	1st	274	–1.83
1937 Masters	2nd	285	–1.75
1937 U.S. Open	1st	281	–2.54
1937 British Open	T-11	300	–0.84
1937 Western Open	1st	288	–2.12
1938 Masters	T-2	287	–1.65
1938 U.S. Open	1st	284	–2.49
1938 Western Open	1st	279	–2.79
1939 Masters	1st	279	–1.84
1940 PGA	semifinals	match play	–2.37

Note: Average Z score: –2.02. Effective stroke average: 69.00.

Masters: 8 starts, 1 win (1939), –4.76
U.S. Open: 15 starts, 2 wins (1937, 1938), –9.43
British Open: 1 start, 0 wins, –0.84
Western Open: 11 starts, 3 wins (1936, 1937, 1938), –9.94
PGA Championship: 5 starts, 0 wins, –6.44
Total (41 starts): –31.41

Year	Score
1931	-0.09
1932	0.87
1933	-1.73
1934	-0.91
1935	0.45
1936	-1.54
1937	-1.65
1938	-2.01
1939	-1.31
1940	-1.22
1941	-0.72
1942	1.60
1946	1.07
1947	0.11
1948	0.32
1949	0.01
1950	-0.71

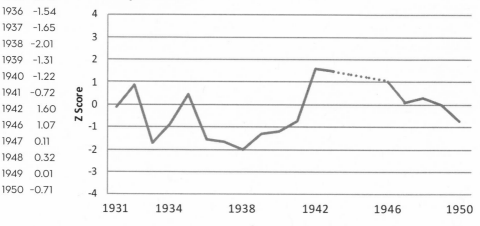

Ralph Guldahl

Byron Nelson

Number 21 Peak, Number 11 Career

Byron Nelson is today recalled as the man who dominated professional golf in 1945, winning a record eleven consecutive tournaments and eighteen overall. Nobody's ever had a season approaching that, and the fact that it occurred during a "war year" only fuels the speculation regarding precisely how good Nelson actually was.

The truth is that Nelson enjoyed his best years immediately prior to World War II, a period when he stood astride a maturing game replete with genuine stars: a young and vibrant Sam Snead, front-rankers Henry Picard and Ralph Guldahl, and veterans such as Harry Cooper, Gene Sarazen, and Craig Wood.

Nelson came out of the Texas ranch country to beat them all with a swing often characterized as close to perfection. He was the picture of

languid repetition, so much so that when the United States Golf Association developed a mechanical golf club and ball tester, it christened
the robot "Iron Byron."

As a youth, Nelson took up caddying at a Fort Worth club, where
he shared bag duties with a young Ben Hogan. Tall and lanky, Nelson's
development paralleled the rise in popularity of steel-shafted clubs as a
replacement for hickory. Nelson always felt one of the keys to his early
success was his quick understanding that the new technology could be
put to greater use by incorporating the larger hip and leg muscles with
a fuller turn rather than the more wristy approach in vogue at the time.
He was pioneering the modern golf swing.

He turned pro at age twenty in 1932, although the professional world
initially took very light notice of the fact. For three years he won nothing
whatsoever, failing to make the cut in his only U.S. Open appearance, in
1933. Nelson finally emerged in 1935 as champion of the New Jersey State
Open, an achievement that impressed Bobby Jones enough to extend
him an invitation to play at that year's Masters. There Nelson surprised
the field—possibly including himself—by tying for ninth place. The Masters proved his springboard. Invited back in 1936, he tied for thirteenth.
That won him a ticket back for 1937, and this time he won, seizing the
opportunity for a two-stroke margin when Guldahl floundered around
Amen Corner in the final round.

The Masters title legitimized Nelson's status and gave him all the confidence he needed. His first credible showing at the U.S. Open—a tie
for twentieth—followed in a few weeks. When the U.S. Ryder Cup team
included the British Open in its schedule that summer, Nelson made his
only appearance in that event and finished fifth, the top American ahead
of teammates Ed Dudley, Snead, Picard, Guldahl, and Shute.

The 1939 U.S. Open at Philadelphia Country Club is recalled today
for Sam Snead's final-hole collapse, but some attention ought to be paid
to Nelson. Snead's fall actually left three players—Nelson, Denny Shute,
and Craig Wood—deadlocked for the championship, forcing what was
supposed to be an eighteen-hole playoff the next day. It turned into a
thirty-six-hole playoff when Nelson and Wood finished the initial eighteen even at 68. There are those who believe Byron effectively decided
the second playoff on the fourth hole, a 453-yard par 4 when his one

iron fairway shot found the bottom of the cup for an eagle 2. He beat Wood by 3 strokes. Four more top-five finishes followed until the war suspended major competitions following the 1942 Masters, won, by the way, by Nelson, in a playoff from his old caddie foe, Hogan. At match play, he had already added the 1940 PGA.

It is often tempting to speculate what great players might have done had not outside forces intervened against their primes, but in Nelson's case the speculation is truly delicious. He was twenty-nine when the United States entered the war, in the absolute prime of his athletic life. A statistical projection of his performance in the major events for the years immediately prior to and following the war suggests Nelson might have consistently posted scores in the range of 96 percent of the field average, and given normal standard deviations for front-rank players of about 0.03, it's fair to assume he would have dipped down to 93 or 94 percent a couple times in the seven stateside majors canceled due to the war. Assuming the field performed as it did in the 1941 tournaments—298 at Augusta and 303 in the Open—that could have brought Nelson in as low as 277, a record in either event. That level of performance generally translates to Z scores in the range of −1.95. Among majors (counting the Western Open) that Nelson routinely played in, there were eleven war-induced cancellations. Give Nelson his projected −1.95 average in those eleven events, and he would leap to fourth on the all-time career chart.

The speculation is moderated only slightly by how Nelson actually did during what remained of the war-reduced tour. In seventy-five starts from 1944 to the end of 1946, he won thirty-four times and finished second sixteen times, climaxed of course by the singular 1945 season. He won the only major held that summer, the PGA, and between 1944 and 1946 finished out of the top ten only once. During the five war-year "majors" that were actually contested—the 1942 Masters, PGA, and Western and the 1944 and 1945 PGA—Nelson's average Z score was −1.33.

Engaged increasingly deeply in his ranching interests, Nelson gradually pulled back from his commitment to professional golf, although the record demonstrates his retreat was not for receding skills. He lost a playoff to Lloyd Mangrum for the 1946 U.S. Open championship, that playoff occasioned by a freak penalty assessed against Nelson during the third round. On the thirteenth hole, one of the marshals holding back the crowd with a rope got closer than he should have to Nelson's ball. Nelson's caddie, fighting through the crowds, ducked under the rope and accidentally kicked the unseen ball, drawing the penalty. After the U.S. Open playoff loss to Mangrum, Nelson limited himself almost exclusively to the Masters. Yet he was good enough to beat the four-round average there annually until 1960, finishing second, 2 strokes behind Jimmy Demaret, in 1947 and eighth in 1948.

Nelson in the Clubhouse

Tournament	Finish	Score	Z score
1937 Masters	1st	283	–2.00
1937 British Open	5th	296	–1.42
1937 PGA	quarterfinals	match play	–1.72
1938 PGA	quarterfinals	match play	–2.36
1939 U.S. Open	1st	284	–1.92
1939 Western Open	1st	281	–2.13
1939 PGA	2nd	match play	–3.08
1940 PGA	1st	match play	–1.58
1941 Western Open	T-2	278	–1.89
1941 Masters	2nd	283	–1.75

Note: Average Z score: –1.98. Effective stroke average: 69.06.

NELSON'S CAREER RECORD (1933–61)

Masters: 23 starts, 2 wins (1937, 1942), –16.87
U.S. Open: 9 starts, 1 win (1939), –0.29
British Open: 2 starts, 0 wins, –0.95
PGA Championship: 9 starts, 2 wins (1940, 1945), –17.07
Western Open: 7 starts, 1 win (1939), –9.71
Total (50 starts): –44.88

Byron Nelson

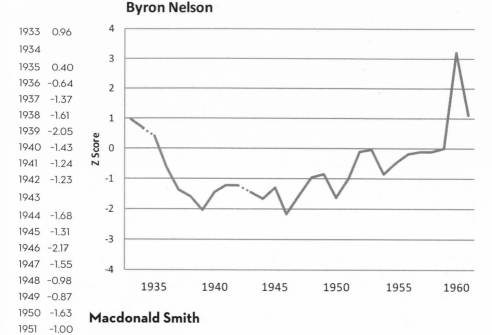

Year	Z Score
1933	0.96
1934	
1935	0.40
1936	-0.64
1937	-1.37
1938	-1.61
1939	-2.05
1940	-1.43
1941	-1.24
1942	-1.23
1943	
1944	-1.68
1945	-1.31
1946	-2.17
1947	-1.55
1948	-0.98
1949	-0.87
1950	-1.63
1951	-1.00
1952	-0.12
1953	-0.05
1954	-0.86
1955	-0.49
1956	-0.18
1957	-0.12
1958	-0.12
1959	0.00
1960	3.21
1961	1.13

Macdonald Smith

Number 14 Career

Is it possible for one bad hole to cost a player several major championships? Herbert Warren Wind, the best-known authority on American golf between 1930 and 1970, thought so. "There is no knowing the heights Mac Smith might have scaled in major championship play if he had seized his first golden opportunity in 1910," Wind wrote in 1948. "A par on either the 71st or 72nd hole would have won the Open for the gauche twenty-year-old boy, but he went one over on each hole."[12] Those bogeys threw Smith into a tie with his brother, Alex, and also with Johnny McDermott. The next day, Macdonald Smith watched big brother run away with the playoff.

Wind's theory is based on the proposition that Smith's failure to close the deal as a twenty-year-old in 1910 scarred him for critical situations going forward. He diagnosed Smith as "harried by some psychic injury sustained in his first mishaps that . . . grew into a complex of such obstinate proportions that the harder he fought to defeat it, the more viciously it defeated him."

Obviously, Wind's premise is debatable; plenty of newcomers who lost big tournaments subsequently won other big tournaments. Macdonald Smith was hardly an emotional wallflower following his playoff defeat. He had the breeding: Alex's 1910 Open title was his second, and both of those succeeded brother Willie's 1899 victory. He proved his toughness by serving in the U.S. Army during World War I, returning to the professional tour in 1924 and winning twenty-four times over the next thirteen seasons. A dozen times he finished in the top five in a major, that total featuring three runners-up in addition to his 1910 playoff defeat. He may have bogeyed those final two holes, but he still shot a closing 71 that brought him from fifth place, 4 strokes behind McDermott, to that playoff moment. Two summers later, he came from 4 strokes off the third-round pace to win the Western Open—a big deal in 1912—by 3 shots, overtaking McDermott among others. In 1913, when Ouimet beat Vardon and Ray at Brookline, Smith was among those in the tie for fourth.

The Great War combined with off-course interests to put Smith's game on hold between 1916 and 1922. In addition to his military service, he worked in a shipyard and following the war tried life without golf for a time. He was thirty-three when he resumed golf combat in 1923, tying for twentieth at the U.S. Open and standing solo third in the British Open. One of the quirks of Smith's record is that although a touring pro through the ensuing fifteen seasons, he never teed it up in the PGA Championship, apparently preferring to focus on the American and British national events. He parachuted in and out of the Western Open, winning for a second time in 1925—this time by six shots—but missing it altogether between 1928 and 1932.

Smith's focus on the Opens was well directed. In 1924 he tied for fourth in the U.S. Open and for third—three strokes behind Walter Hagen—in the British event. When psychologists invite Smith's résumé to their analytical couch, it's his performance at the 1925 British Open they're most likely to cross-examine. Smith carried a 5-stroke advantage over Jim Barnes as the round began . . . but the scenario immediately began to work against him. The tournament was being held that year at Prestwick, by then a small course compared to other tracks of the era, and more than ten thousand fans had turned out, many to watch Smith, who had emigrated to America from Scotland as a youth. The combination created something close to an uncontrollable crush around Smith, who did not handle it well. Knowing he needed merely a 78 to win—his worst previous tournament round had been 76—Smith fumbled through bogey after bogey and made the turn in 42. On the home nine, the crowd's rooting was less impactful than the claustrophobic impact of its mass, as it surged through the inadequate efforts of crowd control. Smith turned in an 82 and claimed fourth place, 3 shots behind Jim Barnes.

When they're finished psychoanalyzing Prestwick, the shrinks eventually will get to Carnoustie, site of the 1931 British Open and, not coincidentally, Smith's boyhood home. This time he was not leading—merely second, three behind Argentinean José Jurado—after fifty-four holes. Yet he came to the sixteenth tee needing to par in for the victory. Instead, he played the holes in 4 over par, and Tommy Armour overtook Jurado for the win. Smith tied for fifth, 3 back.

Other near misses were more forgivable. When Bobby Jones claimed the two professional legs of his 1930 Grand Slam—the U.S. and British Opens—Smith finished second, 2 behind at both Hoylake (in a tie with Leo Diegel) and Interlachen. Following his Carnoustie disaster, he returned for another strong run at the British Open in 1932. Nobody was going to catch Gene Sarazen that year, but Smith's final-round 70 made up 5 strokes on the rest of the field, and he finished alone in second, if 5 behind the victor.

Away from the majors, Smith was borderline dominant. He won four tournaments in 1925, five more in 1926, and at least one annually (save for 1927) between 1924 and 1936.

It was written that Ben Hogan copied Smith's pronated wrists in order to develop his own pronounced draw. Smith must have pronated the heck out of those wrists because surviving videos show him in a pronounced open "body forward" position at impact, one that otherwise would have generated a consistent fade or push. But it worked for Smith.

None of the above establishes that Herbert Warren Wind's estimation of Macdonald Smith was in error. But as with his contemporary Harry Cooper and with Ayako Okamoto, who would follow a half century later on the women's tour, sometimes there simply is no explanation for why unfortunate events constantly combine to undermine a talented player when the stage is brightest.

Smith in the Clubhouse

Tournament	Finish	Score	Z score
1930 U.S. Open	T-2	289	–2.31
1930 British Open	T-2	293	–2.02
1931 U.S. Open	T-10	299	–0.90
1931 British Open	5th	299	–1.50
1932 U.S. Open	T-14	302	–0.67
1932 British Open	2nd	288	–2.13
1933 Western Open	**1st**	**282**	**–2.72**
1934 Masters	T-7	292	–1.02
1934 U.S. Open	T-6	296	–1.55
1935 British Open	T-4	292	–1.77

Note: Average Z score: –1.66. Effective stroke average: 69.53.

SMITH'S CAREER RECORD (1910–37)

Masters: 1 start, 0 wins, –1.02

U.S. Open: 18 starts, 0 wins, –15.92

British Open: 9 starts, 0 wins, –13.64

Western Open: 7 starts, 3 wins (1912. 1925, 1933), –12.57

Total (35 starts): –43.15

Macdonald Smith

Year	Z Score
1910	–1.56
1911	
1912	–2.13
1913	–1.44
1914	
1915	0.94
1916	
1917	
1918	
1919	
1920	
1921	
1922	
1923	–1.23
1924	–1.60
1925	–1.77
1926	–1.23
1927	–0.81
1928	–1.13
1929	–0.29
1930	
1931	–1.20
1932	1-.40
1933	–1.64
1934	–1.45
1935	–0.57
1936	–1.42
1937	0.42

THE TOP-TEN GOLFERS OF ALL TIME FOR PEAK
RATING AS OF THE END OF THE 1930 SEASON.

Rank	Player	Seasons	Z score	Effective stroke average
1.	James Braid	1901–10	–2.18	68.76
2.	Bobby Jones	1926–30	–2.11	68.87
3.	Walter Hagen	1923–27	–2.10	68.88
4.	Harry Vardon	1896–1904	–2.03	68.98
5.	Jim Barnes	1919–23	–1.81	69.31
6.	Jock Hutchison	1916–20	–1.78	69.35
7.	J. H. Taylor	1900–1908	–1.77	69.37
8.	Willie Anderson	1901–6	–1.71	69.46
9.	Ted Ray	1908–20	–1.67	69.51
10.	Gene Sarazen	1926–30	–1.66	69.53

THE TOP-TEN GOLFERS OF ALL TIME FOR CAREER
RATING AS OF THE END OF THE 1930 SEASON.

Rank	Player	Seasons	Z score
1.	Walter Hagen	1913–30	–66.12
2.	Jim Barnes	1913–30	–44.58
3.	Bobby Jones	1916–30	–39.62
4.	J. H. Taylor	1893–1920	–38.70
5.	Harry Vardon	1893–1914	–37.88
6.	Jock Hutchison	1908–30	–34.37
7.	James Braid	1894–1914	–33.63
8.	Willie Anderson	1897–1910	–32.29
9.	Gene Sarazen	1920–30	–30.39
10.	Macdonald Smith	1910–30	–26.80

THE TOP-TEN GOLFERS OF ALL TIME FOR PEAK
RATING AS OF THE END OF THE 1940 SEASON.

Rank	Player	Seasons	Z score	Effective stroke average
1.	James Braid	1901–10	–2.18	68.76
2.	Bobby Jones	1926–30	–2.11	68.87
3.	Walter Hagen	1923–27	–2.10	68.88
4.	Harry Vardon	1896–1904	–2.03	68.98
5.	Ralph Guldahl	1936–40	–2.02	69.00
6.	Gene Sarazen	1929–33	–1.98	69.06
7.	Byron Nelson	1936–40	–1.89	69.19
8.	Jim Barnes	1919–23	–1.81	69.31
9.	Jock Hutchison	1916–20	–1.78	69.35
10.	J. H. Taylor	1900–1908	–1.77	69.37

THE TOP-TEN GOLFERS OF ALL TIME FOR CAREER
RATING AS OF THE END OF THE 1940 SEASON.

Rank	Player	Seasons	Z score
1.	Walter Hagen	1913–40	–73.94
2.	Gene Sarazen	1920–40	–64.13
3.	Jim Barnes	1913–31	–43.58
4.	Macdonald Smith	1910–37	–43.15
5.	Bobby Jones	1916–30	–39.62
6.	J. H. Taylor	1893–1920	–38.70
7.	Harry Vardon	1893–1914	–37.88
8.	Jock Hutchison	1908–30	–34.43
9.	Ralph Guldahl	1930–40	–33.85
10.	James Braid	1894–1914	–33.63

7 Bantam Ben and Slammin' Sam

During the final decade of the nineteenth century, Charles Blair Macdonald fancied himself a pretty good golfer. Although an American by birth, Macdonald had learned the game while studying in Scotland, going so far as to play matches against Young Tom Morris.

Since no golf courses existed in the United States in the 1880s, Macdonald was forced to set his sticks aside. But as the game began to take hold, Macdonald mobilized some buddies and constructed what came to be known as the Chicago Golf Club, the first actual course west of the Alleghenies. In the process, Macdonald established a new American profession, golf course architect, with himself as the guru.

He was, to an extent, stealing from across the sea. Old Tom Morris had been designing golf courses in Scotland and England for decades, and Morris wasn't alone. In the United States, however, the nascent activity was far more rudimentary and haphazard. What Macdonald did was formalize the process, introducing deliberate planning to the design of holes. That "planned" concept saw its first full flower in the United States in 1909 when Macdonald opened the National Golf Links of America on eastern Long Island.

At National, Macdonald's architectural hand could be seen in many of the eighteen holes, which he manipulated around and through sandy coastal land. He designed the par-five seventh and par-three thirteenth holes as replicas and homages to the famed seventeenth and eleventh, respectively, at St. Andrews in Scotland, where he had faced Young Tom. Other holes at National mimicked memorable holes at Royal St. George's, Prestwick, and other popular British-Scottish courses of the day.

Probably more than any other American course, Macdonald's success at National spurred an industry. His collaboration with Seth Raynor led to the Old White at the Greenbrier, the Yale University course, and Mid-Ocean on the island of Bermuda. It also spurred competition.

At Pinehurst in North Carolina, club pro Donald Ross, whose competitive efforts rarely won him more than a fifth-place finish (and a check for eighty dollars) at the 1903 U.S. Open moved into architecture. Ross designed four new courses for his home complex, the reception prompting him to take up the task full-time. He designed Oak Hill in Rochester, Seminole in Florida, and Inverness in Toledo, all of which remain respected today. In the early 1920s, Ross produced Oakland Hills outside Detroit, a layout that gained notoriety when it hosted the 1924 Open at a length of 6,880 yards, more than 300 yards longer than the previous record.

Over the ensuing two decades, golf course planning and design developed into an art. Macdonald died in 1939 and Ross in 1948, but by then A. W. Tillinghast had made his own name at Winged Foot and Alister Mackenzie had opened Cypress Point. In 1934 Mackenzie's collaboration with Bobby Jones produced Augusta National.

The outbreak of World War II stunted course design, as it did other facets of the game, but only temporarily. With its end, Robert Trent Jones emerged to succeed Ross and Mackenzie as the game's foremost designer. Trent Jones opened Peachtree with Bobby Jones in 1948 and the Dunes a year later.

The war had a similar "generational change" effect on the ranks of competitive players. With the exceptions of Sam Snead and Lloyd Mangrum, careers that had flourished before the war ended abruptly. Ralph Guldahl and Byron Nelson both effectively retired. Craig Wood and Lawson Little dabbled seriously in a few of the major postwar events but found that they were no longer factors.

The tour ground along at a halfhearted pace during the war. Rationing of goods and services was one impediment; the loss of some top players to the service was another. Bobby Jones conducted the Masters in 1942 before suspending it, but the U.S. Open was not resumed until 1946.

With the war's conclusion, players whose positions at the cusp of greatness had been slowed or derailed entirely by its arrival—notably Ben Hogan and Jimmy Demaret—marched to the game's forefront. The postwar era also saw the advancement of the professional game across wider reaches of the globe, including Asia, Australia, and Africa. In short order, one man brought those regions into contact.

Bobby Locke

The first true world golfing figure traveled by the rather ungainly name of Arthur D'Arcy Locke. The awkward label proved fitting, for Bobby Locke was an awkward man. He emerged from the South African gold mines to become a player of note in prewar Britain, after the war taking his game to America and then the world. At various times, Locke held the national championships of nine countries on four continents.

On course, Locke was prickly to the point of being annoying. Fellow competitors disliked his personality almost as much as they admired his game, particularly his putting stroke. His professional churlishness may have stemmed from the fact that—as a native South African—he never played in a major competition anyplace near his home. Few appreciated his pace, which was glacial. The odd thing about Locke was that his on-course demeanor was a 180-degree departure from the ukulele-playing, devil-may-care off-course habitué of after-hours spots.

It was said that Locke honed his game as a boy in South Africa by reading Bobby Jones's instructional books. His swing looked like something slapped together across paragraphs: it was wristy, forced, and strikingly inside out, not at all reminiscent of Jones's own. But it worked in South Africa, enabling Locke at the tender age of thirteen to walk away with his homeland's boy's championship. By 1935, still just seventeen, he held the championships of both South Africa and Natal, along with each area's amateur crowns. He reprised the Natal title in 1936 and the South African victory in 1937.

So great was the young Locke's reputation that his employer, the Rand Mining House, shipped him off to its London office, where his light workload gave him time to mingle with an aging Harry Vardon. Locke debuted in the British Open in 1936, catching everybody's attention with an eighth-place finish. Not yet twenty, he turned pro and tried again in the 1937 Open, tying for seventeenth. An established figure in Britain by the war's onset, he played a few tournaments back home in 1940 before enlisting in his nation's air force.

When the war ended, Locke moved to America to give the more lucrative U.S. tour a try. Due in part to his slow pace, he became less than a fully welcome figure. The hook produced by his severe inside-out swing plane—so consistent he was said to line up as much as 45 degrees off target just to account for the natural ball flight—also drew criticism. But the big problem was probably Locke's performance: he was threateningly good. When the British Open resumed in 1946, Locke tied for second behind Sam Snead. In 1947 he tied for third at the U.S. Open. He finished fourth in that event in 1948 and again in 1949 and then returned to Britain to win a playoff with Irishman Harry Bradshaw for the 1949 Open title. This was the famous "battle with the bottle." On the fifth hole of the second round, Bradshaw drove into the rough, the ball coming to rest amid shards of a broken beer bottle. Rather than seek free relief from the outside agency—which the rules would have allowed—Bradshaw chose to play the ball as it lay in the glass. He failed to move it very far, losing a stroke that would eventually prove decisive.

In one thirty-two-month span, Locke played in fifty-nine tournaments, winning eleven, finishing second ten times, third eight times, and fourth five times. He quickly gained a reputation as the sport's best on the greens.

Spurred by his first major win, Locke remained in Britain to play most of the 1950 season, prompting the PGA to suspend him, allegedly for breaking appearance commitments. Locke thumbed his nose at the Americans by repeating his British Open victory that summer, this time by three strokes over Argentinean Roberto De Vicenzo. When the PGA relented in 1951, the South African deigned to come back on a pick-and-choose basis. He finished third to Hogan at the U.S. Open at Oakland Hills in 1951 but otherwise spent most of his time chasing trophies on the European and South African tours. In 1952 he returned for the first time in three years to the Masters, finishing twenty-first. Locke fared decidedly better in Scotland, winning his third British Open championship by a shot over Peter Thomson.

Locke stood out in his appearance and dress as well as in his play. At a time when brilliant golf attire was coming into vogue, Locke dressed almost exclusively in gray flannel knickers, white buckskin shoes, linen dress shirts with neckties, and white Hogan caps. His jowly features and changeless expression earned him the decidedly unflattering nickname of "Muffin Face."

Locke used an old rusty-headed putter with a hickory shaft, addressing the ball at the toe and striking out at it. The result, as bizarre as it
looked, was the same "hook" on the greens that had become his trademark off the tee. "Very early in my career I realized that putting was
half the game of golf," Locke said. "No matter how well I might play
the long shots, if I couldn't putt, I would never win." It is to Locke that
the aphorism "Drive for show and putt for dough" is ascribed. The putter rarely failed him, one of those occasions occurring in 1954. Locke
came to the final hole of the British Open at Royal Birkdale needing to
hole a birdie putt to tie Thomson. He left it just short and had to settle
for second place.

After 1954 Locke largely confined his major appearances to the British Open, which he won for a fourth time in 1957. Although Locke's
play that week at St. Andrews was as solid as ever, fortune and a
kindly rules official had something to do with the victory. Locke
came to the final hole holding a three-shot lead, his second shot
having stopped just a few feet from the cup. It lay, however, in the
direct line of competitor Bruce Crampton's putt. Locke marked his
ball, moving the mark over the length of a putter head in order not
to interfere with Crampton. But when he putted out, Locke failed to
replace his mark in the proper spot. By rule that violation should have
resulted in a penalty, which in turn should have resulted in Locke's
disqualification once he signed for the lower score. But tournament
officials decided to waive the disqualification, finding in essence that
no harm had been done.

This triumph, a few months before his fortieth birthday, combined
with a serious 1959 car accident to mark the end of the most competitive
portion of Locke's career. Locke made largely ceremonial appearances
at the British Open on and off through 1971, none of them noteworthy.

Locke in the Clubhouse

Tournament	Finish	Score	Z score
1948 Masters	T-10	291	−0.87
1948 U.S. Open	4th	282	−1.61
1948 Western Open	3rd	283	−1.40

1949 U.S. Open	T-4	289	-1.44
1949 British Open	**1st**	**283**	**-1.69**
1950 British Open	**1st**	**279**	**-2.02**
1951 U.S. Open	3rd	291	-1.69
1951 British Open	T-6	293	-1.06
1952 Western Open	2nd	282	-1.45
1952 British Open	**1st**	**287**	**-2.36**

Note: Average Z score: -1.56. Effective stroke average: 69.68.

LOCKE'S CAREER RECORD (1936–67)

Masters: 4 starts, 0 wins, -2.79
U.S. Open: 6 starts, 0 wins, -8.43
British Open: 15 starts, 4 wins (1949, 1950, 1952, 1957), -5.28
PGA: 1 start, 0 wins, +0.71
Western Open: 3 starts, 0 wins, -4.37
Total (29 starts): -20.16

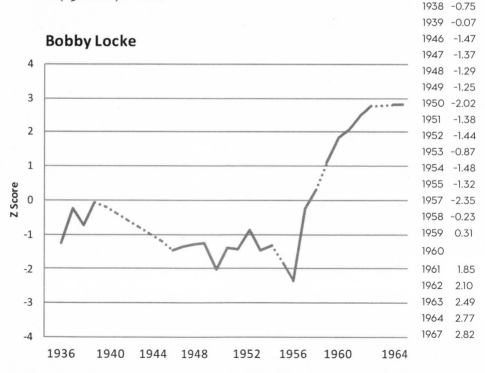

Bobby Locke

Year	Z
1936	-1.24
1937	-0.26
1938	-0.75
1939	-0.07
1946	-1.47
1947	-1.37
1948	-1.29
1949	-1.25
1950	-2.02
1951	-1.38
1952	-1.44
1953	-0.87
1954	-1.48
1955	-1.32
1957	-2.35
1958	-0.23
1959	0.31
1960	
1961	1.85
1962	2.10
1963	2.49
1964	2.77
1967	2.82

Sam Snead

Number 12 Peak, Number 4 Career

With Byron Nelson effectively retired, Lloyd Mangrum at war, and Ben Hogan yet to emerge as a front-rank player, Sam Snead was the face of the U.S. tour as peace resumed. Alone among the great prewar U.S. pros, Snead nurtured and enhanced his reputation into the latter part of the 1940s . . . and well beyond. The result was one of the most lengthy and productive careers in the history of American sport.

Snead emerged as a young pro out of Virginia in 1937 and made an immediate impact. The youngest of five children and a natural athlete, he ran a ten-flat one-hundred-yard dash in high school. He picked up golf watching his older brothers knocking balls around a cow pasture and took a liking to it. A job caddying at the nearby Homestead resort led to an assistant pro's position at the equally tony Greenbrier across the state line in West Virginia. Snead studied golf mechanics hard but never allowed himself to get wrapped up in them. He was a "feel" player. "I try to feel oily," he explained of his swing. At another time he said he knew he was hitting the ball well when "my mind is blank and my body is loose as a goose."

Just twenty-four when he left Greenbrier to try his hand on the tour, Snead was an almost immediate success. In his first full season, 1937, he won the Oakland Open, the Bing Crosby Pro-Am, the St. Paul Open, the Nassau Open, and the Miami Open. Invited to play at the Masters, he turned in a score of 298 that put him in the top twenty. At the U.S. Open at Oakland Hills, the rookie posted a 283 that looked good enough to win and waited to see whether anybody could beat it. Ralph Guldahl did, playing the final eleven holes in 3 under par to consign Snead to runner-up honors.

Still, fans gravitated to Snead in the way they had gravitated to Bobby Jones nearly two decades earlier. "Watching him . . . provided an aesthetic delight," said Herbert Warren Wind. "Here was that rarity, the long hitter who combined power with the delicate manners of shotmaking, this slow-speaking, somewhat timid, somewhat cocky young man from the mountains."[1]

He traveled to Britain with the Ryder Cup team and joined the American delegation at the 1937 British Open, tying for eleventh. Snead won eight more tour events in 1938, although he performed miserably in the majors. But following a second-place finish to Guldahl at the 1939 Masters, Snead entered that summer's U.S. Open as a favorite and held the lead through seventy-one holes. He came to the final one needing just a par for the victory . . . but Snead did not know that. Thinking he needed a birdie, he gambled, made a triple bogey, and shot himself out of a three-way playoff.

Snead won six more times in 1941, and in 1942 he claimed the PGA Championship at match play. A handful of victories on the war-shortened tour followed, and then in 1946 Sam defeated Locke by four strokes in the British Open.

Snead did not return to that event for sixteen years, but the 1946 victory inaugurated what would prove to be his most extended stretch of golf superiority. Even that, however, could not bring him an Open victory. In 1947 he lost in a playoff to Lew Worsham.

Snead opened 1949 by winning the Masters by three strokes over Johnny Bulla and Lloyd Mangrum. In 1949 and 1950 Snead won sixteen tour events, including both Western Opens and the 1949 PGA. It is tempting to argue that more than any other player he benefited from the absence of Hogan, who had been sidelined by a near-fatal car crash in the spring of 1949. But the intimation that Snead could not hold his own against Hogan is plainly invalid. With Hogan's return in 1950, the rivalry resumed, Snead winning the 1951 PGA and both the 1952 and the 1954 Masters. He defeated Hogan in the latter event by one stroke in a playoff.

In more than fifty years as an active competitor, Snead won a record eighty-two official tour events. He led the money list three times, won the Vardon Trophy four times, and played on seven Ryder Cup teams. His final tour victory came in 1965 when, at age fifty-three years and ten months, he beat the field at Greensboro. He was fourth in the PGA Championship at age sixty in 1972 and third in 1974 at age sixty-two.

For a player whose name will be forever attached to the phrase "didn't win the Open," Snead did remarkably well at that event, finishing as runner-up four times. Having said that, Snead's true playground was Augusta National. Not only did he win the Masters three times, but he was also in the top five on four other occasions and beat the field average there seventeen consecutive times between 1939 and 1958. A three-time winner of the PGA at match play, Snead plainly excelled at the one-on-one game.

Snead in the clubhouse

Tournament	Finish	Score	Z score
1947 U.S. Open	2nd	282	−2.26
1948 PGA	quarterfinals	match play	−2.16
1949 Masters	**1st**	**282**	**−2.15**
1949 U.S. Open	T-2	287	−1.85
1949 PGA	**1st**	**match play**	**−2.08**
1949 Western Open	**1st**	**268**	**−2.47**
1950 Masters	3rd	286	−1.85
1950 Western Open	**1st**	**282**	**−1.95**
1951 PGA	1st	match play	−2.34
1951 Western Open	3rd	273	−1.62

Note: Average Z score: −2.07. Effective stroke average: 68.93.

SNEAD'S CAREER RECORD (1937–62)

1937 −0.57	Masters: 23 starts, 3 wins (1949, 1952, 1954), −22.28
1938 0.59	U.S. Open: 22 starts, 0 wins, −17.92
1939 −0.80	British Open: 3 starts, 1 win (1946), −3.56
1940 −0.68	PGA: 22 starts, 3 wins (1942, 1949, 1951), −21.57
1941 −0.21	Western Open: 12 starts, 2 wins (1949, 1950), −3.37
1942 −0.45	**Total (82 starts): −68.69**

1937 −0.57
1938 0.59
1939 −0.80
1940 −0.68
1941 −0.21
1942 −0.45
1946 −0.81
1947 −0.82
1948 −1.39
1949 −2.14
1950 −1.04
1951 −1.49
1952 −0.72
1953 −1.51
1954 −1.53
1955 −1.11
1956 −0.92
1957 −1.35
1958 0.23
1959 −0.84
1960 −0.94
1961 −0.39
1962 −0.21

Sam Snead

Lloyd Mangrum

Number 25 Career

Until Hogan's postwar emergence, the most plausible figure to challenge Snead for supremacy on tour was a dapper, mustachioed man with a steady game. Another in a lengthy line of stars who came out of Texas—think Guldahl, Hogan, and Nelson—Lloyd Mangrum looked more like a leading man than an athlete. But he knew one and only one career path, starting as an assistant to his club pro brother at the age of fifteen and joining the tour at twenty-three.

Following a disheartening debut at the 1936 U.S. Open—he missed the cut—Mangrum picked up experience at minor events. He pushed Hogan to the limit at the 1939 Western Open, eventually losing by a stroke. Invited to the Masters in 1940, he finished second, four strokes behind Jimmy Demaret. He was fifth at the 1940 Open and a consistent top-ten figure from that point until the war intervened.

Mangrum felt its intervention more than most other first-rate athletes. An army sergeant, he saw action in Europe, including the Normandy invasion and the Battle of the Bulge. He acquired a broken arm during the former, shrapnel wounds in the latter. He returned home from the war in 1945 with four battle stars, two Purple Hearts, and no fear whatsoever of facing the tour's biggest names. "I don't suppose that any of the pro and amateur golfers who were combat soldiers, Marines or sailors will soon be able to think of a three-putt green as one of the really bad troubles in life," Mangrum said.[2]

At thirty-two, Mangrum was entering a delayed but rich golfing prime. The 1946 U.S. Open, played at Canterbury Golf Club, east of Cleveland, loomed as a stage for Nelson or Hogan, the co–betting favorites. But when both stumbled down the final stretch, Nelson fell into a playoff with Mangrum and Vic Ghezzi, and Hogan fell out of it. That playoff turned into one of the most laborious and closely contested in major golf history, all three men shooting identical 72s to remain deadlocked after eighteen holes. Under the rules of the time, that forced them into a second eighteen-hole round the same afternoon. On the par-5 553-yard ninth hole—the twenty-seventh playoff hole—Mangrum drove out-of-bounds. But he recovered with a 60-foot putt for a bogey and then followed with three birdies in a four-hole stretch. Mangrum played the final two holes in bogey-bogey as rain and lightning poured from the sky, yet the three back-nine birdies provided just enough cushion. Mangrum won with a 72 to the 73s carded by Nelson and Ghezzi.

Between 1948 and 1950, Mangrum added sixteen tour victories, among them the 1948 Bing Crosby Pro-Am, All-American Open and World Championship of Golf, and the 1949 Los Angeles Open and All-American Open. He was the overlooked playoff loser in Hogan's glorious return from his car-bus accident at the 1950 U.S. Open at Merion.

Mangrum finished third behind Hogan at the 1951 Masters, fourth behind Hogan at that summer's Open, and fourth again at the Western Open. In the top ten at the Masters and Open in 1952, he routed the field at the 1952 Western Open, winning by eight strokes. In 1953 he was third at Augusta, third again at the U.S. Open, and second at the Western Open. The only trip of his career to the British Open that summer yielded his worst performance, a tie for twenty-fourth. In 1954 he was fourth at the Masters, third at the Open, and first at the Western. That gave him four thirds, two fourths, a sixth, and no finish outside the top ten in the Masters and Open alone between 1951 and 1954. Mangrum was the tour's leading money winner and Vardon Trophy winner in 1951, repeating the Vardon award in 1953.

His health eventually did him in. A chain-smoker, Mangrum suffered the first of a series of heart attacks in the mid-1950s. Those attacks reduced his play to occasional appearances after his final victory, at the 1956 Los Angeles Open, and to none at all after 1962. The twelfth attack killed him in 1973. He was not yet sixty.

A grinder who built his reputation on playing in a lot of events and contending in most, Mangrum's results are best illustrated by his performance in the Western Open. He entered all but one between 1938 and 1957, winning twice and finishing second three more times. Only the great Walter Hagen put together a better record at the Western.

Mangrum in the Clubhouse

Tournament	Finish	Score	Z score
1949 Masters	T-2	285	–1.77
1949 PGA	T-3	match play	–2.57

1949 Western Open	T-3	273	−1.79
1950 U.S. Open	2nd	287	−1.66
1950 PGA	quarterfinals	match play	−2.07
1951 Masters	T-3	286	−1.53
1952 Western Open	**1st**	**274**	**−2.44**
1953 Masters	3rd	282	−1.71
1953 U.S. Open	3rd	292	−1.57
1953 British Open	T-24	301	+0.05

Note: Average Z score: −1.71. Effective stroke average: 69.46.

MANGRUM'S CAREER RECORD (1937–62)

Masters: 19 starts, 0 wins, −4.86
U.S. Open: 16 starts, 1 win (1946), −3.14
British Open: 1 start, 0 wins, +0.05
PGA: 9 starts, 0 wins, −8.98
Western Open: 16 starts, 2 wins (1952, 1954), −17.56
Total (61 starts): −34.49

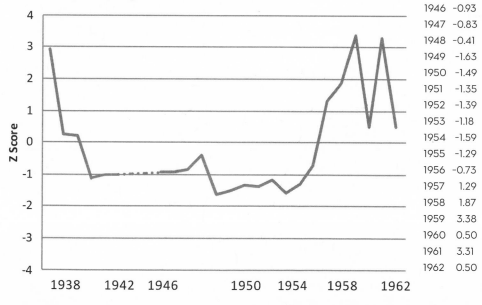

Lloyd Mangrum

1937	2.92
1938	0.24
1939	0.20
1940	−1.12
1941	−1.02
1942	−1.01
1946	−0.93
1947	−0.83
1948	−0.41
1949	−1.63
1950	−1.49
1951	−1.35
1952	−1.39
1953	−1.18
1954	−1.59
1955	−1.29
1956	−0.73
1957	1.29
1958	1.87
1959	3.38
1960	0.50
1961	3.31
1962	0.50

Ben Hogan

Number 9 Peak, Number 10 Career

Certain years take on a magical aspect, and that is certainly true of 1912 in golf. The strange coincidence by which a foursome of golf immortality arrived almost simultaneously actually began on November 22, 1911, when Ralph Guldahl was born in Dallas. Less than three months later, on February 4, 1912, Byron Nelson came to be in Fort Worth. On May 27, Sam Snead arrived in Ashwood, Virginia. That same year produced Ben Hogan, born August 13 in Dublin, Texas. In time the foursome would produce twenty-four major championships, and one can scour calendars from now till the Masters without finding any twelve-month period equaling that total.

Of the four, Hogan was the most prolific, with nine major titles to his credit: four U.S. Opens, two Masters, two PGAs, and a British Open the only time he played in it. This is especially noteworthy because among the four, Hogan was decidedly the latest bloomer and the one initially displaying the least promise.

Moving to Fort Worth at age nine when his father died, Hogan's interest in golf developed out of his experience as a caddie, where he shared the shed with Nelson. He was twenty when he first tested himself professionally in 1932, and the experience nearly ruined him. A long hitter despite his small size, Hogan fought unsuccessfully to control a hook. He missed the cut at the 1934 U.S. Open, went broke, missed the cut at the 1936 Open, and went broke again. By this time, his old caddie tournament foe, Nelson, was the defending Masters champion, while Guldahl held the Open title and Snead was runner-up. A final-round 69 at an obscure tournament in Oakland garnered Hogan $380—badly needed capital—and a shot of confidence. "I played harder that day than I ever played before or ever will again," he said later. His developing practice regimen with tour star Henry Picard also took hold. If there was one thing Hogan could do, it was practice. "Work never bothered me like it bothers some people," he said.

While the results were not instantaneous, they were measurable. Invited to the 1938 Masters, he cobbled together four passable rounds to finish in a tie for twenty-fifth place at 301. The U.S. Open at Cherry Hills, a repeat victory for Guldahl, was another setback. For the third time in three tries, Hogan missed the cut. He did win the Hershey Four-Ball—the first of sixty-four championships he would eventually accumulate—and landed a top-ten finish at the 1939 Masters. His showing at the 1939 Open was unremarkable—a score of 308 and a sixty-second-place standing, 24 strokes behind Nelson—but at least he lasted all four rounds.

The war's intervention obscured Hogan's slow, steady progress, which included top-ten finishes in the final three Masters and two Opens before those events were halted. He missed thirteen major tournaments during the war, most of which were canceled entirely. Based on his prewar performance, projections suggest he might have dominated those events, compiling Z scores in excess of –2.00. That's contender level. Those watching closely could see the signs: between 1940 and 1942, Hogan won thirteen tour titles, although almost all of them were at minor events.

With the war's end, Hogan emerged with a game viewed by many as machinelike. Some ascribed the improvement to a weakened left hand that turned his unpredictable hook into a controlled fade. Hogan was more mysterious, asserting merely that his interminable practice sessions had uncovered "a secret."

The record verified that something was afoot. He won ten times in 1946 alone, including the PGA, Colonial Invitational, and the Western Open, the latter by 4 strokes over Mangrum. Equally impressively, he was second at the Masters and third at the U.S. Open. More of the same followed in 1947, with wins at Los Angeles, Phoenix, Colonial, the World Championship of Golf, and Miami. He was again top five at both Augusta and the U.S. Open and in the fall captained the victorious Ryder Cup team. In 1948 Hogan underscored his breakthrough with an opening 67 at the Open at Riviera, using that as a springboard to a record four-run total of 276 and a 2-stroke victory. Nine more tour victories, including the U.S. Open at Riviera, the PGA, and the Western, strongly suggested that Hogan had supplanted Snead as the game's premier figure.

What such a dominant player entering such a late and full prime might have done in 1949 will forever remain unknown. On February 2, Hogan and his wife, Valerie, were severely injured when a Greyhound bus crashed head-on into their car. He was sidelined for fourteen months, not returning until the 1950 Masters, where he trailed Jim Ferrier by just

2 strokes after three rounds. But a Sunday 76—perhaps attributable to the physical grind—dropped him into a tie for fourth place. It also solidified the suspicion among many that Hogan might never fully return to championship form.

At the U.S. Open that June at Merion, he entered the final thirty-six-hole Saturday in fourth place, 2 shots behind Dutch Harrison. His morning 72 placed him third, 2 shots behind Mangrum, and 1 behind Harrison. Fighting into the lead at the turn of the afternoon session, he felt his knees buckle on number 12, and he wobbled with three straight back-nine bogeys. Hogan came to the final hole, a 454-yard par 4, needing par to force a playoff with Mangrum and George Fazio. He drove the center of the fairway and then struck one of the game's iconic shots—a perfect one-iron to the center of the green—to force the playoff. The next day Hogan shot 69 to win that playoff by 4 shots.

Either befitting his age or as a concession to his injuries, Hogan reduced his playing schedule after 1950. He never again played at the Western Open, and three of his five subsequent victories on the nonmajor portion of the tour came at his home club, Colonial. Yet as Hogan played less, he played better. In 1951 he finally won the Masters and followed that by taming the Oakland Hills "monster" to win his third U.S. Open, this time by 2 strokes. His 1953 season is the equal of any. A 5-stroke victory at Augusta, he humiliated the field at the U.S. Open at Oakmont, recording a 283 that was 6 shots superior to Snead, the runner-up, and 19 below the field average of 302. Then Hogan, who had never played in the British Open before, gave Carnoustie a try. The result was a 4-stroke triumph. For the three majors cumulatively, Hogan recorded a dominance score of 93.2. In 2000, when Tiger Woods won three of the four major events, his dominance score was 94.4. It is at least an arguable proposition that nobody has ever been better in the majors than Hogan was in 1953.

The British Open title was Hogan's ninth and final major victory, but it was not his last shot at contention. Now forty-two, he lost to Snead in a playoff at the 1954 Masters, ran second to Cary Middlecoff at the 1955 Masters, and lost a playoff to club pro Jack Fleck at the 1955 U.S. Open. He lost to Middlecoff by a stroke again in the 1956 Open.

Hogan's career record trails Nicklaus so substantially at least in part due to events out of Hogan's control. The crash cost him a full season and probably reduced the number of his subsequent appearances. The war knocked out most of four more years, and the exigencies of cross-ocean travel and scheduling discouraged him from playing in more than a single British Open. Nicklaus played in 28 British Opens by age fifty and 112 majors overall, twice as many as Hogan. To the extent one chooses to believe projections, they speculate that the combined impact of the war and the 1949 crash cost Hogan the opportunity to participate in 17 major events, at which he might have improved his career Z score by close to 40 points. Hogan presently stands tenth on the career chart; give him those 40 points, and he leaps to second, behind only Nicklaus.

Hogan in the Clubhouse

Tournament	Finish	Score	Z score
1950 Masters	T-4	288	-1.62
1950 U.S. Open	1st	287	-1.66
1951 Masters	1st	280	-2.17
1951 U.S. Open	1st	287	-2.39
1952 Masters	T-7	293	-1.29
1952 U.S. Open	3rd	286	-1.70
1953 Masters	1st	274	-2.60
1953 U.S. Open	1st	283	-2.98
1953 British Open	1st	282	-2.15
1954 Masters	2nd	289	-1.76

Note: Average Z score: -2.13. Effective stroke average: 68.84.

HOGAN'S CAREER RECORD (1938–62)

Masters: 21 starts, 2 wins (1951, 1953), -18.47
U.S. Open: 18 starts, 4 wins (1948, 1950, 1951, 1953), -22.38
British Open: 1 start, 1 win (1953), -2.15
PGA: 8 starts, 1 win (1948), -5.11
Western Open: 7 starts, 2 wins (1946, 1948), -4.98
Total (55 starts): -53.09

Ben Hogan

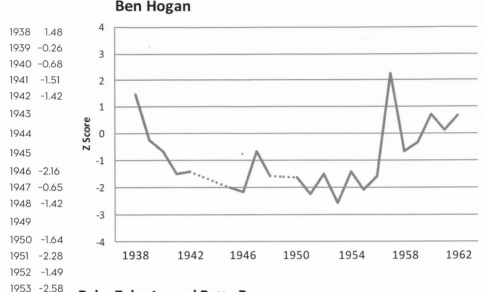

1938	1.48
1939	-0.26
1940	-0.68
1941	-1.51
1942	-1.42
1943	
1944	
1945	
1946	-2.16
1947	-0.65
1948	-1.42
1949	
1950	-1.64
1951	-2.28
1952	-1.49
1953	-2.58
1954	-1.44
1955	-2.08
1956	-1.58
1957	2.26
1958	-0.68
1959	-0.35
1960	0.73
1961	0.14
1962	0.67

Babe Zaharias and Patty Berg

Number 23 Career and Number 3 Career, Respectively

The accomplishments of these two founding figures from the Ladies Professional Golf Association certainly justify separate consideration. Yet their careers were so inextricably overlapping, their competitions so headline grabbing, that the temptation for a joint assessment is overwhelming.

Zaharias was the older of the two by seven years, having been born in 1911 in Port Arthur, Texas. Yet the Babe's international success at her first career—Olympic track and field star—meant they arrived at the attention of the golfing public virtually simultaneously. Following her victories at the 1932 Los Angeles Olympics, Zaharias dabbled in various efforts to translate her fame into some sort of paying proposition before finding that she was a natural at golf. She entered the inaugural Titleholders Championship in Augusta, Georgia, where the field included the nineteen-year-old Berg, an amateur from the University of Minnesota making her own debut on the game's stage. Born February 13, 1918, to a grain merchant who belonged to the Interlachen Country Club, Berg turned her own focus to golf at thirteen and never stopped. She won the Minneapolis City Championship as a sixteen-year-old in 1934, later calling it "my proudest victory ever."

With that as a spur, she placed second to Glenna Collett Vare in the women's amateur in 1935. The veteran was duly impressed. Asked to rank the upcoming cohort of female players, Vare said, "By all means, Patty Berg first . . . in fact quite a distance ahead of the rest."

Berg played the three rounds at Augusta in 1937 in 240 strokes, three ahead of the field and 21 better than the better-known Babe. Suddenly, the hitherto invisible women's game had two dominant personalities, not one.

The Babe, who married wrestler George Zaharias in 1938, soon signed a contract with the Wilson Sporting Goods Company to endorse golf equipment—making her one of the few women pros at the time. In the amateur-driven game that was women's golf, it also made her ineligible for most every tournament in existence at the time . . . including, for a few years, the Titleholders. That, coupled with the intervention of war and injuries, meant the Zaharias-Berg story line idled through several seasons. Berg returned to successfully defend her Titleholders championship in 1938, this time winning by 16 strokes against a field absent the Babe, and won for a third time in 1939, Zaharias again barred by her professional status from participating. The Babe traded on her name by playing exhibitions and occasionally challenging on the men's tour, making one or two cuts. In June 1940 she teed it up in the Women's Western Open—the most prestigious tournament open to women pros at the time—and scorched through five victorious matches without ever being taken to the eighteenth hole. Berg, having left the University of Minnesota to capitalize on her own burgeoning golf reputation, won the same tournament in 1941. Seriously injured in an automobile crash that December, she missed the 1942 season altogether but returned to repeat in 1943, this time as Lieutenant Berg, whose military assignment consisted of raising morale on the golf course. In neither of her wins did she face Zaharias, also idled by injuries and by her eventually successful fight to recoup her amateur status.

That meant their meeting at the 1944 Women's Western was their first since that 1937 introduction at the Titleholders. It also marked the true start of their head-to-head rivalry. Between then and 1953, when Zaharias was sidelined by cancer, the two would collide at eighteen major events, seven at match play and eleven at stroke play, one or the other of them winning twelve of those eighteen. At the 1944 Women's Western, Zaharias exacted a measure of revenge for her defeat by Berg at the 1937 Titleholders, cruising to the title again without ever playing the eighteenth hole. Berg was ousted in the quarterfinals. Zaharias added a third Women's Western title in 1945, despite waking up on the morning of the semifinals to the news that her mother had died the previous night. She was reported to have tried to make emergency plane reservations home, but finding that impossible on the weekend committed to finishing the event. "I knew mother would have wanted me to win this championship," she told reporters following her 4 and 2 finals win over Dorothy Germain.

Responding to interest generated primarily by Berg and Zaharias, the USGA created the Women's Open in 1946, and Berg won it. At the 1947 Titleholders, the Babe—by then an acknowledged professional competing in a more tolerant atmosphere—bested Patty and the full field, winning by five strokes with Berg seven back in fourth. "The great distance she gets with her shots is just too much for the rest of us to contend with, and I don't mind admitting it," Dorothy Kirby, a two-time Titleholders champion, wrote in the *Atlanta Journal-Constitution* following her runner-up finish, five shots behind Zaharias. The two stars jointly dominated the women's tour in 1948, Patty beating the Babe by a stroke at the Titleholders and Zaharias exacting revenge with an eight-stroke win at the Open—by now contested at medal play. Berg finished fourth, 13 back. That season's Western constituted a fitting and epic conclusion, both players marching through the field to a final showdown, which Berg won on the thirty-seventh hole of the scheduled thirty-six-hole distance. The year 1948 was also the year that Zaharias filed papers to enter the men's U.S. Open at Riviera, but tournament officials squelched that effort, citing a "men's only" provision.

Though enthusiastic competitors, Berg and Zaharias also knew when to team up for maximum impact. So it was that in the late 1940s they provided the impetus behind creation of the Ladies Professional Golf Association, an effort to expand professional opportunities for the game's best women players. Both players were at the zenith of their reputations, especially the Babe, whose boisterous personality was a natural promotional tool. "I'm here girls! Who's going to finish second?" she was said to have made a habit of bellowing as she entered the locker room prior to tournaments. In 1950 Zaharias swept all three of the events that would come to be considered women's majors, taking the Titleholders by eight strokes, the Open by nine, and winning the Western after ousting Berg 1-up in the semifinals. It was the Babe's eighth of an eventual ten major championships; Berg by then had nine of her eventual fifteen. Patty added a tenth in 1951, capturing the Western after famously taking out Zaharias 1-up in a pulsating second-round battle punctuated by the Babe's very verbal run-in with photographers. On the second hole, Zaharias drove into a bunker, blasted out, and missed the green with her third. "Okay, I suppose now you'll want another picture," she snapped at a photog she believed had distracted her on her swing. Striking an indifferent approach to the green, she angrily picked up her ball, telling Berg, "You can have this one, Patty; I can't do anything with all this clicking."

Zaharias evened that score at the 1952 Titleholders, beating Betsy Rawls by seven with Berg tied for third, eight back. Berg got her own revenge at the 1953 Augusta event, winning by nine with Zaharias tied for sixth, 18 strokes distant. It was the Babe's final appearance before her cancer diagnosis. Her return in 1954 was triumphant—a third-place finish at the Titleholders, two behind Berg and nine in back of Louise Suggs—followed by an inspirational third U.S. Open victory. Wearing a colostomy bag, the Babe completed 72 holes in 291 strokes, 12 better than the field. "It will show a lot of people that they need not be afraid of an operation and can go on and live a normal life," she said of her comeback. Noted sports columnist Jim Murray later termed it "probably the most incredible athlete feat of all time, given her condition." The enthusiasm, however, proved transitory; the cancer returned, and by 1956 Zaharias was dead. On that day, President Dwight Eisenhower opened his press briefing by heralding her courage.

Berg by then was thirty-eight, still in her prime, a fact she proved by winning the 1955 Titleholders and Western, claiming both again in 1957 and adding a seventh Women's Western in 1958. It was her fifteenth and final major win. She was the LPGA's leading money winner in 1954,

1955, and 1957; won the Vare Trophy for lowest scoring average in 1953, 1955, and 1956; and was three times voted outstanding woman athlete of the year by the Associated Press. She was also the first woman to win $100,000 in career earnings. "The perfect golfer for a woman," Mickey Wright called her.

The performances of Berg and Zaharias between the mid-1930s and the mid-1950s marked the most sustained era of joint dominance since the days of the British Triumvirate. Across the arc of their careers, Zaharias and Berg competed in the same field twenty-two times, fittingly each finishing ahead of the other in eleven. Babe won eight of those twenty-two events, and Patty won seven, leaving just seven others for the field. Between 1946 and 1955, Berg or Zaharias won at least one major championship nine times, the sole exception being 1949.

Zaharias in the Clubhouse

Tournament	Finish	Score	Z score
1946 Women's Western	quarterfinals	match play	–1.66
1947 Titleholders	1st	304	–1.84
1948 U.S. Open	1st	300	–1.58
1948 Women's Western	2nd	match play	–1.74
1949 Titleholders	4th	304	–1.20
1949 U.S. Open	2nd	305	–1.26
1949 Women's Western	quarterfinals	match play	–1.17
1950 Titleholders	1st	291	–2.91
1950 U.S. Open	1st	291	–1.83
1950 Women's Western	1st	match play	–1.35

Note: Average Z score: –1.65. Effective stroke average: 69.54.

ZAHARIAS'S CAREER RECORD (1940–55)

Titleholders: 10 starts, 3 wins (1947, 1950, 1952), –11.48
U.S. Open: 6 starts, 3 wins (1948, 1950, 1954), –7.78
Women's Western Open: 11 starts, 4 wins (1940, 1944, 1945, 1950), –16.51.
Total (27 starts): –35.77

Babe Zaharias

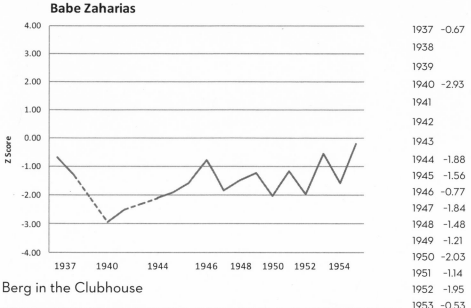

1937	-0.67
1938	
1939	
1940	-2.93
1941	
1942	
1943	
1944	-1.88
1945	-1.56
1946	-0.77
1947	-1.84
1948	-1.48
1949	-1.21
1950	-2.03
1951	-1.14
1952	-1.95
1953	-0.53
1954	-1.57
1955	-0.19

Berg in the Clubhouse

Tournament	Finish	Score	Z score
1953 Titleholders	**1st**	**294**	**-2.62**
1953 U.S. Open	3rd	303	-1.72
1954 Titleholders	2nd	300	-1.49
1955 Titleholders	**1st**	**291**	**-2.29**
1955 Western Open	5th	307	-1.59
1956 LPGA	2nd	291	-1.91
1956 Titleholders	2nd	303	-1.90
1957 Western Open	**1st**	**291**	**-1.92**
1957 Titleholders	**1st**	**296**	**-2.23**
1957 U.S. Open	2nd	305	-1.49

Note: Average Z score: -1.92. Effective stroke average: 69.15.

BERG'S CAREER RECORD (1935-68)

U.S. Amateur: 4 starts, 1 win (1938), -2.39

Titleholders: 23 starts, 7 wins (1937, 1938, 1939, 1948, 1953, 1955, 1957.) -25.27

U.S. Open: 23 starts, 1 win (1946). -13.32.

LPGA: 11 starts, 0 wins, -4.93

Western Open: 23 starts. 7 wins (1941, 1943, 1948, 1951, 1955, 1957, 1958). −27.30.

Total (84 starts): −73.21

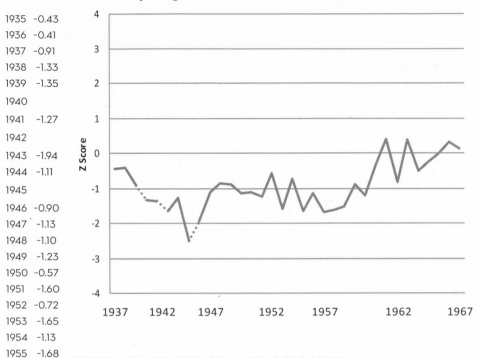

Patty Berg

1935	−0.43
1936	−0.41
1937	−0.91
1938	−1.33
1939	−1.35
1940	
1941	−1.27
1942	
1943	−1.94
1944	−1.11
1945	
1946	−0.90
1947	−1.13
1948	−1.10
1949	−1.23
1950	−0.57
1951	−1.60
1952	−0.72
1953	−1.65
1954	−1.13
1955	−1.68
1956	−1.62
1957	−1.52
1958	−0.88
1959	−1.20
1960	−0.33
1961	0.40
1962	−0.81
1963	0.39
1964	−0.50
1965	−0.24
1966	−0.03
1967	0.32
1968	0.13

THE TOP-TEN GOLFERS OF ALL TIME FOR PEAK RATING AS OF THE END OF THE 1950 SEASON.

Rank	Player	Seasons	Z score	Effective stroke average
1.	James Braid	1901–10	−2.18	68.76
2.	Bobby Jones	1926–30	−2.11	68.87
3.	Walter Hagen	1923–27	−2.10	68.88
4.	Harry Vardon	1896–1904	−2.03	68.98
5.	Ralph Guldahl	1936–40	−2.02	69.00
6.	Sam Snead	1946–50	−2.01	69.01
7.	Byron Nelson	1937–41	−1.984	69.06

8.	Gene Sarazen	1929–33	–1.976	69.06
9.	Ben Hogan	1946–50	–1.86	69.23
10.	Jim Barnes	1919–23	–1.81	69.31

THE TOP-TEN GOLFERS OF ALL TIME FOR CAREER
RATING AS OF THE END OF THE 1950 SEASON.

Rank	Player	Seasons	Z score
1.	Walter Hagen	1913–40	–73.94
2.	Gene Sarazen	1920–50	–57.54
3.	Byron Nelson	1933–50	–46.28
4.	Jim Barnes	1913–31	–44.58
5.	Macdonald Smith	1910–37	–43.15
6.	Bobby Jones	1916–30	–39.62
7.	J. H. Taylor	1893–1920	–38.70
8.	Harry Vardon	1893–1914	–37.88
9.	Sam Snead	1937–50	–34.69
10.	Jock Hutchison	1908–30	–34.43

THE TOP-TEN GOLFERS OF ALL TIME FOR PEAK
RATING AS OF THE END OF THE 1960 SEASON.

Rank	Player	Seasons	Z score	Effective stroke average
1.	James Braid	1901–10	–2.18	68.76
2.	Ben Hogan	1950–54	–2.13	68.84
3.	Bobby Jones	1926–30	–2.11	68.87
4.	Walter Hagen	1923–27	–2.10	68.88
5.	Sam Snead	1947–51	–2.06	68.94
6.	Ralph Guldahl	1936–40	–2.02	69.00
7.	Harry Vardon	1896–1904	–2.03	68.98
8.	Byron Nelson	1937–41	–1.984	69.06
9.	Gene Sarazen	1929–33	–1.976	69.06
10.	Patty Berg	1953–57	–1.92	69.15

THE TOP-TEN GOLFERS OF ALL TIME FOR CAREER
RATING AS OF THE END OF THE 1960 SEASON.

Rank	Player	Seasons	Z score
1.	Walter Hagen	1913–40	–73.94
2.	Patty Berg	1935–60	–69.14
3.	Sam Snead	1937–60	–66.72
4.	Gene Sarazen	1920–51	–58.09
5.	Louise Suggs	1941–60	–55.88
6.	Ben Hogan	1938–60	–54.03
7.	Byron Nelson	1933–60	–46.01
8.	Jim Barnes	1913–31	–44.58
9.	Macdonald Smith	1910–37	–43.15
10.	Bobby Jones	1916–30	–39.62

8   The King, Some Queens, and a Black Prince

The fortuitous combination of factors powering golf's 1950s boom began with the nation's suburban shift. Many of those migrating baby-boom families, seeking a more relaxed ranch-house lifestyle, incorporated visions of a country club, or a reasonable facsimile, into their great American dream.

The arrival of television—and in particular the first telecasts of major golf tournaments in the mid-1950s—fueled this fantasy. So did the emergence of a walking, talking all-American he-man to energize this willing golf audience. Arnold Palmer came out of Wake Forest University in the mid-1950s at precisely the correct instant to energize the game's growing popularity. Palmer sometimes played golf like he was clearing a forest, with a reckless slash-and-grab style that alternately landed him in and out of trouble. But his success conveyed the message to would-be golfers that they need not master all the technical intricacies of the game. Golf, as Palmer demonstrated, could simply be enjoyed.

Pat Ward-Thomas, golf writer for the *Manchester Guardian* during the early 1960s, was among those noting the rare combination of talent and personality. "As a driver and long iron player, he has no peers; his pitching is wonderfully firm and always bold, save when strategy dictates otherwise, and his putting under pressure is superb," Ward-Thomas wrote. "If one adds to this technical ability, an active inquiring mind, that rare blend of immense self-confidence and true modesty, the ability to acquire concentration through a relaxed approach, and a truly formidable desire to win that is never outwardly aggressive, there is a remarkable man." He summed up Palmer as "a delightful friendly human being who commands respect and admiration."[1]

Across America, people driven by their fondness for Palmer began plugging into golf as they never had before. Ratings for the telecast of the 1958 Masters, won by Palmer, soared to 6.2, nearly doubling the 3.4

rating received by the previous year's telecast. They would continue to rise, climbing to 9.0 by 1964. With the ratings came cash. In 1955, the year Palmer debuted on tour, the money leader cashed $63,000. During Palmer's prime, that figure rose thusly: 1960, $75,000; 1965, $140,000; 1968, $205,000; 1971, $245,000; and 1972, $430,000.

Arnold Palmer

Number 4 Peak, Number 22 Career

Palmer lacked the cool expertise of a Hogan or a Snead, but he possessed more flair than any player since Hagen. As telegenic as Palmer was, he accumulated a throng of fans wherever he played; in short order this fan base acquired a name, Arnie's Army. The connection between player and fan was more method than happenstance. "I tried to look the whole gallery in the eye," he said.[2]

The son of a club pro, Palmer always wanted to be a golfer. He attended college on a golf scholarship and climaxed his amateur career by winning the 1954 U.S. Amateur. Ready or not, the pro circuit was next.

Palmer's arrival on that circuit could not have been better timed . . . and not merely because people across the country had begun tuning in. The tour itself was on the cusp of profound change. Ben Hogan, its preeminent figure and the winner of three majors in 1953, had reduced his playing schedule to a handful of tournaments. Sam Snead remained active, but in his late forties he was no longer the threat he had been a half-dozen years before. Into that looming void stepped . . . nobody in particular. Journeymen Ed Furgol and Jack Fleck won the 1954 and 1955 U.S. Opens. An amateur, Ken Venturi, nearly claimed the 1956 Masters, losing at the end to the telegenic but unreliable Jack Burke Jr.

Palmer's initial forays into big-time competition had been disasters; as an amateur, he missed the cut at both the 1953 and the 1954 U.S. Opens. But in his first major professional test, at the 1955 Masters, he finished in a tie for tenth place. His showing two months later at the Open at Olympic was reputable, a tie for twenty-first with Masters champion Cary Middlecoff. He was seventh to Middlecoff at the 1956 Open at Oak Hill and seventh again at the 1957 Masters behind Doug Ford. He approached the 1958 Masters with a kind of brash confidence. As his game demonstrated—a one-stroke victory over Ford—that swagger was merited. Although in 1959 he won nothing more significant than the Thunderbird Invitational, a third-place finish at Augusta and a fifth at the Open ushered in one of the most dominant stretches of success ever strung together by one golfer.

Between 1960 and 1964, Palmer lifted his own play and that of the game as well. At the 1960 Masters, his 282—built upon birdies at the final two holes—not only outlasted Venturi by 1 but was 13 strokes below the field average. He fired a final-round 65 at the Open at Cherry Hills to defeat Jack Nicklaus by 2 strokes, following that with a second-place finish in the British Open and a seventh at the PGA. He should have won the 1961 Masters as well but gave it away to Gary Player with a careless double bogey from the middle of the fairway on the final hole. Palmer made up for it with a brilliant performance at the British Open at Birkdale, recording a seventy-two-hole score of 294 that was 15 strokes below the field average. "Throughout the day he attacked the hole," observed John Stobbs, the *Observer*'s golf writer. "He seemed to have no fear of banging his approach putts far enough past to raise feelings of horror in the bellies of ordinary golfers. Not, though, in his."[3]

He won a three-way playoff at the 1962 Masters, again posting a total that bettered the tournament average by 13 strokes. At the U.S. Open played at Oakmont, Palmer and Nicklaus battled to a draw—again 13 strokes ahead of the field average—although this time Nicklaus bested Palmer in the playoff. Back in Britain, Palmer routed the field at Troon, winning by 6 shots over Kel Nagle. On a course that drove the average four-round total to a 9-over-par 297, Palmer fashioned a 12-under-par 276. At the 1964 Masters, he won a fourth green jacket, this time 6 shots ahead of Dave Marr. His 276 was 15 shots below the field average.

Palmer's résumé included sixty-two tour events and seven professional major championships, six of them during that magical 1960–64 run. With a piercing draw and distinctive knock-kneed putting stance, he was an easy player to envision.

He lost as memorably as he won, never more so than at the 1966 U.S. Open at Olympic. Leading by 7 shots with nine holes to go, he set his cap toward Hogan's Open record. Instead, his gambling style allowed veteran

Bill Casper to catch him by shooting a 32 on the back nine to Palmer's go-for-it 39. In the next day's playoff, Palmer again led at the turn, this time by 2 strokes, only to fall apart on the final nine holes. Casper's fifty-foot birdie putt on the thirteenth put him in front, and he won the playoff by 4 strokes.

As it turned out, that Open was Palmer's last best chance at major glory. He never did win a PGA Championship, the one major whose omission haunted him. But his game had yet further highlights. He battled Nicklaus at the 1967 U.S. Open, eventually finishing second, and he made a brave run at the 1970 PGA title, losing by 2 to Dave Stockton. When the U.S. Open came to Pebble Beach in 1972, the forty-three-year-old Palmer finished third to Nicklaus in his prime. His last tour title came at the 1973 Bob Hope Desert Classic.

Palmer in the Clubhouse

Tournament	Finish	Score	Z score
1960 Masters	1st	282	–2.27
1960 U.S. Open	1st	280	–1.97
1960 British Open	2nd	279	–1.87
1961 British Open	1st	284	–2.24
1962 Masters	1st	280	–2.30
1962 U.S. Open	2nd	283	–2.25
1962 British Open	1st	276	–3.15
1963 U.S. Open	T-2	293	–1.72
1964 Masters	1st	276	–2.87
1964 PGA	T-2	274	–2.44

Note: Average Z score: –2.31. Effective stroke average: 68.57.

PALMER'S CAREER RECORD (1955–80)

Masters: 26 starts, 4 wins (1958, 1960, 1962, 1964), –12.81
U.S. Open: 26 starts, 1 win (1960), –9.02
British Open: 15 starts, 2 wins (1961, 1962), –9.96
PGA: 22 starts, 0 wins, –4.30
Western Open: 1 start. 0 wins, –0.58
Total (90 starts): –36.67

Arnold Palmer

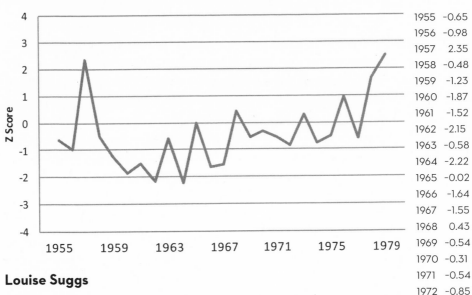

1955	-0.65
1956	-0.98
1957	2.35
1958	-0.48
1959	-1.23
1960	-1.87
1961	-1.52
1962	-2.15
1963	-0.58
1964	-2.22
1965	-0.02
1966	-1.64
1967	-1.55
1968	0.43
1969	-0.54
1970	-0.31
1971	-0.54
1972	-0.85
1973	0.29
1974	-0.75
1975	-0.50
1976	0.96
1977	-0.60
1978	1.63
1979	2.49

Louise Suggs

Number 6 Career

Unlike Patty Berg and Babe Zaharias, whose apexes largely anticipated the arrival of an organized ladies professional golf tour, Louise Suggs came to the golf party almost precisely on time. A twenty-five-year-old defending U.S. and British Women's Amateur champion when the LPGA formed in 1948, she fitted naturally at the tour's forefront. In fact, Suggs already owned three "major" titles before even turning pro, the 1946 Titleholders in her home state of Georgia and the 1946 and 1947 Women's Western Open. In the Western triumphs, she ousted Berg both times, 2-up in the 1946 final and 1-up in the 1947 semifinals. She wasted little time ensuring her professional reputation, claiming the 1949 Women's Western—again defeating Berg in the semis—and the Women's Open by 14 strokes over Zaharias. The Open victory was especially meaningful for Suggs, who resented Zaharias's aura of superiority. "We butted heads," she confessed, describing Zaharias as "your typical barroom brawler. But she couldn't put anything over on me. I'd look her right in the eye. I was just as competitive as she was."[4] A third

Western Open championship in 1949 included a third elimination of Berg, again by 1-up in the semis.

Suggs lacked the flash of Zaharias or the natural appeal of Berg, but she was more than their equal in every other way. Hogan said her swing "combines all the desirable elements of efficiency, timing and coordination . . . appears to be completely effortless." Yet he added, "she is consistently as long off the tee and through the fairway as any of her feminine contemporaries."[5]

Suggs was a consistent presence near the top of the LPGA leader boards throughout the 1950s. She finished second behind Rawls at the 1951 Open and was third at the 1953 Titleholders. That summer she shot 288 to win the Tampa Open, fracturing her own seventy-two-hole LPGA scoring record.

She won the Titleholders again in 1954, this time by 7 strokes over Berg and 9 over Zaharias. A third at the 1954 Open preceded runner-up finishes in three of the four women's majors of 1955. In the fourth, the Titleholders, she had to settle for fourth place. That tournament fell her way again in 1956, as did the 1957 LPGA. So consistent was her performance that of forty-three majors played between 1951 and 1965, Suggs turned in only three four-round cards above the field average.

Suggs loved competition, including events that crossed gender lines. She was among the first to advance the notion that while men were superior physically to their female opponents, women could compete equally in non-distance-related aspects of the game. In 1961 she won a three-day tournament on a par-3 course that included a dozen PGA tour pros, among them Sam Snead.[6]

Whether Suggs might have continued to dominate the tour into the 1960s is problematic. By 1958 a second generation of emerging women stars, led by Mickey Wright and Kathy Whitworth, threatened her standing. But Suggs was not done in by the competition; her early 1960s break with the tour grind—she would henceforth only play in majors—occurred over a fine levied against her for failure to keep a commitment. "I would have paid for her myself," remarked Betsy Rawls, then the

LPGA president, of Suggs's departure over what she viewed as an issue of principle. "I forever regretted it for her, and I thought it was one of the saddest things in the LPGA history."[7] Sad, perhaps, but Louise Suggs could point to a résumé that featured eleven major titles and seventy tour championships.

Suggs in the Clubhouse

Tournament	Finish	Score	Z score
1955 U.S. Open	2nd	303	–1.45
1955 Western Open	2nd	294	–1.26
1956 U.S. Open	T-7	307	–1.02
1956 Titleholders	1st	**302**	**–2.08**
1956 Western Open	2nd	308	–1.48
1957 LPGA	1st	**285**	**–2.18**
1958 Western Open	3rd	299	–1.31
1959 Titleholders	1st	**297**	**–1.90**
1959 U.S. Open	2nd	289	–2.7
1959 LPGA	3rd	290	–1.59

Note: Average Z score: –1.63. Effective stroke average: 69.57.

SUGGS'S CAREER RECORD (1948–72)

Titleholders: 14 starts, 3 wins (1954, 1956, 1959), –12.15
U.S. Open: 23 starts, 2 wins (1949, 1952), –20.60
LPGA: 16 starts, 1 win (1957), –12.91
Western Open: 14 starts. 1 win (1953), –15.87
Total (67 starts): –60.31
Note: Suggs also won the 1946 Titleholders and the 1946 and 1947 Women's Western Opens as an amateur.

Louise Suggs

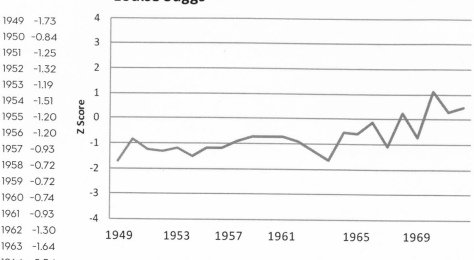

1949	-1.73
1950	-0.84
1951	-1.25
1952	-1.32
1953	-1.19
1954	-1.51
1955	-1.20
1956	-1.20
1957	-0.93
1958	-0.72
1959	-0.72
1960	-0.74
1961	-0.93
1962	-1.30
1963	-1.64
1964	-0.54
1965	-0.57
1966	-0.11
1967	-1.09
1968	0.23
1969	-0.71
1970	1.11
1971	0.28
1972	0.47

Betsy Rawls

Jacqueline Nolte Pung was a good-natured and more than slightly over-weight (she admitted to 235 pounds) Hawaiian who frequented the fringes of contention on the women's golf tour during the 1950s. Professionally, it was a no-frills existence, the entire stakes often amounting to a few thousand dollars and with even a top-ten finish potentially netting less than $100. The field for those small purses was shallow but stacked with dominant talents. Suggs, Berg, and (for a time) Zaharias claimed most of the loot.

Against such competition Jackie Pung was usually good enough to just miss. In her first "major," the 1953 Titleholders Invitational, she placed fifth, trailing Berg by 16 shots. Pung followed with a 71-77 playoff loss in the Open held that June, claiming $1,250 instead of the $2,000 grand prize for a tourney in which only the top dozen professionals cashed any sort of check at all.

Her record made Pung a functional afterthought as ninety-six players teed it up for the 1957 title at Winged Foot in late July. Yet as she came to the eighteenth hole, the Hawaiian journeywoman needed a par 4 to post a 72 for a four-round total of 298 that would claim the championship by a stroke. She made the par, turned in her card showing her correct total, and enjoyed on-green celebrations and photographs befitting a new champion. Then all heck broke loose.

The precipitant was USGA president Dick Tufts's discovery that Pung's scorer had mistakenly credited Pung with a 5 rather than the 6 she had actually made on a hole early in the round. The error, undiscovered by Pung, had not been reflected in the total shown on the card, which had been correct. But as every club championship competitor knows, a golfer is held accountable for the hole-by-hole scores, not for his or her addition. And if a golfer turns in a score on any hole that is lower than he or she actually makes, the penalty is disqualification.

So in a show of adherence to the letter of the rules that would have made the Inquisition proud, USGA officials dismissed Pung from the tournament even though she had submitted her correct, winning eighteen-hole score. Instead, they presented the championship trophy and $1,800 on the eighteenth green to the runner-up, as Pung sat literally within touching distance of the trophy.

What does any of that have to do with Betsy Rawls? She was the runner-up who became the winner.

The opposite of Pung in many ways, Rawls hardly qualified as a surprise champion. Joining the tour shortly after its founding, she remained a perennial front-runner for the better part of two decades. Eventually, that dedication would yield fifty-five career victories—a total ranking fourth on the career list—and four U.S. Women's Open championships, as many as Mickey Wright.

Winning the 1949 Texas Amateur at age twenty-one, Rawls trailed only Zaharias in the 1950 Women's Open. Those showings provided the impetus to turn pro, and again Rawls was a virtual overnight success. At the 1951 U.S. Open, Rawls shot to fame with a four-round total of 293 that was 5 strokes ahead of Suggs and 6 better than Zaharias.

It was no fluke. At the 1952 Titleholders, she placed second to Zaharias, following that up by winning the Western Open, contested at match play at the time. In 1953 she claimed her third major and second Open, defeating Pung in an outcome that presaged their fated 1957 encounter.

As it happened, Rawls's 1957 victory served as the springboard to her greatest period of sustained success. On tour she won four times that year, twice in 1958, and nine times in her best season, 1959. Those titles included her first of two PGA crowns, beating out Berg by a stroke. She breezed to the Western Open championship by 6 shots over Berg and a rising amateur named JoAnne Gunderson. (As JoAnne Carner, she would emerge as one of the tour stars of the 1970s and 1980s.) Rawls nearly made it three majors in 1959, losing to Suggs by a single shot in the Titleholders.

Her fourth women's Open, then a record, came in 1960, a year when she won four times in all. In 1961, the year when Wright proved virtually unstoppable, Rawls was the only reliable competition. She tied Wright for second in the Western, finished third to her in the LPGA, and was runner-up to her at the Open. Although past her prime and limited to a handful of events in the late 1960s, the forty-one-year-old Rawls still had enough game left to thrill nostalgia buffs with a 4-stroke victory over Carol Mann and Susie Maxwell Berning at the 1969 LPGA.

After her retirement, Rawls reduced her success to almost metaphysical, mind-over-matter terms. "I thought I was going to be a winner, and as I went along, winning became easier and easier," she said. "I don't take much credit for it, but I could perform under tense situations."[8]

When she retired from tournament golf in 1975, Rawls became a tournament director for the LPGA and later took over as executive director of the McDonald's LPGA Championship.

Rawls in the Clubhouse

Tournament	Finish	Score	Z score
1956 Titleholders	3rd	306	–1.35
1957 Titleholders	T-7	305	–0.51
1957 U.S. Open	1st	299	–2.08
1959 Titleholders	2nd	298	–1.77
1959 Women's Western	1st	293	–2.10
1959 LPGA	1st	288	–1.84
1959 U.S. Open	7th	297	–1.63
1960 U. S. Open	1st	292	–1.66
1960 Western Open	T-5	306	–0.94
1960 LPGA	3rd	301	–1.31

Note: Average Z score: –1.61. Effective stroke average: 69.60.

RAWLS'S CAREER RECORD (1951–75)

Titleholders: 17 starts, 0 wins, –11.20
U.S. Open: 25 starts, 4 wins (1951, 1953, 1957, 1960), –3.02
LPGA: 20 starts, 2 wins (1959, 1969), –1.65
Western Open: 17 starts, 1 win (1959), –12.93
Total (79 starts): –28.81

Betsy Rawls

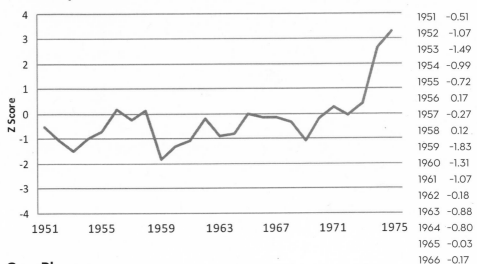

Year	Z Score
1951	-0.51
1952	-1.07
1953	-1.49
1954	-0.99
1955	-0.72
1956	0.17
1957	-0.27
1958	0.12
1959	-1.83
1960	-1.31
1961	-1.07
1962	-0.18
1963	-0.88
1964	-0.80
1965	-0.03
1966	-0.17
1967	-0.15
1968	-0.33
1969	-1.09
1970	-0.21
1971	0.27
1972	-0.07
1973	0.42
1974	2.65
1975	3.29

Gary Player

Number 16 Career

However much he might have wished to lift golf's public profile, Arnold Palmer would have found that task difficult by himself. He did not, however, star in a solo performance. The rise to costarring stature first of Gary Player, then of Jack Nicklaus, intensified the on-course drama. Nicklaus, who had surpassed Palmer as a star by the mid-1960s only to retreat and then reemerge as a more dominant player in the early 1970s, is more properly assessed in the context of the latter era. While Player's career, like Nicklaus and Sam Snead before him, was noteworthy in part for its sheer longevity, his greatest glory days largely overlapped Palmer's.

Physically, Palmer and Player were different figures. At just five-foot-seven and 160 pounds, Player could not boast a classic athlete's physique. Yet Player possessed two aspects in common with Palmer that lifted his golf stature. The first was energy, the other determination. "I had a great deal of talent," he was fond of saying. "But talent alone will only take you so far."[9] In his 1991 autobiography he described himself as "an animal when it comes to achievement and wanting success. There is never enough success for me."[10] Palmer admired Player's ability to get the most out of his relatively small stature. "Watch him closely and you'll see that he's in fine balance when he comes to the ball and that he swings right through it," Palmer wrote of his adversary.[11]

A native of Johannesburg, South Africa, he took up golf following his mother's death when he was eight, and he turned professional in 1953 at age eighteen. Despite his lack of size, Player found it was something he could well. By age twenty, he had won two tournaments in Africa, and at twenty-one he qualified for the British Open. Dressing in head-to-toe black as a source of empowerment, he surprised the veteran international field with a four-round total of 291, good for fourth place.

His arrival in America for the following season turned out to be a reality check. Taken aback by the sheer distance off the tee generated by the best tour players, Player hit the weight and exercise rooms hard. The work paid off when he won the Kentucky Derby Open in May 1958 and finished second to Tommy Bolt at the U.S. Open that June. "Son," Ben Hogan told the twenty-three-year-old, "you are going to be a great player."[12]

Hogan proved prophetic. At the 1959 British Open, Player's 284 was good for a 2-stroke victory. He won at Augusta in 1961, benefiting from Palmer's unexpected double bogey of the final hole. To that point, the only thing marring the South African's résumé was consistency. When not in contention, the young Player displayed a tendency to disappear into the middle of the pack. But that was about to change, the drive to excel and the challenge posed by both Palmer and Nicklaus spurring Player. "Gary, as much as anyone I ever saw, has that thing inside him that champions have," Nicklaus would observe.[13]

At the 1962 Masters, the defending champion put together a stunning 280—a total that would have won any of the last five Masters—only to lose to Palmer in a three-way playoff that also included Dow Finsterwald. His total, although not good enough for the trophy, was 13 strokes below the field average for the week. He placed sixth at the U.S. Open and then won the PGA. From 1962 into 1964, he finished in the top ten in six straight majors.

His brilliant 280 in the 1965 Masters—tying Palmer for second—was easy to overlook in the shadow of Nicklaus's eye-catching 271. But there was no losing sight of the 282 he shot two months later at the U.S. Open at Bellerive, a testing layout on which Nicklaus managed only a 299 and Palmer failed to make the cut. It earned Player a playoff with Kel Nagle, which he won, becoming just the third player ever to win all four majors in his career.

Since his 1959 victory at Muirfield, the British Open—with a missed cut, a withdrawal, and two middle-of-the-pack finishes—had become Player's toughest challenge. He met it in 1966, placing fourth, following with a third-place finish at the PGA. Into his thirties, Player's physical regimen and mental toughness kept him competitive at a stage when contemporaries had lost their edge and contributed to five major titles after age thirty, including the 1978 Masters, when he was forty-two. Player began the final round 7 strokes behind leader Hubert Green, shot 34 on the front side, and then toured the back in 30 for a 1-stroke victory.

Before he was through, Player could lay claim to 163 tournament victories around the world—including 24 PGA tour wins. For twenty-seven straight years, from 1955 to 1982, Player won at least one sanctioned tournament somewhere. His diverse field of accomplishments included titles on every continent where golf is played, a circuit he completed by winning the 1972 Brazilian Open.

Player in the Clubhouse

Tournament	Finish	Score	Z score
1965 Masters	T-2	280	–1.96
1965 U.S. Open	**1st**	**282**	**–2.20**
1966 British Open	T-4	286	–1.49
1966 PGA	T-3	286	–1.60
1967 Masters	T-6	287	–1.22
1967 U.S. Open	T-12	286	–0.94
1967 British Open	T-3	284	–1.51
1968 Masters	T-7	282	–1.13
1968 British Open	**1st**	**289**	**–2.09**
1969 PGA	2nd	277	–2.09

Note: Average Z score: –1.62. Effective stroke average: 69.59.

PLAYER'S CAREER RECORD (1956–84)

Masters: 27 starts, 2 wins (1961, 1974), –14.75
U.S. Open: 27 starts, 1 win (1965), –10.67
British Open: 27 starts, 3 wins (1959, 1968, 1974), –1.24
PGA: 23 starts, 2 wins (1962, 1972), –14.12
Total (104 starts): –40.78

Gary Player

1956	-1.57
1957	0.22
1958	0.08
1959	-1.07
1960	-0.82
1961	-1.00
1962	-1.13
1963	-1.12
1964	-0.69
1965	-1.52
1966	-0.97
1967	-1.22
1968	-1.25
1969	-0.22
1970	0.37
1971	-1.09
1972	-1.24
1973	-0.31
1974	-1.88
1975	0.23
1976	-0.24
1977	-0.43
1978	-0.76
1979	-0.77
1980	0.92
1981	0.66
1982	1.98
1983	1.59
1984	0.30

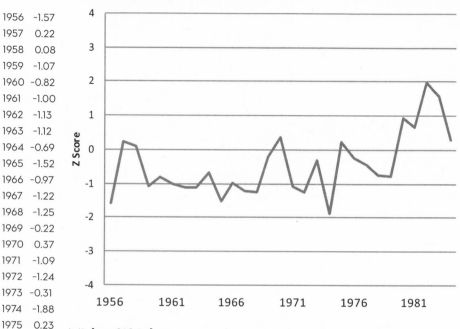

Mickey Wright

Number 13 Peak, Number 7 Career

They called Mickey Wright the female Arnold Palmer in part because her career success ran parallel to Palmer's, in part for their mutual determined attitudes on the course, but also in part simply because of a striking physical resemblance. To many, Wright resembled Palmer's sister.

The one difference may have been in how the two stars handled the remarkable success that came their way at such a young age. Palmer relished his role as the tour's leading man, to the extent of continuing to grasp for it even when it was clear that several of his cohorts—Nicklaus most obviously—had supplanted him. Wright, the face and inspiration of the women's tour through the 1960s—never did truly adjust. As a result, virtually at the top of her game, Wright effectively retired, a victim of what would come to be called burnout.

"The pressure was so great," remembered Kathy Whitworth. "Sponsors threatened to cancel their tournaments if she didn't play. And, knowing that if they canceled, the rest of us wouldn't be able to play, Mickey would always play."[14]

And play well. Over fourteen years of active participation, Wright won eighty-two tournaments. She was the tour workhorse, competing in thirty-three tournaments in 1962, another thirty in 1963, and twenty-seven in 1964. She won thirty-four of those ninety tournaments. But after a few more years of living the demanding tour life, Wright chucked it all, declaring that "I'm not real good as far as wanting to be in front of people. . . . It finally got to where it wasn't tolerable to me." She was just in her midthirties, often a golfer's prime years.[15]

At least Wright left little unaccomplished. A four-time champion of both the U.S. Women's Open and the LPGA Championship, she won the Vare Trophy five times, was the leading money winner four times, twice had winning streaks of four straight tournaments, and held LPGA records for lowest round (62), lowest nine-hole score (30), and most birdies in a round (9). Noted golf writer Herbert Warren Wind described her as Hogan-like in her technical simplicity.

A Californian who took to golf naturally, Wright broke 100 at age twelve, shot 70 as a fifteen-year-old, and attended Stanford, only to leave after her freshman year when the national stage beckoned. As a nineteen-year-old in 1954, she reached the finals of the Women's Amateur, finished fourth in Babe Zaharias's remarkable Open comeback from cancer surgery, and won the World Amateur.

She broke into the pro tour winner's circle at the 1956 Jacksonville Open, adding top-five finishes in three of that season's majors to boot. Wright reprised her Jacksonville victory in 1957 and added two other championships. Barely twenty-three, she won both the U.S. Open (by 5 strokes over Suggs) and LPGA (by 6 over Fay Crocker) titles in 1958, the same season, coincidentally, that Palmer won his first major title. She would add at least one major—frequently more—in each of the next six seasons.

At the 1959 U.S. Open, Wright and Suggs staged a brilliant two-woman battle. On a course that frustrated most of the forty-player field—the average four-round score approached 309—Wright shot 287 to beat Suggs by 2 strokes. She bested Suggs again, by 3 strokes, at the 1960 LPGA, her 292 a full 22 strokes below the field average.

Wright's best year was 1961, when the twenty-six-year-old coasted through the most important women's tournaments. She won the Open by 6 shots over Rawls, took the Titleholders over Ruth Jessen in a play-off, and swept through the LPGA 9 strokes ahead of Suggs. All that stood between her and a women's Grand Slam was a runner-up finish in the Western Open, where she tied with Rawls 6 strokes behind Mary Lena Faulk. She beat Faulk in a playoff to win the 1963 Western and added a fourth LPGA by 2 strokes over Suggs. The Open title came her way for a fourth time in 1964, and a third Western Open championship followed in 1966.

Of the nineteen women's majors in which Wright played between 1958 and 1962, she won nine and finished outside the top five just three times. Wright largely limited her play to the majors beginning in 1969. "She could have won 100 tournaments if she hadn't quit early," Whitworth contended.[16]

Wright in the Clubhouse

Tournament	Finish	Score	Z score
1958 U.S. Open	1st	290	–2.23
1958 LPGA	1st	288	–1.71
1959 U.S. Open	1st	287	–3.01
1960 LPGA	1st	292	–2.22
1961 U.S. Open	1st	293	–2.18
1961 Titleholders	1st	295	–1.66
1961 Western Open	T-2	296	–1.57
1961 LPGA	1st	287	-2.76
1962 Titleholders	1st	299	–1.62
1962 Western Open	1st	295	–1.60

Note: Average Z score: –2.06. Effective stroke average: 68.94.

Titleholders: 12 starts, 2 wins (1961, 1962), –12.76

U.S. Open: 17 starts, 4 wins (1958, 1959, 1961, 1964), –18.91

LPGA: 17 starts, 4 wins (1958, 1960, 1961, 1963), –15.59

Western Open: 11 starts. 3 wins (1962, 1963, 1966), –14.96

Dinah Shore: 1 start, 0 wins, 2.55 (Wright won the Shore in 1973, before it was recognized as a major)

Total (58 starts): –59.67

Mickey Wright

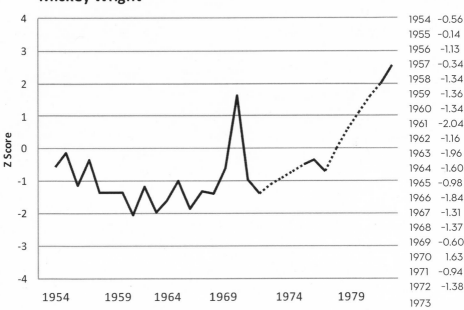

Year	Z Score
1954	-0.56
1955	-0.14
1956	-1.13
1957	-0.34
1958	-1.34
1959	-1.36
1960	-1.34
1961	-2.04
1962	-1.16
1963	-1.96
1964	-1.60
1965	-0.98
1966	-1.84
1967	-1.31
1968	-1.37
1969	-0.60
1970	1.63
1971	-0.94
1972	-1.38
1973	
1974	
1975	
1976	
1977	-0.33
1978	-0.69
1979	
1980	
1981	
1982	
1983	
1984	2.55

Tony Lema

Before Payne Stewart had ever been heard from, there was Tony Lema, possibly the preeminent story of golf talent struck down too soon since Young Tom Morris.

A Marine Korean War vet and club-shop pro, Lema was an Oakland area protégé of Eddie Lowery—yes, the grown-up version of Francis Ouimet's caddie at the 1913 U.S. Open. A wealthy businessman in the 1950s Bay Area, Lowery underwrote Lema's early golf training in exchange for a portion of the winnings, a gesture that paid off when Lema won the 1957 Imperial Valley Open, his coming-out party.

But hard times followed: Lema's pro earnings fell from $10,000 in 1958 to $5,000 a year later and then $3,000 in 1960. By 1962 Lema owed Lowery more than $11,000. His lifestyle contributed to the slump: Lema was widely known on tour as a "live for today" kind of guy, a habitué of whatever club bar happened to be handy. He missed the cut at the 1962 U.S. Open in June, but a victory at the Sahara Invitational that September helped offset his mounting financial losses. When Lema followed by winning at Orange County a month later, he bought a round of champagne for the press corps as a victory celebration. From that moment on, he was "Champagne Tony." From that moment on, he was also a success.

Invited to the 1963 Masters, Lema battled Jack Nicklaus furiously, posting a final round of 70 for a score of 287 and only missing out on a playoff when Nicklaus dropped a three-foot par putt on the seventy-second hole. At that summer's U.S. Open, he finished fifth, 2 shots out of a three-way playoff involving Palmer, Jackie Cupit, and eventual champion Julius Boros. He skipped the long flight to Scotland for the British Open but finished in a tie for thirteenth at the PGA.

Following top-twenty placements at the 1964 Masters and U.S. Open plus victories in three of his preceding four Tour appearances, Lema decided at the last moment to take in that season's British Open, being played at St. Andrews. On his first trip to Europe, Lema arrived in time for just nine holes of practice. His lack of preparation appeared to show when Lema shot an opening 76, putting him 5 strokes off the lead. But a good night's sleep plus plenty of sage advice from Tip Anderson, erstwhile caddie for Arnold Palmer who signed on with Lema when Palmer decided not to make the trip, turned him around. Back-to-back 68s left Lema 7 shots ahead of Nicklaus entering the final round, and he closed the deal with a final round of 70, winning by 5. Britishers, many of whom had barely heard of Lema, were seduced. "It is a pleasure in these days of efficiency and power to see a golfer who combines both with rare grace and elegance of style," the golf writer for the *Guardian* gushed.[17]

The victory marked the high point of a stretch that saw Lema finish among the top ten eight times in thirteen majors and never worse than twenty-second. He added two more tour championships in 1965 and a third in 1966, the last coming in May at Oklahoma City. It was his twelfth title. A few weeks later at the Casper-Palmer U.S. Open at Olympic, Lema tied for fourth.

Lema's strength was his ability to handle tension. Peter Alliss said he combined "an elegant swing of rare beauty" with "grace under pressure" that Alliss compared to Bobby Jones's coolness.[18]

In August 1966, Lema and his wife, Betty, boarded a small plane at Firestone Country Club in Akron, Ohio, where he had finished in a tie for thirty-fourth in the PGA Championship, for a flight to suburban Chicago. He was to take part in a charity event and clinic there the following day. A few miles short of its destination, the plane ran out of fuel, crashing in a golf course water hazard. The player, his wife, the pilot, and copilot were all killed. Champagne Tony Lema was just thirty-two years old.

Lema in the Clubhouse

Tournament	Finish	Score	Z score
1963 Masters	2nd	287	–1.58
1963 U.S. Open	T-5	295	–1.42
1963 PGA	T-13	287	–0.93
1964 Masters	T-9	287	–0.73
1964 U.S. Open	20th	293	–0.42
1964 British Open	**1st**	**279**	**–2.84**
1964 PGA	T-9	282	–0.98
1965 U.S. Open	T-8	289	–1.08
1965 British Open	T-5	289	–1.40
1966 U.S. Open	T-4	286	–1.52

Note: Average Z score: –1.29. Effective stroke average: 70.07.

LEMA'S CAREER RECORD (1962–66)

Masters: 4 starts, 0 wins, –2.74

U.S. Open: 5 starts, 0 wins, –1.70

British Open: 3 starts, 1 win (1965), –4.20

PGA: 4 starts, 0 wins, –0.88

Total (16 starts): –9.52

Tony Lema

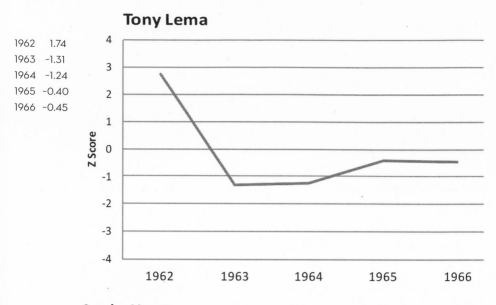

1962	1.74
1963	-1.31
1964	-1.24
1965	-0.40
1966	-0.45

Sandra Haynie

Number 13 Career

For more than decade, nobody on the LPGA Tour was consistently better than Sandra Haynie. Then, still very much in her prime, she gave up the game. But her career was a refutation of Fitzgerald's axiom that there are no second acts in American life. She returned following a three-year exile, having lost little if anything in the way of touch or skill.

The first act was hard to top. Not yet twenty when she arrived on tour, she was an immediate hit, winning two tournaments as a rookie in 1962, adding the prestigious Phoenix Thunderbird in 1963 and winning three more tour titles in 1964. That gave Haynie six by the time she was able to vote. She nearly had a major as well, tying Louise Suggs for second at the 1963 U.S. Open.

Success piled upon success. After top-five finishes at the 1964 Open and LPGA and the 1965 Women's Western Open, Haynie came to the LPGA ranked just behind Clifford Ann Creed—winner of two of the three most recent tour events—as a tourney favorite. They stood tied with each other at 9 under par entering the final round, Haynie outlasting Creed at the finish for a 1-stroke victory. A multiple-event winner every year but one of the next nine, Haynie approached the 1974 season as a tour star.

In her mind, however, Haynie had already begun to question her commitment to the game. The years of practice were one aspect of it. Competitive since age twelve, her hand ached from arthritis brought on by the steady pounding of club on ball. The beginnings of an ulcer, attributable to tour pressure, also stirred. "I'd come out to the course and wish I were someplace else," she said later.[19]

Initially, Haynie's problems did not show up in her game. In many respects, 1974 was her best season. In April she lost the Dinah Shore in a playoff to JoAnne Prentice. In mid-June she survived a four-hole playoff against Gloria Ehret to claim the Lawson's LPGA crown, and a week later she won her second LPGA Championship, by 2 strokes, over JoAnne Carner. It was a dominating performance; her 288 four-round total was nearly 15 strokes below the field average for the tournament.

A month later, Haynie added her first U.S. Open title, this time by a stroke over Beth Stone and Carol Mann. Between June 16 and September 15, Haynie entered nine LPGA Tour events and won six of them, including both majors.

Haynie could hardly have been expected to maintain such a pace, but she gave it a good run. In 1975 she won four more tour events, finished sixth at the Open, and missed winning her third LPGA title by a stroke to Kathy Whitworth. Not until 1976 did her medical problems take a toll on her game, and although she still mustered two runner-up finishes in eighteen starts, Haynie walked away from golf that September, her career seemingly over.

Instead of playing, she threw herself into coaching. Haynie worked with tennis player Martina Navratilova, who was on the way to her first Wimbledon singles victory in 1978. Haynie had been known as a cerebral golfer; now she labored to teach Navratilova the art of winning. The effort had an unexpected by-product; teaching Haynie valuable lessons in self-control. Gradually, as her body rested and heeled, Haynie's interest in competitive golf resumed. After more than two seasons on the sidelines, she tested herself at the 1979 Dinah Shore, but rounds of 75-75-72-77 for a forty-fourth-place finish indicated she had not yet fully regained her competitive spirit. New tests came in 1980, Haynie playing seven early events but garaging her game again after disappointing results.

"'Do I really want to do this all over again?'" she later told the *New York Times* she asked herself. "All the traveling, all the pressure of tournaments . . . 'Are you that crazy?'" She characterized the answer as "Absolutely." So after a cameo appearance on the 1980 fall women's tour, Haynie enlisted for a full competitive season in 1981. Results didn't follow automatically, but her performance in 1982 rivaled everything she had done eight years earlier. Tying for second at the U.S. Open, she fell to a tie for seventh at the LPGA, but entered the season's final major, the du Maurier in Canada, having won the previous week at Rochester. At the du Maurier, the issue resolved itself to a ten-foot par putt on the final hole. Make it and Haynie had her fourth major; miss and she would be thrown into a playoff with Beth Daniel. Even from that distance, the hole, she said, "looked huge. As soon as I hit the putt, I knew it was good."[20]

That victory cemented her comeback. For five more years, Haynie dabbled with the tour, but ongoing physical ailments and age reduced her success. Shortly before her retirement, she passed the $1 million mark in career earnings and then left, having captured four majors and thirty-eight additional tour titles. Not to mention one Wimbledon.

Haynie in the Clubhouse

Tournament	Finish	Score	Z score
1963 U.S. Open	T-2	292	−2.02
1964 LPGA	T-5	281	−1.29
1964 U.S. Open	5th	295	−1.36
1965 Titleholders	T-5	302	−0.78
1965 Women's Western	3rd	297	−1.60
1965 LPGA	**1st**	**279**	**−2.07**
1966 U.S. Open	T-5	306	−1.16
1967 Women's Western	2nd	292	−2.07
1967 LPGA	6th	293	−1.22
1967 U.S. Open	T-4	297	−1.42

Note: Average Z score: −1.50. Effective stroke average: 69.76.

HAYNIE'S CAREER RECORD (1961–89)

Titleholders: 5 starts, 0 wins, −1.12

U.S. Open: 18 starts, 1 win (1974), −13.72

LPGA: 18 starts, 2 wins (1965, 1974), −19.64

Western Open: 5 starts. 0 wins, −4.81
Dinah Shore: 4 starts, 0 wins, 0.00
du Maurier: 4 starts, 1 win (1982), −4.33
Total (54 starts): −43.61

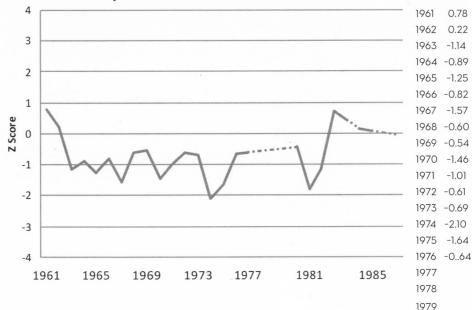

Sandra Haynie

Year	Value
1961	0.78
1962	0.22
1963	−1.14
1964	−0.89
1965	−1.25
1966	−0.82
1967	−1.57
1968	−0.60
1969	−0.54
1970	−1.46
1971	−1.01
1972	−0.61
1973	−0.69
1974	−2.10
1975	−1.64
1976	−0..64
1977	
1978	
1979	
1980	
1981	−0.44
1982	−1.79
1983	−1.16
1984	0.71
1985	
1986	0.15
1987	
1988	
1989	−0.05

THE TOP-TEN GOLFERS OF ALL TIME FOR PEAK
RATING AS OF THE END OF THE 1970 SEASON.

Rank	Player	Seasons	Z score	Effective stroke average
1.	Arnold Palmer	1960–64	−2.31	68.57
2.	Jack Nicklaus	1962–66	−2.23	68.69
3.	James Braid	1901–10	−2.18	68.76
4.	Ben Hogan	1950–54	−2.13	68.84
5.	Bobby Jones	1926–30	−2.11	68.87
6.	Walter Hagen	1923–27	−2.10	68.88
7.	Sam Snead	1947–51	−2.07	68.93
8.	Mickey Wright	1958–62	−2.06	68.94
9.	Harry Vardon	1896–1904	−2.03	68.98
10.	Ralph Guldahl	1936–40	−2.02	69.00

THE TOP-TEN GOLFERS OF ALL TIME FOR CAREER
RATING AS OF THE END OF THE 1970 SEASON.

Rank	Player	Seasons	Z score
1.	Walter Hagen	1913–40	–73.94
2.	Patty Berg	1935–68	–73.21
3.	Sam Snead	1937-62	–68.69
4.	Louise Suggs	1948-70	–62.05
5.	Gene Sarazen	1920–51	–58.09
6.	Mickey Wright	1954–70	–56.58
7.	Ben Hogan	1938–62	–53.09
8.	Arnold Palmer	1955–70	–49.70
9.	Byron Nelson	1933–60	–44.88
10.	Jim Barnes	1913–31	–44.58

9 The Golden Bear Market

Large presences dominated American golf during the 1970s. First among these, of course, was Jack Nicklaus, who emerged from a modest late-1960s pause in his brilliance to dominate the men's tour even more decisively than he had done in wresting attention from Arnold Palmer. He was not, however, alone.

The marvelously entertaining and skilled Lee Trevino chased—and often caught—Nicklaus through the period. In mid-decade Tom Watson rose from his Midwest roots by way of Stanford to stage a series of memorable battles. The most memorable: their classic performance at the 1977 British Open when the two men surged jointly away from the rest of the field.

The women's tour, meanwhile, grew its own personalities and for the first time matured into a stable sports enterprise. The smallest winner's pure on the women's tour virtually doubled—from $11,200 to $22,200—during the 1980s. The largest grew from $37,500 (to the winner of the Dinah Shore) in 1979 to $80,000 in 1989. At the same time, two media darlings with starkly contrasting approaches vied for attention on the tour. Longtime amateur champion JoAnne Gunderson Carner turned pro and took advantage of her power. Then from out of the New Mexican desert, young Nancy Lopez arrived in 1978, smilingly playing her way to nine victories that season alone, five of them in succession.

The intensity of the Nicklaus-Trevino rivalry surfaced during their memorable duel at Merion for the 1971 U.S. Open title. "Jack is the greatest golfer who ever picked up a club," Trevino said of Nicklaus.[1] Theirs was a mutual-admiration society. His one wish going into the tournament, Nicklaus famously said, was that "Trevino never finds out how good he is."[2] Word evidently got to Trevino, who shot a final-round 69 to post a score of even par 280, tying Nicklaus for first. Jack missed a fourteen-foot birdie putt on his final hole, setting up an eighteen-hole playoff on Monday.

This was the famous "rubber snake" playoff in which Trevino tossed the toy at Nicklaus as they waited on the first tee. Both players had a good laugh over it, but if the moment reduced tensions, it didn't immediately show. Trevino bogeyed the first hole, and then Nicklaus bogeyed the second and third. Trevino said later that his big break came from the weather; a storm rolled in as the players completed the fifth hole, delaying action and softening the greens. That helped Trevino, whose lower ball flight was more susceptible in dry conditions to the vagaries of Merion's hard, fast greens. "As soon as it started raining, I was saying, 'keep it up, baby, keep it up,'" Trevino told reporters afterward. When play resumed, the competition ramped up. Trevino birdied the eighth hole, Nicklaus answered with a birdie at eleven, and Trevino birdied the twelfth. A final birdie at fifteen extended the margin to its final three shots, Trevino posting 68 to Nicklaus's 71.

Jack Nicklaus

Number 3 Peak, Number 1 Career

What separates the great players from the golfing pack is often a four- or five-year window of dominance. The history of modern professional golf is laced with talented players—Scott Simpson, Larry Nelson, and Ken Venturi—who capped solid careers with one or even two major titles. But they were frequently in-and-outers. Simpson followed his 1987 U.S. Open title by tying for sixty-second at the British Open a month later. Two months before winning the 1983 U.S. Open, Nelson missed the cut at the Masters. Between that Open victory and 1987, Nelson would add one PGA Championship—but he would also miss seven more cuts. In the five seasons following his fabled 1964 Open victory at Congressional, Venturi made the top five in just one more major.

The great players not only win but dominate over a sustained period. What distinguishes Jack Nicklaus's record from the stellar pack is not merely that he dominated over a sustained period but that he did it twice.

Between 1962 and 1966, Nicklaus was nearly the equal of Arnold Palmer. Arnie won six majors, but so did Jack. Palmer won more tour titles over that 1960–66 period, but the bulk of those came prior to 1963, when Nicklaus was just beginning to burnish his reputation. "It is frightening to think what this boy may do in the years to come," Byron

Nelson told reporters following Nicklaus's 1965 Masters victory.[3] Nicklaus's peak rating for 1962–66—the average standard deviation of his ten most dominant performances in major tournaments for that period—is –2.27. If in 1966 anybody had thought to calculate a Z score for golfers, Nicklaus would have stood second on the all-time list for peak performance, barely trailing Palmer's 1960–64 peak of –2.30.

It would be an overstatement to suggest that Nicklaus's performance slackened dramatically between 1966 and 1970. He did, after all, win both the 1967 U.S. Open and the 1970 British Open, and he consistently beat the field averages in those seasons' majors. But in comparison with the standards he had set, there was a slowdown. Between 1962 and 1966, Nicklaus won six majors with four runners-up and thirteen top fives; between 1967 and 1970, he won two, finished second three times, and made seven top fives. This relative retreat sparked speculation that the man known as the Golden Bear for his physique and blond hair had lost his edge.

Nicklaus may have sensed the same thing, for in capturing the 1970 Open at St. Andrews—surviving a playoff with Doug Sanders—he sounded simultaneously energized and refocused. "There is no place in the world I would rather win an Open championship than here," he told the playoff spectators. Then he added, in what turned out to be a portent, "It is some while since I won a championship . . . and I have never been so excited in my life."[4]

Excited and energized. Between 1971 and 1975, Nicklaus compiled a performance résumé even steadier and stronger than what he had done a decade earlier. He added six more major titles and twenty more tour championships, improving his 1962–66 Z score. "Nicklaus has now reached a pinnacle of achievement comparable only to those of Bobby Jones and Ben Hogan," remarked Pat Ward-Thomas, adding, in a concession to the obvious, "In every sense of the term Nicklaus is the world's greatest golfer."[5]

So dominant was Nicklaus that if you considered only his ten *worst* performances in majors between 1971 and 1975, his Z score would still be a very respectable –1.33, roughly the equal of Tony Jacklin's best.

Jack Nicklaus had done something that is rarely accomplished in athletics. He had set a full, mature, lofty, and functionally complete standard of performance . . . then starting from scratch he had bettered it. This was the kind of determination that by the mid-1970s led many golf experts to refer to Nicklaus as the greatest player who ever lived. "He plays a game with which I am not familiar," Bobby Jones famously observed following Nicklaus's romp at the 1965 Masters. Jones was referring both to the immensity of Nicklaus's power and to the immensity of his competitive determination. His could be a crushing presence.

Mathematicians estimate that in any set of data—say, tournament golf scores—only about 3 percent of scores will fall more than two standard deviations below the tournament's average performance level. In a field of fifty players, that means maybe one or two players might shoot such a strikingly low score. For the twenty majors played between 1962 and 1966, Nicklaus reached the 2-standard-deviation indicator of dominance eight times, his best being a −3.48 during that 1965 Masters that awed Mr. Jones. Then between 1971 and 1975, he topped even that, with ten such exceptional performances . . . three of them in 1975 alone. For his career, Nicklaus recorded twenty-seven such performances in the majors.

Born January 21, 1940, in Columbus, Ohio, Nicklaus was introduced to golf early. The relationship took. He won the 1956 Ohio State Open at age sixteen and then won the U.S. Amateur in both 1959 and 1961. In between, he tied for second behind Palmer at the 1960 U.S. Open.

Nicklaus came to the pro tour as a stout dynamo with a mighty upright swing that allowed him to hit the ball high, long, and straight. But the game had seen bombers before. Nicklaus could also hit devastatingly precise long irons, such as his clinching one-iron to the final hole of the 1967 U.S. Open at Baltusrol. His putting touch was considered unusually consistent.

Playing Nicklaus, tour players sometimes felt as if they had no chance. Why should they feel otherwise? Between 1962 and 1986, he won seventy official events, a total that remains second all time behind only Sam Snead. He won twenty majors—two U.S. Amateurs, a record six Masters, a record-tying four U.S. Opens, three British Opens, and a record-tying five PGAS. That's a triple Grand Slam, plus change.

What many consider Nicklaus's best season unfolded in 1972. He won the Masters in April and the U.S. Open at Pebble Beach, both by three strokes over Bruce Crampton, then finished just one stroke back of Trevino at the British Open. Statistically, however, his best was yet to come. In 1973 he won the PGA, finished no worse than fourth in the majors, and averaged a −2.05 Z score, the best of his career. But it was not by much: he opened 1975 with a one-stroke victory over Johnny Miller and Tom Weiskopf at Augusta, followed with seventh- and third-place finishes at the Opens, and then won the PGA by two over Crampton, averaging −2.04.

Nor did he retreat much as age reduced his physical skills. For twenty-two consecutive seasons well into the 1980s, Nicklaus unfailingly beat the field scoring average in major events. He did so without exception in the British Open annually between 1963 and 1982, a twenty-year window of performance. During the same twenty-year window, he beat the field average eighteen times at the Masters, seventeen times at the U.S. Open, and sixteen times at the PGA. Merely to equal Nicklaus's run, a player starting out today would have to beat the field average performance in the majors every season through 2037. It is a daunting thought, indeed.

Nicklaus only scored worse than the field average in 22 of his 111 majors between 1962 and 1989, 12 of those coming after 1982. You won't find many players who can string together ten consecutive seasons with Z scores better than −1.14. Between 1972 and 1981, Jack Nicklaus did.

Nicklaus in the Clubhouse

Tournament	Finish	Score	Z score
1971 U.S. Open	2nd	280	−2.00
1971 PGA	1st	281	−2.40
1972 U.S. Open	1st	290	−2.72
1972 British Open	2nd	279	−2.31
1973 Masters	T-3	285	−1.98
1973 British Open	4th	280	−2.21
1973 PGA	1st	277	−2.27
1974 British Open	3rd	287	−2.08
1975 Masters	1st	276	−2.47
1975 PGA	1st	276	−2.57

Note: Average Z score: −2.30. Effective stroke average: 68.59.

NICKLAUS'S CAREER RECORD (1962–89)

Masters: 27 starts, 6 wins (1963, 1965, 1966, 1972, 1975, 1986), –31.56

U.S. Open: 28 starts, 4 wins (1962, 1967, 1972, 1980), –19.62

British Open: 28 starts, 3 wins (1966, 1970, 1978), –31.39

PGA: 28 starts, 5 wins (1963, 1971, 1973, 1975, 1980), –21.98

Total (111 starts): –104.55

Jack Nicklaus

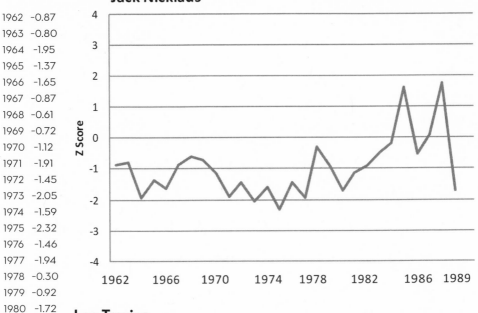

Year	Score
1962	-0.87
1963	-0.80
1964	-1.95
1965	-1.37
1966	-1.65
1967	-0.87
1968	-0.61
1969	-0.72
1970	-1.12
1971	-1.91
1972	-1.45
1973	-2.05
1974	-1.59
1975	-2.32
1976	-1.46
1977	-1.94
1978	-0.30
1979	-0.92
1980	-1.72
1981	-1.13
1982	-0.92
1983	-0.49
1984	-0.19
1985	1.62
1986	-0.51
1987	0.07
1988	1.76
1989	-1.70

Lee Trevino

Of the men who arose at various times to challenge Nicklaus's superiority, the most colorful was Lee Trevino. "The Merry Mex" emerged from the obscurity of South Texas municipal courses to place fifth at the 1967 U.S. Open won by Nicklaus and ratified that newfound fame by winning the following year's Open at Oak Hill. In the process, he defeated Nicklaus by four shots.

Trevino fitted nobody's formula for a golf genius. Born in 1939, he was raised in a three-room Dallas shack, not a suburban development, and spent his time working the cotton fields, not the country club. "I thought hard work was just how life was," he said. His biggest break was geographic: as modest as the family's home was, it happened to be just a hundred yards from the seventh fairway of the Dallas Athletic Club. By the time Trevino was eight, he had wangled a job caddying. "That's where I learned my killer instinct, playing games with the caddies and betting everything I had earned that day," he wrote. It also toughened him to tournament pressure. "Pressure," he once famously remarked, "is when you play for $5 and you've got $2 in your pocket."[6] He quit school in eighth grade to work at a driving range, where he would hit hundreds of balls a day. Lessons? Trevino taught himself, manufacturing balls and clubs out of whatever material could be brought to the task.

The experiences Trevino acquired came in handy when he joined the Marines and was assigned to what in effect was the golf team. A natural hustler, he took his discharge papers and set out to find money games around Dallas and El Paso, one of which included his hitting the ball around a par-three course with a Dr. Pepper bottle.

Trevino's signature move was a controlled fade. It gave him a distinctive swing, dominated by a strong grip, a body alignment well left of his target, and a consistent blocking action of his left side. It was a case of three wrongs somehow making a right. "Who knows, maybe my method is best," Trevino said.

Trevino was a virtual overnight success. By 1971, just five years after winning tour privileges, he held two U.S. Open titles, one British Open championship, and eight more tour championships. He added a second British Open in 1972, chipping in from off the green at the seventy-first hole of what had evolved into a head-to-head showdown to beat Tony Jacklin at Muirfield. His tour résumé included five Vardon trophies: 1970, 1971, 1972, 1974, and 1980.

Where Trevino's fade bias frequently caught up with him was Augusta National, a place noted as favoring the right-to-left player. Between 1970 and 1977, he skipped the Masters four times and on the occasions when he did play only once did well. That was in 1975, when he shot 286 to tie for tenth. In 1971, following a second consecutive no-show, Jack Nicklaus took Trevino aside for something between a pep talk and a lecture. "You can win anywhere," Nicklaus told him. It turned out to be one of the few times in his professional life that Nicklaus was wrong. Trevino returned to the Masters and finished in a tie for thirty-third, 14 strokes behind Nicklaus.

Perhaps oddly, considering how far removed the roots of his game were from the classical British model, Trevino often saved his best showings for the British Open. In addition to winning in 1971 and 1972, he finished third in 1970 and second in 1980. In twenty-three British Opens played during his prime—between 1969 and 1992—Trevino missed just one cut.

Trevino in the Clubhouse

Tournament	Finish	Score	Z score
1968 U.S. Open	1st	**275**	**−2.62**
1968 PGA	T-23	288	−0.64
1969 Masters	T-19	290	−0.18
1970 U.S. Open	T-8	294	−0.97
1970 British Open	T-3	285	−1.87
1971 U.S. Open	1st	**280**	**−2.00**
1971 British Open	1st	**278**	**−2.37**
1972 U.S. Open	T-4	295	−1.82
1972 British Open	1st	**278**	**−2.49**
1972 PGA	T-11	286	−1.22

Note: Average Z score: −1.62. Effective stroke average: 69.59.

TREVINO'S CAREER RECORD (1966–92)

Masters: 20 starts, 0 wins, +13.31
U.S. Open: 23 starts, 2 wins (1968, 1971), +11.63
British Open: 23 starts, 2 wins (1971, 1972), −11.60
PGA: 20 starts, 2 wins (1974, 1984), −1.95
Total (86 starts): +4.26

Lee Trevino

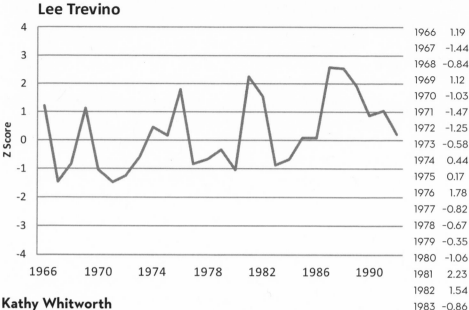

Year	Z Score
1966	1.19
1967	-1.44
1968	-0.84
1969	1.12
1970	-1.03
1971	-1.47
1972	-1.25
1973	-0.58
1974	0.44
1975	0.17
1976	1.78
1977	-0.82
1978	-0.67
1979	-0.35
1980	-1.06
1981	2.23
1982	1.54
1983	-0.86
1984	-0.68
1985	0.07
1986	0.09
1987	2.57
1988	2.51
1989	1.92
1990	0.86
1991	1.02
1992	0.22

Kathy Whitworth

Number 24 Career

As of the end of 2017, Tiger Woods still needed three tournament titles to equal Sam Snead's PGA tour record of eighty-two. But if or when he does pass Snead, Woods will still be a half-dozen wins short of the all-time professional record, Kathy Whitworth's remarkable eighty-eight LPGA tour victories between 1963 and 1985.

Whitworth's secret was consistency. "I never had a golf swing," she said, incorrectly, for she was a competent technician.[7] In the eleven seasons from 1963 to 1973, she led the money list eight times and stood second twice and third the other year. During that stretch, she won the Vare Trophy and Player of the Year honors seven times each.

A native of the Southwest, Whitworth started playing golf at fifteen. Two years later, she won the first of two consecutive New Mexico State Amateur titles. But she initially struggled on the LPGA tour, winning less than $1,300 in her rookie season. Whitworth's big break may have been the sisterly attitude that pervaded the tour at the time. She credited Mickey Wright, Betsy Rawls, Gloria Armstrong, and Jackie Pung all with boosting her flagging confidence, and with offering useful tips. By 1963 Wright and Rawls may have come to regret their beneficence. Previously winless, Whitworth won eight times that year and counted the Titleholders among eight more championship trophies in 1965. In 1968 she topped even that with eleven tournament titles. By then she'd already claimed a second Titleholders as well as the 1967 LPGA and Western Open.

Confidence? Momentum? Whitworth suddenly had it. "When I won eight tournaments in 1963, I was living on a high," she said. "I got in a winning syndrome. Nothing bothers you."[8]

Whitworth was only just entering her competitive prime. Following her LPGA triumph in 1967, she lost in a playoff to Sandra Post in 1968, lost to Shirley Englehorn in another playoff in 1970, and got her second victory by four strokes over Kathy Ahern in 1971. Although she did not win any of the three Opens between 1969 and 1971, Whitworth compiled an unmatched record. She finished third by two strokes to Donna Caponi in 1969, lost again to Caponi by two in 1970, and was runner-up to JoAnne Carner in 1971.

What Whitworth never showed was weakness. During her professional prime, roughly 1963 to 1977, she competed in forty-seven LPGA majors. In addition to winning six of them—the last being the 1975 LPGA—she beat the field average in forty-four of those tournaments, thirty-two in succession. She missed just one cut.

By then Whitworth was focused on passing Wright, holder of the women's championship record, and Snead, both of whom had eighty-two titles. She matched them at the 1981 Kemper Open and passed them with a victory at the 1982 Lady Michelob. "Winning got harder as I got older and there were more players," she said. Yet despite her record victory total, Whitworth is not persuaded those eighty-eight victories put here among the game's elite. "I still say that if Mickey Wright hadn't quit playing so early, there's no telling how many tournaments that woman would have won," she said.[9]

Her final victory came at the 1985 United Virginia Bank Classic. In retirement Whitworth stayed active in golf as vice president, and eventually president, of the LPGA.

Whitworth in the Clubhouse

Tournament	Finish	Score	Z score
1967 Western Open	1st	289	–2.36
1967 LPGA	1st	284	–2.06

1968 U.S. Open	T-5	296	-1.22
1968 LPGA	2nd	294	-1.83
1969 U.S. Open	3rd	296	-1.62
1969 LPGA	T-6	300	-1.23
1970 U.S. Open	T-4	289	-1.40
1970 LPGA	2nd	285	-1.89
1971 LPGA	**1st**	**288**	**-1.89**
1971 U.S. Open	2nd	295	-1.78

Note: Average Z score: -1.73. Effective stroke average: 69.43.

WHITWORTH'S CAREER RECORD (1959-89)

Titleholders: 7 starts, 2 wins (1965, 1966), -6.90

U.S. Open: 28 starts, o wins, -8.15

LPGA: 22 starts, 2 wins (1967, 1971), -13.19

Western Open: 7 starts. 1 win (1967), -5.46

Dinah Shore: 7 starts, o wins (Whitworth won in 1977 before the tournament was considered a major), -2.01

du Maurier: 10 starts, o wins, +1.03

Total (81 starts): -34.68

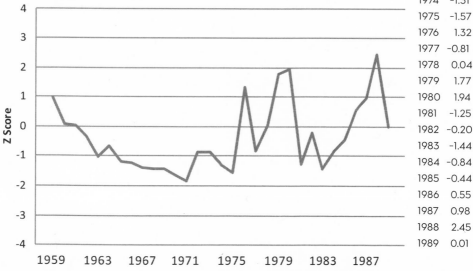

Kathy Whitworth

Year	Value
1959	0.97
1960	0.06
1961	0.02
1962	-0.33
1963	-1.02
1964	-0.65
1965	-1.18
1966	-1.24
1967	-1.39
1968	-1.44
1969	-1.43
1970	-1.65
1971	-1.84
1972	-0.85
1973	-0.85
1974	-1.31
1975	-1.57
1976	1.32
1977	-0.81
1978	0.04
1979	1.77
1980	1.94
1981	-1.25
1982	-0.20
1983	-1.44
1984	-0.84
1985	-0.44
1986	0.55
1987	0.98
1988	2.45
1989	0.01

Tom Weiskopf

There was a time when the young Tom Weiskopf looked like he might be the next Jack Nicklaus. Both were tall sluggers from Ohio State, Weiskopf arriving in Columbus just as Nicklaus was starring there. Weiskopf came to the pro tour in 1964, just as Nicklaus's star was poised to supersede Arnold Palmer's, and the legitimate prospect loomed that the two Buckeyes might soon challenge one another for the top of the money chart.

For various reasons—some ascribed it to inexperience, others to Weiskopf's occasionally volcanic temper—that challenge never truly took hold. Weiskopf started more than seventy tournaments before finally winning—at the 1968 San Diego Open—in the process finishing no higher than fifteenth at any of the handful of majors for which he actually qualified. That San Diego win kick-started a 1968 campaign that was lucrative by comparison: he tied for sixteenth in his first appearance at the Masters, tied for twenty-fourth at the U.S. Open, and in July won a second event, the Buick. At the following spring's Masters, Weiskopf came to the seventy-first hole in a tie for the lead with George Archer, only to bogey and fall back into a tie for second. In the years to come, he would conduct a flirtatious romance with the Masters, finishing second four times but never winning.

Weiskopf's stride may have been delayed in coming, but when it arrived—in 1972—it was impressive. He again tied for second at Augusta—although this time three strokes behind Nicklaus—finished eighth at the U.S. Open and tying for seventh at the British Open. Third behind Johnny Miler's remarkable closing 63 at the 1973 U.S. Open, he flew to Troon for that summer's British Open as one of the favorites. Weiskopf shot an opening 68, led start to finish, and posted a record-tying total of 276. It was exactly how everybody had always envisioned he would play.

"The game was easy, fun. I was relaxed," Weiskopf said. "I had unbelievable confidence, and I kept working, pushing." The champion also drew inspiration from the death of his father the previous March. "I felt like I'd let him down [with my play]."[10]

The Troon win was Weiskopf's only major trophy but hardly his only moment in the spotlight. Coming off a bout with tendinitis that hampered his swing during the winter tour in 1974, he tied for second a third time at Augusta, this time 2 strokes behind Gary Player. One spring later, Weiskopf led the Masters after three rounds, only to be overtaken by Nicklaus's final-round 66. Weiskopf came to the eighteenth hole needing birdie to force an eighteen-hole playoff and watched an eight-foot downhill putt slide by on the right side.

Weiskopf was fast becoming Mr. Near Miss. His fifth runner-up finish in a major unfolded at the 1976 U.S. Open at the Atlanta Athletic Club when he finished 2 strokes behind Jerry Pate. He was third at the 1977 Open, and fourth in both 1978 and 1979. That gave him a dozen finishes of fourth or better in PGA Tour majors, yet only one victory. "I had a great run, with four consecutive top-4 finishes (in the Open) from 1976 through 1979," he would say later. "But I couldn't get it done." Why not? Weiskopf could only speculate. "I had trouble dealing with the fame," he acknowledged.[11]

His tour résumé still showed sixteen career victories and sixty-eight finishes in the top three. But Weiskopf began reducing his playing schedule after 1980 and essentially quit the tour in 1984 to focus on what was becoming a burgeoning golf course design business. Assessing his career, *Golf* magazine saw "a golf swing to die for, a mixture of grace and power" that was occasionally derailed by a bad temper and a knack for becoming flustered. It described him as "a linear perfectionist who somehow didn't attain the greatness expected of him."

Weiskopf never disagreed. Asked by the magazine whether he had maximized his potential, Weiskopf replied, "Emphatically, no." Taking no exception with that self-critique, a lot of PGA Tour regulars would love to put together a résumé that includes one major championship, five runner-up finishes, a dozen placings in the top five, and twenty-one in the top ten, all accompanied by sixteen career tour victories and more than $2.2 million in winnings.

Weiskopf in the Clubhouse

Tournament	Finish	Score	Z score
1973 U.S. Open	3rd	281	–1.88
1973 British Open	**1st**	**276**	**–2.90**
1973 PGA	T-6	283	–1.25
1974 Masters	T-2	280	–1.44

1974 British Open	T-7	293	–1.11
1975 Masters	T-2	277	–2.28
1975 PGA	3rd	279	–2.05
1976 U.S. Open	T-2	279	–2.05
1976 PGA	T-8	284	–1.24
1977 U.S. Open	3rd	281	–1.56

Note: Average Z score: –1.80. Effective stroke average: 69.32.

WEISKOPF'S CAREER RECORD (1965–92)

Masters: 16 starts, 0 wins, –5.20

U.S. Open: 17 starts, 0 wins, –8.23

British Open: 17 starts, 1 win (1973), +9.66

PGA: 17 starts, 0 wins, +9.94

Total (67 starts): +6.17

Year	Value
1968	0.60
1969	–0.61
1970	0.68
1971	0.53
1972	–0.70
1973	–1.40
1974	–1.11
1975	–1.29
1976	–1.13
1977	–0.32
1978	–1.17
1979	1.46
1980	0.41
1981	–0.34
1982	1.36
1983	–0.03
1984	1.54
1985	
1986	
1987	
1988	
1989	3.96
1990	3.37
1991	1.51
1992	2.61

Tom Weiskopf

Tom Watson

Number 8 Peak

There was an aw-shucks quality to Tom Watson, a fair-haired kid from Kansas City who came out of Stanford to compete with, and eventually supplant, Nicklaus as the tour's most predictable winner. Even more than his alter ego, Trevino, Watson was especially deadly in Britain, winning the British Open five times, a total exceeded only by Harry Vardon. They were among his eight major championships and thirty-nine tour titles.

Watson was a made golfer. At Stanford, he established a decent but not especially noteworthy reputation on the links, actually doing better in the classroom, where professors predicted a fine career for him in psychology. Watson, however, had other ideas. He took his college golfing experience to the tour, working and working to hone his game. "Tom would never tolerate a weakness," said Lanny Wadkins. "He'd go to the practice tee and beat at it until the darn thing went away."[12]

The "darn thing" didn't go away easily. At the 1974 U.S. Open at Winged Foot, Watson, trying for his first professional victory, took a 1-stroke lead into the final round. A 79 dropped him to fifth. Victory a week later at the Western Open may have been some consolation. At the 1975 U.S. Open, Watson held the thirty-six-hole lead but finished 78-77 to fall into a tie for ninth. "I learned how to win by losing and not liking it," he said later in his career.[13]

His solution was more effort. Making his debut at the British Open that summer at Carnoustie, Watson stood over a twenty-foot birdie putt on the seventy-second hole to get into a playoff with Jack Newton. He made the putt and then beat Newton by a stroke the next day.

From that point on, England and Scotland were virtual second homes to Watson . . . especially if he was battling Nicklaus.

Their personal duel reached its first of several high points in 1977. Watson had already taken Nicklaus's measure at that spring's Masters, birdieing four of the final six holes to defeat Jack by two strokes. In the British Open at Turnberry that July, the two renewed the Augusta showdown, engaging in what some have called the most intense and highest-caliber sustained battle in the history of major championship golf.

Jointly tied for second with Lee Trevino at 68 after the opening round, and with Hubert Green and Trevino after two rounds, they flew from the field on Saturday with matching 65s. It was the third successive day on which they had tied each other.

As Sunday dawned, 10 strokes separated them from third place. Nicklaus got the first edge with a birdie at the second and moved 3-up with a birdie at the third, while Watson bogeyed. Watson birdied the fifth, seventh, and eighth to draw even, and then Nicklaus regained the lead at the ninth when Watson bogeyed. By the turn on that final day, they were 8 and 7 shots ahead of their nearest challenger. A long putt boosted Nicklaus's lead to two shots at the twelfth. But Watson drew even again with birdies of his own at the thirteenth and fifteenth, the latter on a 60-footer.

The break came at seventeen when Nicklaus failed to birdie the 500-yard par 5. Watson did and led by 1. At eighteen, Nicklaus drove into the gorse, then improbably thrashed out of it and onto the green leaving a 20-foot putt. Watson, meanwhile, played straight down the middle and knocked an iron just a few feet from the hole. Nicklaus, needing his long putt for an unlikely birdie to retain any prospect of tying, holed out to the delight of a roaring throng for a 66. But Watson tapped in his as well for a 65 and a 1-shot win in a head-to-head duel for the ages. Watson would repeat as British Open champion in 1980, 1982, and 1983.

Watson added the 1981 Masters to his laurels, and then his personal wrestling match with Nicklaus resumed at the 1982 U.S. Open at Pebble Beach. There Jack aimed for a record fifth title. Nicklaus led until Watson chipped in from the fringe on the seventeenth hole for an improbable birdie to take the lead. His follow-up birdie at eighteen made the margin of victory 2 strokes.

By the time he retired from regular tour competition in the late 1990s, Watson had won thirty-nine events and six Player of the Year awards and had led the money list five times.

Watson in the Clubhouse

Tournament	Finish	Score	Z score
1977 Masters	1st	276	−2.40
1977 British Open	1st	268	−3.38
1977 PGA	T-6	276	−1.24
1978 Masters	2nd	278	−1.75
1978 U.S. Open	T-6	289	−1.22
1978 PGA	T-2	276	−2.56
1979 Masters	T-2	280	−1.86

1980 U.S. Open	T-3	276	-1.83
1980 British Open	1st	271	-3.26
1981 Masters	1st	280	-2.04

Note: Average Z score: -2.17. Effective stroke average: 68.78.

WATSON'S CAREER RECORD (1973-99)

Masters: 25 starts, 2 wins (1977, 1981), -12.94

U.S. Open: 28 starts, 1 win (1982), +2.63

British Open: 24 starts, 5 wins (1975, 1977, 1980, 1982, 1983), -4.59

PGA: 27 starts, 0 wins, -1.91

Total (104 starts): -16.81

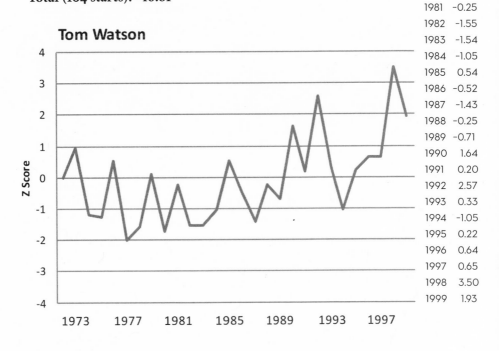

Tom Watson

Year	Z Score
1972	-0.02
1973	0.93
1974	-1.18
1975	-1.27
1976	0.54
1977	-2.01
1978	-1.59
1979	0.12
1980	-1.71
1981	-0.25
1982	-1.55
1983	-1.54
1984	-1.05
1985	0.54
1986	-0.52
1987	-1.43
1988	-0.25
1989	-0.71
1990	1.64
1991	0.20
1992	2.57
1993	0.33
1994	-1.05
1995	0.22
1996	0.64
1997	0.65
1998	3.50
1999	1.93

JoAnne Carner

Number 15 Career

Throughout the 1970s and into the 1980s, fans of women's golf might have debated who—Whitworth, Nancy Lopez, Sandra Haynie—was the best player. But the choice, whoever it might have been, always ended up being compared to the oversize, overenergetic, and overtalented Carner.

A precocious teen amateur with a soaring reputation when she initially rose to fame in 1959, the girl known at the time as JoAnne Gunderson (or more simply "the Great Gundy") offered a first demonstration of her talent at the 1959 Western Open. There, while still a teenager, Gunderson battled the tour's best on equal terms, finishing in a tie with Patty Berg for second place, behind only Betsy Rawls and ahead of such established stars as Louise Suggs and Marlene Hagge.

For years following that debut, Gunderson contented herself with dominating the amateur ranks. Between 1956, when she lost to Marlene Stewart, and 1968, Gunderson—Carner after her 1963 marriage to her coach and business manager—won the Women's Amateur title five times and was runner-up in seven more. The match-play format seemed to especially suit Carner's gallery-pleasing personality.

Both in her dominance and in her crowd-friendly nature, Carner drew comparisons to legends of the stripe of Babe Ruth and Walter Hagen. Away from the course, though, Garner exhibited far simpler tastes than Hagen or the Babe. No fancy suites for her; she often traveled to events in a Gulfstream driven by her husband, who used it to catch fish for dinner while she was on the course. "I play better golf living in our trailer," Carner explained.[14]

Finally, in 1969, Carner forsook the amateur life for that of a professional, where she was the immediate hit everybody predicted she would be. She dominated the field at the 1971 U.S. Open, defeating Whitworth by 7 strokes and posting a score of 288 that was 21 strokes below the field average for the week. In classic Ruthian form, power was her trademark. "The ground shakes when she hits it," Sandra Palmer said of Carner.[15]

She was on her way to forty-one championships—including an encore victory at the 1976 U.S. Open, this time in a playoff over Palmer. Three times she was Player of the Year and five times the Vare Trophy winner, and she consistently led in body language and crowd reaction. In the process, the kid once known as "the Great Gundy" acquired a new nickname: Big Momma. Carner wallowed in the interaction.

"Concentration and getting involved with the shot are important," she said, "but if I get too serious I can't play." Unlike many players who tend to cocoon themselves from galleries, Carner seemed at times almost to be her own gallery. "If the ball is going for the pin or in the cup, I am the first one to yell," she conceded.[16]

Perhaps befitting a stage personality, Carner was at her best in the big events. In her thirty-eight U.S. Open or LPGA appearances between 1970 and 1989, "Big Momma" made every cut but one and beat the field average twenty-seven times. Carner's first appearance in the LPGA's year-old major, the 1980 du Maurier (then called the Peter Jackson Classic), saw her wage a marvelous duel with Pat Bradley, eventually losing by a stroke.

Carner in the Clubhouse

Tournament	Finish	Score	Z score
1980 LPGA	T-3	289	-1.60
1980 du Maurier	2nd	278	-2.63
1981 LPGA	T-5	284	-1.63
1982 LPGA	2nd	281	-1.98
1982 du Maurier	T-3	283	-2.18
1982 U.S. Open	T-2	289	-1.61
1983 du Maurier	T-2	279	-1.94
1983 U.S. Open	T-2	291	-1.77
1984 Nabisco	T-5	284	-1.65
1984 du Maurier	5th	284	-1.60

Note: Average Z score: -1.86. Effective stroke average: 69.23.

CARNER'S CAREER RECORD (1970-88)

Titleholders: 1 start, 0 wins, -0.79
U.S. Open: 18 starts, 2 wins (1971, 1976), -18.95
LPGA: 18 starts, 0 wins, -10.96
Nabisco Dinah Shore: 6 starts, 0 wins, -3.89
du Maurier: 8 starts, 0 wins, -8.45
Total (51 starts): -43.04

JoAnne Carner

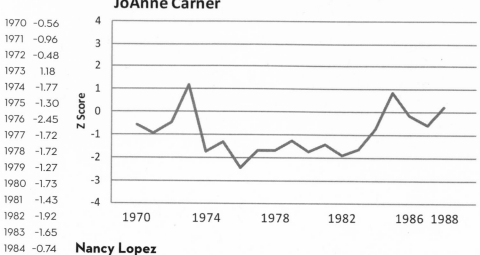

Year	Z Score
1970	-0.56
1971	-0.96
1972	-0.48
1973	1.18
1974	-1.77
1975	-1.30
1976	-2.45
1977	-1.72
1978	-1.72
1979	-1.27
1980	-1.73
1981	-1.43
1982	-1.92
1983	-1.65
1984	-0.74
1985	0.87
1986	-0.16
1987	-0.58
1988	0.24

Nancy Lopez

Nancy Lopez' explosion on tour in 1978 could not have been better timed. A wave of LPGA stars had either retired (Wright, Rawls, Suggs, Haynie) or were past their prime (Berg, Hagge). Whitworth, although a superb shot maker, was perceived as largely colorless. Jan Stephenson had plenty of personality but had not yet established the consistent game. That left only JoAnne Carner as a figure around whom women's golf could mobilize interest.

Then sprang Lopez with a background almost as unlikely as Lee Trevino's to snare all the attention the tour could have hoped for. The daughter of a Roswell, New Mexico, shop owner, Lopez was a prodigy. In 1970, at age twelve, she won the New Mexico Women's Amateur. Because her high school did not have girls' golf, she joined the boys' team and led it to two state championships. At Tulsa she became an All-American, and in 1975 she won the Mexican Amateur. That same year she came to the tour as a National Collegiate Athletic Association (NCAA) champion, qualified for the U.S. Open, and tied Carner for second behind Sandra Post.

By 1977 Lopez's successes persuaded her to leave Tulsa and try the women's tour. In her first event, the Women's International, she tied for fortieth. Her second start, the 1977 Open, went a bit better; she finished second again, two shots behind Hollis Stacy. In her third start, two weeks later, she posted another runner-up finish. In February 1978, Lopez, who had just turned twenty, won for the first time, edging JoAnn Washam by a single shot at Bent Tree.

That was the start of one of the most remarkable runs in the history of women's golf. A week later Lopez won a second time, defeating Debbie Austin by a stroke at the Sun Star Classic. A week after that at the Kathryn Crosby, she lost a playoff to Sally Little. In May and June, she added five more titles, including the LPGA Championship by a stifling 6 shots over Amy Alcott. Lopez played the four rounds in 13 under par, including a second-round 65 that was 2 strokes better than anybody else managed all week. Her total was a full 20 shots below the field average of 295 strokes. Seemingly, LPGA events had suddenly become flighted competitions, with Lopez in the first flight and everybody else in the second.

Before the year was out, Lopez added two more championships to her résumé along with another playoff loss. Her card for the year showed nine victories. Eight more tour wins followed in 1979. So did an unprecedented amount of endorsement money and publicity for a successful young girl with a natural and infectious smile and an evident love of the game. She had plainly overcome her biggest fear—of failure. "After my first year I thought, 'I could be a flash in the pan,' and I was also determined to prove I was not," Lopez has said. "I was determined not to fall on my face, though it is easy enough to choke yourself to death trying to win."[17]

The amazing thing was that looking strictly at her performance in the majors, Lopez could have been even better. Aside from the 1978 LPGA victory, she largely had to content herself with close calls in the tour's biggest events. Lopez did win two more LPGA Championships, in 1985 and 1989. But she never got closer to a U.S. Open title than those two early runner-up finishes, and her second place to Stephenson at the 1981 du Maurier was her best showing in that major. She was runner-up there three times.

Overall, Lopez finished second seven times in recognized LPGA majors, the last at the 1997 U.S. Open when the thirty-nine-year-old's last-gasp effort at the event that most frustrated her included shooting four rounds in the 60s. Lopez was the first women to do that, yet she still lost by 1 stroke to Alison Nicholas.

The golf nation hung on every shot of that drama, pulling for the popular veteran, a three-time Vare Trophy winner. "I'd love to have won the Open," Lopez once said. "But I've had enough good things in life that I won't be shattered because I don't."[18]

Lopez in the Clubhouse

Tournament	Finish	Score	Z score
1985 Nabisco	T-11	285	–1.13
1985 LPGA	**1st**	**273**	**–3.58**
1985 U.S. Open	T-4	288	–1.51
1988 Nabisco	T-5	282	–1.61
1988 LPGA	T-24	291	–0.45
1988 U.S. Open	T-12	288	–0.82
1989 Nabisco	T-18	291	–0.73
1989 LPGA	**1st**	**274**	**–3.30**
1989 U.S. Open	2nd	282	–1.75
1989 du Maurier	9th	283	–1.46

Note: Average Z score: –1.63. Effective stroke average: 69.57.

LOPEZ'S CAREER RECORD (1977–2006)

Nabisco Dinah Shore: 21 starts, 0 wins (Lopez won the Shore in 1981, before it was classified as a major), +5.03

U.S. Open: 21 starts, 0 wins, –2.01

LPGA: 25 starts, 3 wins (1978, 1985, 1989), –1.50

du Maurier: 11 starts, 0 wins, –9.51

Total (78 starts): –7.99

1978	-2.01
1979	-1.27
1980	-1.19
1981	-1.90
1982	-0.68
1983	-0.90
1984	-0.61
1985	-2.08
1986	
1987	-0.05
1988	-0.62
1989	-1.81
1990	1.27
1991	-0.17
1992	0.58
1993	-0.96
1994	-0.45
1995	-0.81
1996	-0.11
1997	-0.86
1998	0.62
1999	1.53
2000	0.75
2001	1.90
2002	2.97
2003	3.08
2004	2.69
2005	3.30
2006	2.86

Nancy Lopez

Pat Bradley

Number 22 Peak

Pat Bradley was not a long hitter, a great putter, or a crowd favorite. But she was consistent and determined, and she rarely hurt herself. Beyond that, Bradley savored the challenge of teeing it up. The combination brought her riches beyond any previous women's golfer. It also brought her as close to completing the single-season professional Grand Slam as any other player has come.

Workaholic? Between 1974 and 2000—essentially her golfing prime—Bradley competed in 627 tournaments and finished in the top ten 312 times and in the top five 208 times, with thirty-one victories. On the way, she became the first woman golfer to surpass the $2 million (1986), $3 million (1990), and $4 million (1991) marks in career earnings. When she won three of the women's majors in 1986, Bradley became the first modern woman to complete the career Grand Slam.

Although Bradley came to the tour virtually at the same time as Lopez and Beth Daniel, she did not share their quick success. For her, it was a building process. Her potential surfaced in 1977, when the twenty-six-year-old in her fourth season on tour tied veteran Judy Rankin and Jane Blalock for fifth at the Colgate Dinah Shore. She made a serious run at two majors, shooting 282 at the LPGA to tie Rankin and Sandra Post for second and a few weeks later at the U.S. Open tying Jan Stephenson and Amy Alcott for fourth.

Bradley made a second run at the Shore in 1979, tying Donna White for third. The close misses proved to be dress rehearsals for the 1980 Peter Jackson Classic, when Bradley withstood Carner's final-round charge to win by 1 stroke to win at 277, 15 under par. It was a case of honesty paying off; at the seventh hole, Bradley—seeing her ball move imperceptibly as she addressed it—had imposed a 1-stroke penalty on herself. A five-foot birdie putt at the sixteenth gave her the lead she barely held onto when Carner missed her own thirty-foot birdie putt on the final hole. An Open title followed in 1980, Bradley beating Daniel by a stroke.

In 1986 Bradley entered the first major, the Shore, off a winter run that included two runner-up finishes, a fourth, and a third the previous week at Tucson. She won by two over Val Skinner, following that with another runner-up and then a victory at the s&h Golf Classic in late April.

Bradley claimed her fourth second place at the Corning Classic, a prelude to the LPGA Championship in June. Again she won, this time with an imposing score of 277, 11 under par and 1 better than Patty Sheehan. With the Nabisco and LPGA titles, Bradley could lay claim to the career slam, having captured the Open in 1981 and the du Maurier in 1985. Four behind Sally Little entering the final round of the U.S. Open, she was among a tight group of nine players with a chance to win on Sunday afternoon. Bradley pieced together a closing 69, but Jane Geddes's own 69 and Little's 71 left her in a tie for third, 3 strokes away from her third major of the year. Geddes won a playoff with Little the next day.

Two weeks later, Bradley defeated Ayako Okamoto in a playoff at the du Maurier, giving her four of the last five Grand Slam events. Her average Z score for that season's majors was –2.16. "I honestly wish everyone could experience what I did in that dream-come-true year," she would say later. "I was invincible."[19]

The 1988 death of her father, and her own medical problems, cut into Bradley's success in 1987 and 1988, although she still managed a third place at the 1987 Nabisco. But she returned in 1989 with a season rivaling 1986 in consistency, if not in hardware. Virtually written off when the season began, she finished sixth in the Shore, fourth in the LPGA, third in the Open, and second in the du Maurier.

Three more victories followed in 1990 and then four more in 1991, enough to ensure her entrance into the LPGA Hall of Fame. After 1991 Bradley was only an occasional threat on tour, although she maintained a full schedule through 2000.

Bradley in the Clubhouse

Tournament	Finish	Score	Z score
1985 LPGA	T-3	284	–1.57
1985 du Maurier	1st	278	–2.15
1986 Nabisco	1st	280	–2.39
1986 LPGA	1st	277	–2.32
1986 U.S. Open	T-5	290	–1.50
1986 du Maurier	1st	276	–2.43

1987 Nabisco	3rd	284	–2.10
1989 LPGA	T-4	283	–1.70
1989 du Maurier	T-2	280	–2.03
1989 U.S. Open	T-3	283	–1.58

Note: Average Z score: –1.98. Effective stroke average: 69.06.

BRADLEY'S CAREER RECORD (1974–2000)

Nabisco Dinah Shore: 18 starts, 1 win (1986), –12.38

U.S. Open: 26 starts, 1 win (1981), –3.64

LPGA: 26 starts, 1 win (1986), –14.28

du Maurier: 21 starts, 3 wins (1980, 1985, 1986), –1.81

Total (91 starts): –32.11

Pat Bradley

Year	Z Score
1974	1.61
1975	–0.20
1976	–0.21
1977	–1.58
1978	0.03
1979	–0.70
1980	–1.38
1981	–1.67
1982	–0.45
1983	–1.14
1984	–1.36
1985	–1.46
1986	–2.16
1987	0.05
1988	1.85
1989	–1.63
1990	–0.98
1991	–1.62
1992	–0.45
1993	1.00
1994	–0.47
1995	0.87
1996	–0.31
1997	0.61
1998	1.36
1999	0.55
2000	1.48

THE TOP-TEN GOLFERS OF ALL TIME FOR PEAK RATING AS OF THE END OF THE 1980 SEASON.

Rank	Player	Seasons	Z score	Effective stroke average
1.	Arnold Palmer	1960–64	–2.31	68.57
2.	Jack Nicklaus	1971–75	–2.302	68.59
3.	James Braid	1901–10	–2.18	68.76

4.	Ben Hogan	1950–54	–2.13	68.84
5.	Bobby Jones	1926–30	–2.11	68.87
6.	Walter Hagen	1923–27	–2.10	68.88
7.	Sam Snead	1947–51	–2.07	68.93
8.	Mickey Wright	1958–62	–2.06	68.94
9.	Harry Vardon	1896–1904	–2.03	68.98
10.	Ralph Guldahl	1936–40	–2.02	69.00

THE TEN GOLFERS OF ALL TIME FOR CAREER RATING
AS OF THE END OF THE 1980 SEASON.

Rank	Player	Seasons	Z score
1.	Jack Nicklaus	1962–80	–101.71
2.	Walter Hagen	1913–40	–73.94
3.	Patty Berg	1935–68	–73.21
4.	Sam Snead	1937–62	–68.69
5.	Mickey Wright	1954–80	–62.22
6.	Louise Suggs	1948–72	–60.31
7.	Gene Sarazen	1920–51	–58.09
8.	Ben Hogan	1938–62	–53.09
9.	Byron Nelson	1933–60	–44.88
10.	Jim Barnes	1913–31	–44.58

10 Metallurgy

In early May 1981, a little-known touring pro won a rain-shortened second-level tournament . . . and forever changed the way golf was played.

Ron Streck, a twenty-six-year-old journeyman out of the University of Tulsa, shot a third (and final) round 62 to beat Hale Irwin and Jerry Pate by 3 strokes at the rain-truncated Michelob Houston Open. Streck was the definitional journeyman. From 1977 to 1986, he kicked around the minor stops, picking up checks where he could. His only top-ten finish in any major was at the 1979 PGA, when he came home fourth, 4 strokes behind champion David Graham. There'd be no reason to run a peak Z score for Streck, but if you did it would encompass the years 1979–83, include a missed cut at the 1979 Masters, and come out to +0.64. In other words, he was a below-average tour player

What made Streck's 1981 Houston victory profound wasn't his talent but his equipment: he won it using metal woods.

From virtually the game's dawn until the late 1970s, professionals and amateurs alike had used woods that were made of the eponymous material. The wood in question was usually persimmon, but it might also be cherry or hickory. Of course, players, perpetually in search of an advantage, tinkered. Back in May 1924, Sir Harold Delf Gillies, a noted plastic surgeon, showed up for his opening-round match in the British Amateur at St. Andrews with two pieces of equipment that were nothing if not innovative. The first was a nine-inch-long wooden tee with a rubber tip. The second was a driver with a three-inch-high face. When a thorough scan of the rules produced nothing prohibiting the use of such outlandish implements, tournament officials conceded Sir Gillies's right to tee off . . . although before he did so they issued a strongly worded memo encouraging "all players" to abide by the spirit as well as the letter of the equipment rules then in effect. Sir Gillies won his match. The next morning, presumably having heard a few earfuls from his fellow competitors, he shelved the gargantuan driver and tee—and lost 3 and 1.

By the time of Streck's arrival on tour, a start-up equipment company called Taylor Made had begun marketing something designed by a fellow named Gary Adams—a "wood" that was made of metal. Adams persuaded Streck and a handful of other pros—generally underachieving ones with little to lose—to try the club in competition.

Within weeks of Streck's Houston victory, other pros began using the metal woods, and amateurs naturally followed. They benefited from the fact that metal clubs could be made lighter with larger heads and a greater coefficient of restitution, providing both enhanced accuracy and greater clubhead speed. That translated to greater ball speed, which in turn translated to distance. Because the PGA Tour was only then beginning to measure driving distance, we do not know the precise extent of the gain. But we do know this: Taylor Made quickly eclipsed makers of wooden clubs in market share, and in short order "woods" made of actual wood were all but obsolete.

The replacement of wood by metal was only one of several vital alterations taking place during that time in one of the most basic aspects of golf, the club. A year or two after the metal wood showed up, Karsten Solheim, already well known as the inventor of the Ping putter, introduced perimeter-weighted, cavity-backed irons. Different from traditional iron designs, where the metal (and therefore the weight) was more or less evenly distributed across the clubhead, Solheim's cavity-backed irons focused the weight on the club's perimeter. That translated to a more forgiving result, both in distance and in accuracy, for shots struck off center.

In short order, the pros discovered what hackers around the world were also learning: a bag equipped with metal woods and perimeter-weighted irons made them both longer and more accurate.

Seve Ballesteros

Severiano Ballesteros was a dashing, dark-haired Spaniard with wild eyes and a wild game. This Don Quixotish figure not only tilted at windmills but was a threat to hit them. But whether playing from the fairway or the parking lot, Ballesteros did it with a continental flair.

Ballesteros's play was intense in the way the Armada was intense, the difference being he often won. His recurring strategy was high risk, relying on his fabled imagination. His incessant reliance on "Seve shots," unorthodox, intemperate, and often spontaneous hacks along questionable flight lines, may not have suited technicians, but they brought Ballesteros five major championships and trophies from more than seventy professional tournaments around the world.

The golf community knew nothing of Ballesteros when he qualified for the 1975 British Open as an eighteen-year-old. He missed the cut. They knew little more of him when he qualified for the event again in 1976. This time Ballesteros opened their eyes with consecutive 69s to take a 2-stroke lead after thirty-six holes. Despite a third-round 73, he still led Johnny Miller by 2 entering Sunday play when the pressure finally caught up to him. He shot 74, Miller shot 66, and Ballesteros faded into a tie for second with Jack Nicklaus. The knowledgeable looked past the collapse to the accomplishment: a nineteen-year-old from a country with no golf tradition had just tied the great Nicklaus and made a legitimate run at winning the game's most historic event.

Seve Ballesteros had arrived.

That Open won Ballesteros an invitation to the 1977 Masters. He could not repeat his success. But he did learn, and the experience acquired playing both in the United States and internationally paid off when Ballesteros came to Royal Lytham for the 1979 British Open. Late in the tournament, leading Nicklaus by 2 shots, he drove the ball well off course and into a parking lot. No problem for Ballesteros, who knocked his second shot from amid the cars onto the green and holed out for a birdie on his way to a 3-stroke victory. He became the first continental European to win the championship since Arnaud Massy in 1907.

Seve returned to Augusta for the Masters in 1980, but this time as British Open champion, and won by 4 strokes. In 1982 he missed a playoff with Craig Stadler, the eventual winner, and Dan Pohl by 1 shot. A year later there were no misses; Ballesteros cruised to a 4-shot win over Ben Crenshaw and Tom Kite, his 280 total equaling the best since his own 275 in 1980. His second British Open title came in 1984, a 2-stroke victory over Tom Watson and Bernhard Langer at St. Andrews.

He came to the final round of the 1988 British Open back at Lytham in contention for a fifth major win and displayed the full variety of his game. The closing 65 included an amazing eleven-hole stretch: two pars, two bogeys, six birdies, and an eagle. From behind the eighteenth green, Ballesteros finished off a still-hopeful Nick Price with a chip that stopped inches from the cup for a tap-in birdie and a 2-stroke win. By year's end, he had climbed to number 1 in the Official World Golf Ranking.

Always more committed to the European than American tour, Ballesteros capped his career by winning the 1995 Spanish Open. After 1995 he confined his major appearances to the Masters and British Open, and even those soon became largely ceremonial, Ballesteros last making the cut in 1995. Soon after his final Masters appearance in 2007, he was diagnosed with brain cancer, the disease that killed him in 2011.

The long, slow decline of his play muddies Ballesteros's career Z score, which deteriorated from +0.17 in 1994 to +54.48 by his last Masters appearance.

Ballesteros in the Clubhouse

Tournament	Finish	Score	Z score
1983 Masters	1st	280	–2.24
1983 U.S. Open	T-4	286	–1.76
1984 British Open	1st	276	–2.65
1984 PGA	5th	279	–1.59
1985 Masters	T-2	284	–1.58
1985 U.S. Open	T-5	281	–1.42
1986 Masters	4th	281	–1.46
1986 British Open	T-6	288	–1.42
1987 Masters	T-2	285	–1.56
1987 U.S. Open	3rd	282	–1.52

Note: Average Z score: –1.72. Effective stroke average: 69.44.

BALLESTEROS'S CAREER RECORD (1975–2007)

Masters: 28 starts, 2 wins (1980, 1983), +17.25

U.S. Open: 17 starts, 0 wins, +11.27

British Open: 27 starts, 3 wins (1979, 1984, 1988), +16.20

PGA: 13 starts, 0 wins, +9.76

Total (85 starts): +54.48

Seve Ballesteros

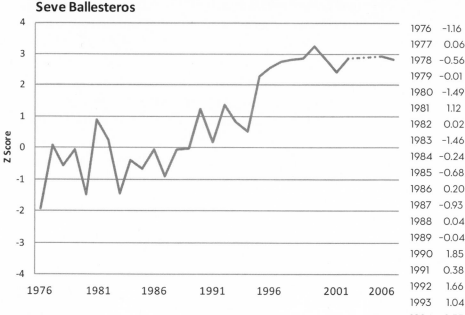

1976	-1.16
1977	0.06
1978	-0.56
1979	-0.01
1980	-1.49
1981	1.12
1982	0.02
1983	-1.46
1984	-0.24
1985	-0.68
1986	0.20
1987	-0.93
1988	0.04
1989	-0.04
1990	1.85
1991	0.38
1992	1.66
1993	1.04
1994	0.55
1995	2.39
1996	2.57
1997	2.76
1998	2.81
1999	2.86
2000	3.25
2001	2.82
2002	2.43
2003	2.86
2004	
2005	
2006	2.93
2007	2.84

Ayako Okamoto

(Tie) Number 15 Peak

When golf experts confront the question of "best player never to have won a major," their attentions generally fall on a small coterie of names: Lee Westwood, Luke Donald, and, until the 2017 Masters, Sergio Garcia. None of those answers are even on the right continent. They're also sexist. Hands down the best player never to have won a major was a slightly built Japanese woman few recall today.

The striking aspect of Ayako Okamoto's record is how consistently and how narrowly she missed that coveted major title.

For the nine-season period between 1983 and 1991, Okamoto finished among the top ten in more than half the contested women's majors, that record including six runner-up finishes and a dozen placements among the top five. Twice she lost majors in playoffs. Between 1986 and 1987, Okamoto finished among the top five in seven consecutive LPGA majors without winning any of them. In the four 1987 majors, she never finished below fifth place, and only nine strokes separated her from completing a Grand Slam.

Okamoto came to golf from a unique background for a touring pro: softball. As a youth, she was rated the best left-handed pitcher in Japan. One day a friend tossed a golf ball in her path, handed her a right-handed club, and suggested she have a whack. Okamoto did, and within a few months she had qualified for the Japanese tour. She finished just outside the top ten in her first professional competition, won the 1979 Japanese LPGA Championship, and by 1981 was—with eight victories and six seconds—clearly the country's best player.

Eager for tougher challenges, Okamoto qualified for the U.S. tour on her first attempt and a few months later claimed her first U.S. victory, the Arizona Copper Classic. By 1984, boosted by a second-place finish in the du Maurier and three tour victories, Okamoto rang up $251,000 in earnings, third best on the U.S. tour.

Through it all, Okamoto was modest about her easygoing success. "I've been very lucky," she told reporters at the height of her popularity in the mid-1980s. In that respect, Okamoto proved a far poorer analyst than player, for her achievements were too consistent to be influenced by mere fortune. She won twice more in 1986 and narrowly missed claiming the du Maurier, losing to Pat Bradley in a sudden-death playoff. Achieving millionaire status during a four-victory 1987 season, she continued her frustrating pursuit of a major win, losing the U.S. Open in another playoff, this one to Laura Davies and also including JoAnne Carner. She lost the du Maurier by two strokes to Jody Anschutz, finished four behind Betsy King at the Dinah Shore, and came in three behind Jane Geddes at the LPGA.

Today, given the international nature of the modern LPGA Tour, it seems odd to consider that Okamoto's success did not spur a generation of aspiring young imitators in Japan, as Se Ri Pak's 1998 arrival soon would in Korea and eventually throughout Asia. But it did not. During the decade in which Okamoto was an active tour member, she never competed regularly against a fellow Asian LPGA member. She returned to Japan in 1993, and her name quickly faded into relative obscurity. Still she could point to seventeen victories on the LPGA tour and sixty-two worldwide. Not bad for a left-handed pitcher.

Okamoto in the Clubhouse

Tournament	Finish	Score	Z score
1985 LPGA	T-5	286	–1.21
1986 LPGA	T-3	279	–1.99
1986 U.S. Open	T-3	288	–1.81
1986 du Maurier	2nd	276	–2.43
1987 Nabisco Dinah Shore	T-5	287	–1.64
1987 LPGA	T-3	278	–1.81
1987 US Open	T-2	285	–2.18
1987 du Maurier	2nd	274	–2.81
1988 LPGA	T-3	284	–1.54
1989 LPGA	2nd	277	–2.77

Note: Average Z score: –2.02. Effective stroke average: 69.00.

OKAMOTO'S CAREER RECORD (1982–2000)

Nabisco Dinah Shore: 16 starts, 0 wins, +3.41
U.S. Open: 14 starts, 0 wins, –8.31
LPGA: 15 starts, 0 wins, –12.19
du Maurier: 8 starts, 0 wins, –8.39
Total (53 starts): –25.48

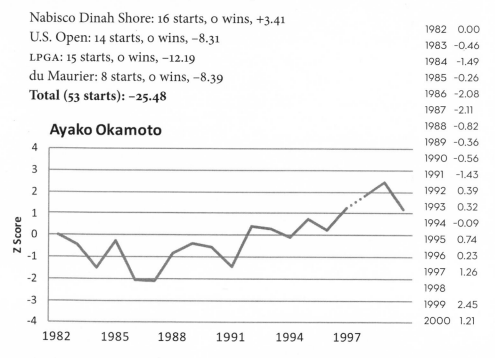

Ayako Okamoto

1982	0.00
1983	–0.46
1984	–1.49
1985	–0.26
1986	–2.08
1987	–2.11
1988	–0.82
1989	–0.36
1990	–0.56
1991	–1.43
1992	0.39
1993	0.32
1994	–0.09
1995	0.74
1996	0.23
1997	1.26
1998	
1999	2.45
2000	1.21

Nick Faldo

(Tie) Number 24 Peak

England proper—and is there any other kind?—produces frontline international golfers in numbers that are disproportionately small relative to its importance to the game. For more than three decades following Max Faulkner's 1951 victory, only one Englishman, Tony Jacklin, laid claim to the British Open golf championship. Then in an eight-year span beginning with Sandy Lyle's victory at St. George's, Englishmen won four championships. The other three all went to Nick Faldo, at his peak the best English golfer since Harry Vardon.

Faldo was a technocrat in the Ben Hogan mold. Never an especially long hitter, he tried to make up for physical shortcomings with the precision of his swing, his approach to the course, and its translation to the scorecard. In that sense, possibly the defining round of any golfer's career was Faldo's final one at the 1987 British Open at Muirfield. On a day when he needed to shoot par golf to claim his first major title, Faldo not only did it but did it meticulously—with pars on every one of the eighteen holes.

When he was a youngster, Faldo's athletic propensities were hard to miss. At six-foot-three, he excelled at sports and seemed to show a special fondness for cycling. His parents bought him an expensive racing bike. But they had not reckoned with Faldo's other proclivity, the one that involved figuring out how things work. Faldo proceeded to dismantle the bike. He was, observers often said, the same way with his golf swing . . . forever taking it apart and putting it back together. Faldo credited watching Charles Coody win the 1971 Masters on television with spurring his interest in golf. By 1975 his game had developed to the point where he was good enough to win ten amateur titles. He joined the European tour in 1976, the same year he debuted at the British Open, finishing in an anonymous but perfectly credible tie (with, among others, Gary Player) for twenty-eighth place. Faldo won $603.

Over the next five years, Faldo became a familiar face in European golf circles, although his visibility in America was largely limited to whatever exposure he gained from the British Open. That exposure could be more than casual. He tied for seventh place in 1978 and in 1982 tied for fourth, just 2 strokes behind Tom Watson's winning 284. His 1978 show-ing qualified him to fulfill his youthful dream by playing at the Masters, where he made the cut but was not a factor in the outcome. In 1981 he began to split time between the European and American tours, playing about a dozen events here and winning just under $50,000.

It was not until his 1987 victory at Muirfield that Faldo leaped to Amer-ican attention. But that victory marked his arrival both as a celebrity and as a player. Between 1987 and 1995, Faldo won six major championships, three Masters, and three British Opens. His name was perennially near the top of the leader board. Beginning with the 1988 U.S. Open and continuing through the 1992 PGA, Faldo landed in the top twenty in nineteen consecutive major events.

Possibly because of his technical virtuosity, Faldo seemed impervious to the pressure that affected other players. His par-heavy winning round at the 1987 British Open was one illustration. At the 1989 Masters, he won in sudden death with a long putt at the second extra hole. In 1990 he beat Ray Floyd in another playoff. In 1992 at Muirfield, Faldo lost a 5-stroke lead on Sunday but rallied with late birdies to win his third British Open by 1. He was ranked number 1 in the world at the conclu-sion of both the 1992 and the 1993 seasons.

The epitome of Faldo's tenacity was the 1996 Masters, when he trailed Greg Norman by 6 strokes entering the final day's play. Other players might have pressed, but Faldo let Norman do that. The tactic worked; Norman's early mistakes built some self-imposed pressure, which Faldo exacerbated with a couple of birdies. By day's end, his 6-stroke deficit had turned into a 5-stroke victory.

There was no such suspense at the 1990 British Open, when Faldo dismantled St. Andrews with a four-round total of 270, 18 under par, winning by 5.

Always a man of the golfing world, Faldo cut back his U.S. appear-ances substantially after 2002 to concentrate on the European tour, a workload he reduced again after the 2005 season to focus on television analysis and other teaching endeavors.

Faldo always performed superbly on his home soil. In thirty British Opens between 1976 and 2005, he beat the field average twenty-two times, including nineteen straight between 1978 and 1996.

Historically, Faldo is one of the first players for whom there are some individual skills data that can be correlated with his results. The data, however, are from the proto era of tour stat analysis, the pre–Strokes Gained period, and, as noted in chapter 1, those data just aren't very refined. The second problem is that because Faldo was an on-and-off competitor on the American tour, the data are only partial and generally biased toward the end of his career. For what it's worth, the data are in line with the characterization of Faldo as a mechanic. Between the early 1980s and mid-1990s, his driving distance was generally a bit below average. Accuracy was another matter. In 1989 Faldo hit fairways at an exceptional rate of 76.11 percent, 1.8 standard deviations better than the tour average of 64.74 percent. In 1995 he hit 77.81 percent of fairways—the tour average was 69.5 percent—and followed that up by hitting 68.55 percent of greens, nearly a full standard deviation better than the tour average for that skill. He also scrambled for pars or better at a rate nearly 2 standard deviations better than the field average. As he aged, Faldo's correlational skills declined. By 1998 he was below average in all of them except fairway accuracy, where he never did lose his edge.

Faldo in the Clubhouse

Tournament	Finish	Score	Z score
1989 Masters	1st	283	–1.82
1989 British Open	T-11	281	–1.05
1990 Masters	1st	278	–2.40
1990 U.S. Open	T-3	281	–1.48
1990 British Open	1st	270	–3.09
1992 U.S. Open	T-4	291	–1.29
1992 British Open	1st	272	–2.54
1992 PGA	T-2	281	–1.68
1993 British Open	2nd	269	–2.36
1993 PGA	3rd	273	–1.91

Note: Average Z score: –1.96. Effective stroke average: 69.09.

FALDO'S CAREER RECORD (1976–2006)

Masters: 23 starts, 3 wins (1989, 1990, 1996), +7.97

U.S. Open: 18 starts, 0 wins, +9.09

British Open: 31 starts, 3 wins (1987, 1990, 1992), −12.18

PGA: 22 starts, 0 wins, +2.45

Total (94 starts): +7.32

Nick Faldo

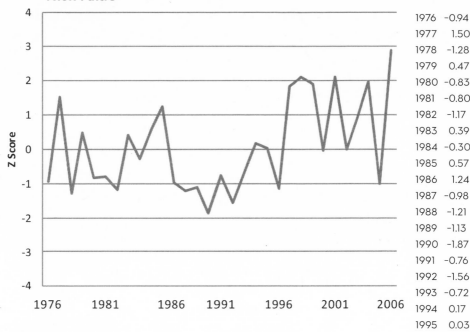

Year	Value
1976	-0.94
1977	1.50
1978	-1.28
1979	0.47
1980	-0.83
1981	-0.80
1982	-1.17
1983	0.39
1984	-0.30
1985	0.57
1986	1.24
1987	-0.98
1988	-1.21
1989	-1.13
1990	-1.87
1991	-0.76
1992	-1.56
1993	-0.72
1994	0.17
1995	0.03
1996	-1.15
1997	1.83
1998	2.11
1999	1.88
2000	-0.04
2001	2.10
2002	-0.02
2003	0.97
2004	1.96
2005	-1.02
2006	2.88

Greg Norman

Anywhere outside the United States, Greg Norman's was as fearsome a presence as his nickname, the Great White Shark, suggests. In America it was often a different story. Norman sometimes appeared baffled by the U.S. game.

That was as much a matter of perception as reality. After all, he did win eighteen times over fourteen seasons in North America. And they weren't all cheapies: Norman won the 1984 Kemper and Canadian Opens, the 1988 MCI Heritage, the 1990 Doral and Memorial, the 1994 Players Championship, and the 1997 World Series of Golf.

But in the majors, Norman's reputation rose and fell depending on which side of the Atlantic he happened to be playing. In England or Scotland, he won two Opens and beat the field average in thirteen consecutive championships between 1983 and 1996. He ran up a career Z score of –13.32 in the world's oldest ongoing major golf competition. Elsewhere, the picture was different. Norman's career Z score was +7.62 in the three U.S.-based majors. He never won any of them, and some of the failures raised the question, "What shark?"

Born in Queensland in 1955, he was raised in a golfing family; his mom was club champion. That and a reading of Jack Nicklaus's 1970s instructional book moved him to take up the game seriously, starting as an assistant pro.

The club pro's life, though, was never what Norman had in mind. He joined the Australian-Asian tour and was an immediate flash, winning the Westlakes Classic at age twenty-one. With almost no world-level experience, he qualified for the 1978 British Open and managed to tie four players, among them Lee Trevino, for twenty-ninth place. At the 1979 U.S. Open, Norman tied for forty-eighth. His tenth-place finish at the British Open a month later was debutant level. In 1981 his flashy appearance at the Masters won him the nickname that would stay with him; his game won him fourth place and $16,000.

Now Norman was going somewhere. Both aggressive and charismatic, he parlayed the fame that came to him into regular appearances on the U.S. tour, a labor that would produce $10 million in career earnings and three Vardon Trophies (1988, 1989, and 1994) in addition to those twenty victories. He was Player of the Year in 1995. At the end of seven different seasons—1986, 1987, 1989, 1990, 1995, 1996, and 1997—he was ranked number 1 in the world.

There was an "agony and ecstasy" element to Norman's game. It first surfaced at the 1984 U.S. Open at Winged Foot when he battled Fuzzy Zoeller for the title. Coming to the final hole needing a par to get into a playoff, Norman faced a fifty-foot putt . . . which he promptly made. So impressed was Zoeller, waiting in the final fairway, that he memorably waved a white towel in mock surrender. In the playoff, though, it was Norman who surrendered, shooting 75 to Zoeller's 67.

Norman's fate in the United States and Britain was superbly summed up in his adventures during 1986. He won one major that year and could with not much more luck or effort have won all four. In fact, he led going into Sunday play in all of them. At the Masters, Jack Nicklaus's memorable final-round 65—with a back nine of 30—overtook Norman, who even so came to the eighteenth hole needing only a par to tie. He missed the green with his approach and made bogey instead. At the U.S. Open at Shinnecock Hills, Norman shot two rounds in the 60s to lead Lee Trevino by 1 entering Sunday play. But a final-round 75 sent him sputtering back to a tie for twelfth, 6 strokes behind champion Ray Floyd. At the PGA in August, a closing 76 allowed Bob Tway to erase most of a 4-stroke deficit coming to the final hole at Inverness. When Tway dropped his third stroke from a bunker in front of the final green for a birdie 3, Norman was consigned to runner-up status again. He did win the British Open at Turnberry, opening up 5 shots on the field with a second-round 63. Despite the final-day failures, Norman's 1986 record works out to a seasonal Z score of −1.92, the best of his career.

His bad luck continued in 1987. At that year's Masters, Larry Mize holed a long chip at the second playoff hole to defeat Norman for the green jacket. In 1993 Norman defeated his recent major demons, besting Nick Faldo by 2 strokes at the British Open at St. George with a closing 64. That victory marked the beginning of Norman's best stretch of play in the majors. Between the British Opens of 1993 and 1996, Norman's thirteen major appearances showed just one victory, but three runner-ups and nine top-ten finishes.

Yet even that stretch yielded frustration and embarrassment. He lost a playoff to Paul Azinger for the 1993 PGA title. Then in April 1996 Norman seemed finally assured of a major win on U.S. soil, shooting an opening 63 and carrying a 6-stroke advantage into the final round at the Masters. Instead, he turned in one of the worst closing rounds of his career, a 78 that let Faldo pass him comfortably. "The best way to put it; I played like crap," Norman said afterward.[1]

"Sometimes I think I have an almost perverse love of being down, even being defeated," he wrote of the failures. "I know it will spur me on to greater things." They may not have always been greater, but they were always more interesting.[2]

Norman in the Clubhouse

Tournament	Finish	Score	Z score
1993 British Open	1st	267	−2.73
1993 PGA	2nd	272	−2.11

1994 U.S. Open	T-6	283	−1.32
1994 PGA	T-4	277	−1.51
1995 Masters	T-3	277	−1.65
1995 U.S. Open	2nd	282	−1.80
1995 British Open	T-15	287	−1.11
1996 Masters	2nd	281	−1.77
1996 U.S. Open	T-10	283	−1.32
1996 British Open	T-7	277	−1.25

Note: Average Z score: −1.66. Effective stroke average: 69.53.

1977	1.97
1978	0.03
1979	−0.07
1980	3.29
1981	−0.70
1982	−0.22
1983	0.11
1984	−0.86
1985	0.83
1986	−1.92
1987	0.18
1988	−1.08
1989	−1.10
1990	0.21
1991	1.08
1992	−0.89
1993	−0.20
1994	−0.99
1995	−1.26
1996	−1.30
1997	1.21
1998	3.36
1999	0.55
2000	2.35
2001	1.63
2002	0.51
2003	1.05
2004	2.81

NORMAN'S CAREER RECORD (1977–2004)

Masters: 22 starts, 0 wins, +1.89

U.S. Open: 17 starts, 0 wins, +5.39

British Open: 24 starts, 2 wins (1986, 1993), −13.32

PGA: 22 starts, 0 wins, +0.11

Total (85 starts): −5.93

Greg Norman

Betsy King

(Tie) Number 24 Peak

For a dozen years in the 1980s and 1990s, no woman golfer in America was consistently better than Betsy King.

That would have come as a profound surprise to those who saw King grind out a golf living through the 1970s and early 1980s. Playing ten tournaments in 1977, King won just $4,000, netting nothing higher than a tie for fifteenth. In 1978 she played a full schedule of twenty-nine events, reaching the top ten eight times and winning $44,000, but never contending for a trophy. In thirty-two events in 1979, she managed eight more top tens, one of them a playoff loss at Wheeling, and $54,000. But she backslid in 1980, with just one top-ten finish in thirty-two tournaments and just $27,000 in winnings. The 1981 season produced five top tens, including another runner-up finish, and restored her earnings power to about $55,000. Still, the most you could say of King was that she had become part of the field.

That didn't change until the 1984 Women's Kemper Open when King, twenty-eight, held off Pat Bradley by a stroke. A month later she won by 2 at Orlando, this time over Alice Miller. That season's LPGA amounted to a breakthrough when she broke par by a stroke and finished in a tie for seventh place. The Women's Open gave her another confidence boost: she tied Patty Sheehan for fifth in her best big-stage showing to date. The du Maurier followed by two weeks, and King did better still, taking third, just 2 shots behind Juli Inkster. From virtually zero visibility, she had claimed three top-ten finishes in majors, two of them in the top five. She finished the year as the LPGA's leading money winner and won its Player of the Year Award.

Suddenly, King had something going. In 1987 she beat Sheehan in a playoff for the Shore, her first major victory. She capped a solid 1989 with a 4-stroke win over Lopez at the U.S. Open and then in 1990 enjoyed a season reminiscent of Bradley's rush through 1986 and Lopez's spectacular 1978. It began at the Nabisco, which King entered on the heels of second- and third-place finishes the previous two weeks. She built a

5-stroke lead after three rounds, and though she staggered home with a closing 75, it was enough for a 2-stroke win. At the Open in July, King won again, this time making up 9 strokes on Patty Sheehan over the final thirty-six holes. A fifth at the LPGA preceded two more tour championships and a net gain to her purse of more than $650,000. Between 1984 and 1990, Betsy King had won twenty-six tournaments, going from winless to the winningest player, man or woman, active in top-level professional golf.

And once having reached the top, King broached no letdown. In 1992 she mounted a historic performance at the LPGA, routing the field by 11 strokes with a four-round score of 267, 17 under par. Her total was 3.52 standard deviations below the average for the week, a level that has been surpassed just eight times in the history of men's and women's professional majors. She was 22 strokes below the field average for the tournament and led runner-up JoAnne Carner by as much as Carner led the five players who tied for thirty-fifth place.

King won her thirtieth championship, qualifying her for the LPGA Hall of Fame, in 1995. She was forty-one when the 1997 season began, but age had never been her problem. So it should not have surprised anyone when she won the Nabisco a third time—her sixth career major.

Since King joined the tour in the mid-1970s and peaked between 1987 and 1991, all of our individual skills correlative data postdate her prime. From 1993 onward, King was a relatively long driver, averaging 0.8 of a standard deviation longer than her competitors. She missed fairways at a rate 0.4 of a standard deviation more often than her fellow pros, but the average standard deviation of her performance in hitting greens in regulation during those seasons was consistently close to the upper third. King's late-career performance on the greens was acceptable if not remarkable, averaging 0.334 standard deviations better than average.

King continued to play at least ten events per year until reaching her fiftieth birthday in 2005. By then her skills had eroded. Indeed, after 1997 King never beat the field stroke average in majors and missed the cut in ten of the last twenty-eight major events she started. Age is hell . . . but then for King, so was youth. That middle part was pretty sweet, though.

King in the Clubhouse

Tournament	Finish	Score	Z score
1986 U.S. Open	T-3	288	−1.81
1986 du Maurier	T-3	281	−1.69
1987 Nabisco Dinah Shore	**1st**	**283**	**−2.25**
1987 LPGA	2nd	276	−2.15
1987 du Maurier	7th	280	−1.69
1987 U.S. Open	T-4	289	−1.54
1989 du Maurier	T-2	280	−2.03
1989 U.S. Open	**1st**	**278**	**−2.41**
1990 Nabisco Dinah Shore	**1st**	**283**	**−2.13**
1990 U.S. Open	**1st**	**284**	**−1.92**

Note: Average Z score: −1.96. Effective stroke average: 69.09.

KING'S CAREER RECORD (1977–2005)

Nabisco Dinah Shore: 23 starts, 3 wins (1987, 1990, 1997), +0.14

U.S. Open: 28 starts, 2 wins (1989, 1990), +10.66

LPGA: 28 starts, 1 win (1992), +0.42

du Maurier: 20 starts, 0 wins, −15.16

British Open: 3 starts, 0 wins, +5.98

Total (102 starts): +2.04

Betsy King

Year	Value
1977	3.85
1978	0.03
1979	2.09
1980	0.95
1981	−0.09
1982	−0.54
1983	−0.11
1984	−1.30
1985	0.35
1986	−0.35
1987	−1.91
1988	−0.42
1989	−1.75
1990	−1.60
1991	−0.99
1992	−0.88
1993	−1.58
1994	−0.77
1995	−1.32
1996	2.31
1997	−0.92
1998	0.70
1999	1.46
2000	0.81
2001	2.41
2002	1.50
2003	2.56
2004	1.17
2005	2.42

Laura Davies

Number 19 Peak

For a time following her arrival on the American tour, Laura Davies seemed capable of taking over. As a big woman who hit big drives, she always had the intimidation factor going for her. Davies was capable of backing up her appearance with action; in fact, she won the U.S. Open before qualifying as an LPGA Tour member. So imposing was Davies's growing reputation that the LPGA—judging its regular tour needed Davies to draw fans—simply rewrote its eligibility requirements to make her immediately eligible for events without having to go through the usual qualifying process.

The most successful player in the history of British women's professional golf, Davies made a name for herself at regional and national tournaments. She qualified for the British Curtis Cup team in 1984, turned pro in 1985, and led the European women's tour in money winnings that season and again in 1986. She also won the Women's British Open, although at the time the event had not gained a stature anywhere near comparable with its masculine sibling.

Having established a continent-wide reputation, the twenty-three-year-old Davies branched out in 1987, committing to play in the Nabisco and the U.S. Open. Her 287 in the Open tied JoAnne Carner and Ayako Okamoto for first place, and Davies produced a 71 in the playoff for a 2-stroke victory over Okamoto, 3 over Carner.

Davies joined the tour regularly in 1988 and played in twenty events, winning two of them. But consistency avoided her. Davies missed the cut in the LPGA and then finished second in the du Maurier. She bobbed and weaved into and mostly out of contention in major events for the next five seasons.

Her game clicked into place in 1994. After finishing second in the Nabisco, Davies won the LPGA in May with a final-round 68. The leading money winner on the U.S. tour that season (at slightly more than $687,000), she claimed victories on five tours worldwide that year. Davies missed repeating her LPGA title by 1 shot in 1995 when Kelly Robbins fired her own final-round 68, but made it two titles in three seasons in 1996 in an event shortened to three rounds by weather. Davies won four times in the United States that season and nine times worldwide.

Davies's skills are firmly etched in the numbers. Between 1994 and 1998—her peak—her drives averaged 259.2 yards, beating the 233.6-yard field average by 2.8 standard deviations, that is, way out on the good edge of the bell curve. She built on that advantage by hitting 69.4 percent of her greens in regulation; the tour average was 62.6 percent. Davies was never much for fairways, hitting them at a less than normal rate every season between her debut in 1993 and 2011. But with her length and ability to find greens, driver accuracy didn't matter.

The rise to prominence of Annika Sorenstam did matter. It sent Davies's reputation into something of an eclipse after 1996. She won one 1997 event and finished fourth in the LPGA, but her earnings fell by more than half. In 1999 she went winless in the United States for the first time in seven seasons, claiming only two top-five finishes in a major after that while missing twenty cuts.

The effect is to give Davies one of the least complementary sets of ratings of any big-name player. Her peak score, measured by her ten best tournaments between 1994 and 1998, approaches −2.00, according her top-twenty status all-time. Yet her +49.27 career score is poor. Her career graph describes Davies's performance in a way that words cannot: a deep midcareer trough giving way to more than a decade of nondescript paycheck collecting.

Davies in the Clubhouse

Tournament	Finish	Score	Z score
1994 Nabisco Dinah Shore	2nd	277	−2.32
1994 LPGA	1st	279	−2.37
1995 Nabisco Dinah Shore	T-3	287	−1.65
1995 LPGA	2nd	275	−2.72
1996 LPGA	1st	213	−2.16
1996 U.S. Open	6th	281	−1.47
1996 du Maurier	1st	277	−2.54

1997 LPGA	T-4	284	–1.89
1998 Nabisco Dinah Shore	T-3	283	–1.88
1998 U.S. Open	T-11	295	–0.91

Note: Average Z score: –1.99. Effective stroke average: 69.04.

DAVIES'S CAREER RECORD (1986–2013)

Nabisco Dinah Shore: 26 starts, 0 wins, +0.69

U.S. Open: 25 starts, 1 win (1987), +22.54

LPGA: 24 starts, 2 wins (1994, 1996), +6.91

du Maurier: 12 starts, 1 win (1996), +1.74

British Open: 10 starts, 0 wins, +14.37

Evian Masters: 1 start, 0 wins, +3.02

Total (98 starts): +49.27

1986	0.90
1987	–1.07
1988	0.30
1989	–0.15
1990	1.16
1991	–0.29
1992	1.42
1993	–0.58
1994	–1.39
1995	–0.23
1996	–1.76
1997	–0.17
1998	–0.74
1999	1.25
2000	0.07
2001	0.29
2002	1.42
2003	1.12
2004	0.24
2005	0.55
2006	1.45
2007	0.75
2008	2.07
2009	–0.02
2010	0.76
2011	1.91
2012	2.72
2013	2.23

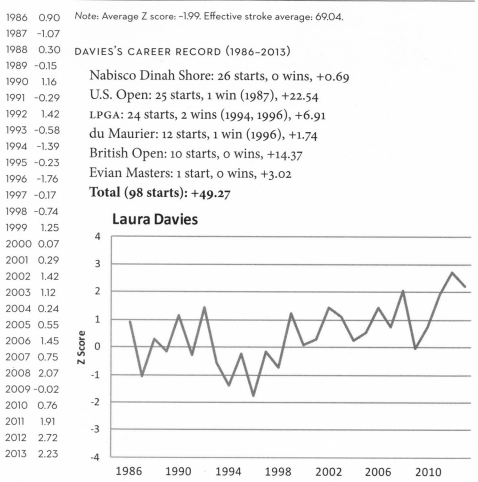

Laura Davies

Juli Inkster

Number 19 Career

What a marvelous beginning to Juli Inkster's professional career . . . a victory in only her fifth start and two major championships in barely a year. And what a conclusion . . . four major titles after her thirty-ninth birthday.

The ostensible prime? That was occasionally shaky. But Inkster could cite a legitimate excuse: motherhood.

Few players arrived with expectations as ratcheted as Inkster, who came out of Northern California to win three Women's Amateur titles between 1980 and 1982. A collegiate All-American at San José State, she was a member of the 1982 Curtis Cup team.

Inkster joined the tour in 1983, winning the Safeco Classic less than two months later. Her first major as a pro—she had played in five U.S. Opens as an amateur—was memorable enough; Inkster beat Pat Bradley in a playoff to pocket the $55,000 first-place check at the 1984 Dinah Shore. Later in the summer she added the du Maurier in her debut at that event. This golf business is easy.

After 1984 the rest of the tour caught up with the young star, although victories continued to come Inkster's way in lesser tournaments. She won once in 1985, added the Women's Kemper and McDonald's Championship in 1986, and repeated in the Safeco in 1988. By 1989 she had twelve tour trophies counting that season's Nabisco, which she won by a comfortable 5 strokes over JoAnne Carner and Tammie Green.

Motherhood complicated the picture in 1990. "Until I had kids, for almost my whole life my whole day was being Juli Inkster," she said later. "It was about me. And then that all changed."[3] Inkster tried to play through the obvious division of interests, but her game showed the effects of diminished attention. That year she missed the cut in the U.S. Open, LPGA, and du Maurier. She missed the Open cut again in 1991. In 1992 Inkster rebounded but lost both the Nabisco and the U.S. Open in playoffs, the first to Dottie Pepper and the second to Patty Sheehan. The playoff failures initiated a five-year victory drought that continued until the 1997 Samsung World Championship. This was due in part at least to the reduced schedule she accepted in deference to the needs of her two young children. In 1994 Inkster played in just sixteen tournaments.

Inkster turned thirty-nine in 1999, but given the time she had laid away from many of the game's competitive stresses, it was a young thirty-nine. She proved it that June with a 5-stroke victory in the U.S. Open. Later in the month, Inkster shot 68 in the opening round of the LPGA, a round played on her birthday. Rounds of 66, 69, and 65 followed, giving her a 4-shot win over Lisolette Neumann and a more substantive gift, the winner's check for $210,000. It also completed the career Grand Slam.

These back-to-back major titles would have been impressive as valedictory performances . . . but Inkster was only just hitting her professional stride. She reprised her LPGA Championship in 2000, surviving a two-hole playoff against Stefania Croce. At the 2002 Open at Prairie Dunes, her experience guided her to a 2-stroke victory over Annika Sorenstam on a course that maximized the importance of cerebral play. Fourth a few weeks later at the LPGA, she added an eighth place showing at the 2003 Open. Inkster was forty-three at the time, but her game had never been better.

During those prime seasons of 1999 through 2003, Inkster was strong in every measured facet of the game. At that peak, Inkster was 1.24 standard deviations longer off the tee than the average LPGA pro and 0.64 standard deviations more accurate. She hit greens at a rate 1.46 standard deviations better than the norm and was 1.13 standard deviations better than the field average in putts taken. It's an extraordinarily balanced portfolio for any tour pro, much less one entering her forties, which Inkster was when her prime began.

Inkster in the Clubhouse

Tournament	Finish	Score	Z score
1999 Nabisco Dinah Shore	6th	283	−1.23
1999 Women's Open	1st	272	−3.11
1999 LPGA	1st	268	−2.61
1999 du Maurier	3rd	283	−1.65
2000 LPGA	1st	281	−2.73
2000 du Maurier	T-5	286	−1.78
2002 LPGA	T-4	285	−1.78
2002 U.S. Open	1st	276	−3.39
2003 U.S. Open	8th	287	−1.31
2003 British Open	T-43	291	+0.31

Note: Average Z score: −1.93. Effective stroke average: 69.13.

Nabisco Dinah Shore: 23 starts, 2 wins (1984, 1989), −22.20

U.S. Open: 24 starts, 2 wins (1999, 2002), +2.11

LPGA: 24 starts, 2 wins (1999, 2000), −13.68

du Maurier: 16 starts, 1 win (1984), −7.21

British Open: 7 starts, 0 wins, +2.64

Total (94 starts): −38.34

Juli Inkster

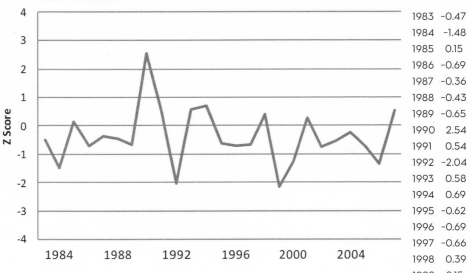

1983	−0.47
1984	−1.48
1985	0.15
1986	−0.69
1987	−0.36
1988	−0.43
1989	−0.65
1990	2.54
1991	0.54
1992	−2.04
1993	0.58
1994	0.69
1995	−0.62
1996	−0.69
1997	−0.66
1998	0.39
1999	−2.15
2000	−1.26
2001	0.26
2002	−0.74
2003	−0.54
2004	−0.22
2005	−0.72
2006	−1.36
2007	0.52

Payne Stewart

When sports figures die before their careers have ended, it is tempting to ponder what might have been. In the case of Payne Stewart's golfing life, what might have been probably parallels what was.

Stewart was forty-two years old when he perished aboard that oxygen-starved aircraft in October 1999. He had won the U.S. Open the previous June, but otherwise his recent career had not been memorable. Since 1994 Stewart's twenty-one other major appearances had produced one top-ten finish—second at the 1998 U.S. Open—two other showings in the top twenty, and five missed cuts. Aside from the Open victory, he had won twice in official tour events, the 1995 Shell Houston Open and the 1999 AT&T. But his five-season peak Z score, –1.49 between 1989 and 1993, was only –0.76 from 1995 onward.

Yet Pinehurst showed that he remained capable, as most on tour are, of winning in any given week. Thus, there exists a residue of wonderment.

Even during his best seasons Stewart's tour record always tended to veer toward the haphazard. One of his best seasons, 1993, was bracketed by two of his worst. In 1992 he missed the cut at the Masters, performed unremarkably at the other majors, and accumulated a seasonal Z score of +1.27. In 1994 Stewart missed the cut in each of the first three majors.

Even during those peak seasons of 1989 to 1993, that was Stewart's modus. He might deliver big, but he was a shaky bet. His 1989 PGA title capped one of Stewart's better seasons: a tie for twenty-fourth at the Masters, for thirteenth at the U.S. Open, and for eighth at the British Open. His average 1989 Z score of –1.05 was fourth best among those who played at least three majors, behind only Scott Hoch, Faldo, and Norman.

The 1990 season was less memorable. Stewart followed a lackluster performance at the Masters, tying for twenty-sixth, by shooting 73-75 at the U.S. Open and failing to make the cut. He did salvage a runner-up showing at the British Open, but it was 5 strokes behind Faldo. His average 1990 Z score was +0.49. Another uneven season followed in 1991: a missed cut at the Masters, then his first U.S. Open win, then placing thirty-second and thirteenth at the Brit and the PGA.

Stewart's +22.83 career score reflects the up-and-down nature of his résumé. Unlike peak Z scores—which count only the best performances within a defined high point of a player's chart—career scores encompass the good and bad equally. That means they can get pretty bloody, and Stewart's does. It's a trait he shares, by the way, with an unusual number of players from his era. Tom Kite, Nick Price, Davis Love, Paul Azinger, Ian Woosnam, José María Olazábal, and Curtis Strange, all from the 1980s and 1990s, all also produced career Z scores in excess of +15.0.

He had a second trait that tended to hurt his overall record, an aversion to Augusta National Golf Club. Stewart teed it up there fourteen times and beat the field average only five of those times. He missed the cut more times (three) than he hit the top 10 (two), and his average finish on the eleven occasions he did play the weekend was twenty-ninth.

Stewart in the Clubhouse

Tournament	Finish	Score	Z score
1989 U.S. Open	T-13	284	–0.89
1989 British Open	T-8	280	–1.21
1989 PGA	**1st**	**276**	**–1.87**
1990 British Open	T-2	275	–1.98
1990 PGA	T-8	292	–1.08
1991 U.S. Open	**1st**	**282**	**–2.32**
1991 PGA	T-13	285	–0.93
1993 Masters	T-9	285	–0.98
1993 U.S. Open	2nd	274	–2.32
1993 British Open	12th	276	–1.10

Note: Average Z score: –1.47. Effective stroke average: 69.81.

STEWART'S CAREER RECORD (1981–99)

Masters: 14 starts, 0 wins, +12.30
U.S. Open: 16 starts, 1 win (1999), –0.95
British Open: 17 starts, 0 wins, –0.41
PGA: 18 starts, 1 win (1989), +7.55
Total (65 starts): +18.49

Payne Stewart

1981	1.60
1982	3.83
1983	1.39
1984	3.14
1985	–1.01
1986	–0.95
1987	0.84
1988	–0.73
1989	–1.05
1990	0.35
1991	0.16
1992	1.27
1993	–1.04
1994	2.52
1995	–0.35
1996	1.19
1997	0.12
1998	0.35
1999	–0.03

THE TOP-TEN GOLFERS OF ALL TIME FOR PEAK
RATING AS OF THE END OF THE 1990 SEASON.

Rank	Player	Seasons	Z score	Effective stroke average
1.	Arnold Palmer	1960–64	–2.31	68.57
2.	Jack Nicklaus	1971–75	–2.302	68.59
3.	James Braid	1901–10	–2.18	68.76
4.	Tom Watson	1977–81	–2.17	68.78
5.	Ben Hogan	1950–54	–2.13	68.84
6.	Bobby Jones	1926–30	–2.11	68.87
7.	Walter Hagen	1923–27	–2.10	68.88
8.	Sam Snead	1947–51	–2.07	68.93
9.	Mickey Wright	1958–62	–2.06	68.94
10.	Harry Vardon	1896–1904	–2.03	68.98

THE TOP-TEN GOLFERS OF ALL TIME FOR CAREER
RATING AS OF THE END OF THE 1990 SEASON.

Rank	Player	Seasons	Z score
1.	Jack Nicklaus	1962–89	–104.86
2.	Walter Hagen	1913–40	–73.94
3.	Patty Berg	1935–68	–73.21
4.	Sam Snead	1937–62	–68.69
5.	Louise Suggs	1947–72	–60.31
6.	Mickey Wright	1954–84	–59.67
7.	Gene Sarazen	1920–51	–58.09
8.	Ben Hogan	1938–62	–53.09
9.	Tom Watson	1972–90	–45.05
10.	Byron Nelson	1933–60	–44.88

11 Millennials

Since the PGA and LPGA Tours began keeping records of such things, only three men and four women have compiled season-long scoring averages that were at least one stroke lower than all of his or her competitors. The three men who did that were: Tiger Woods in 2000, Tiger Woods in 2007, and Tiger Woods in 2009. The four women were Annika Sorenstam annually from 2002 through 2005.

As a practical matter, the question of whether Tiger Woods is the best golfer in history ultimately comes down to whether he was better than Annika Sorenstam at her peak or Jack Nicklaus over the course of his career.

The Tiger Woods story is well-enough known that its details need only be touched upon here. How he was raised as the only child of an American military man and an Asian woman. How his golf skills first went on display on *The Mike Douglas Show* at the age of three. How relentless training, both physical and mental, gave him the skill and will to dominate junior golf. How he became the youngest winner in the history of the U.S. Amateur and then won it twice more in succession. How he focused, from the effective start of his life, on becoming a golf champion. How he dominated. Finally, how it all somehow came apart just at the moment when it appeared Woods would become generally recognized as the greatest ever at his sport.

Woods was not alone in his exceptionality. Sorenstam dominated the women's tour almost in parallel fashion. She won 72 of her 307 career starts—that's 23 percent—competitive with Woods's 24.5 percent. Jack Nicklaus, by comparison, won 12 percent of his events, Sam Snead won 14 percent, and Lorena Ochoa won 16 percent. In 2004 Sorenstam started eighteen LPGA tournaments and won eight of them—by an average of three strokes. Sorenstam's worst finishes that season were a pair of ties for thirteenth place in fields of 99 and 124. More than 160 LPGA Tour members played for $42.075 million in purses in 2004; Sorenstam won $2,544,707, or 6 percent, of the total purse.

Tiger Woods and Annika Sorenstam

Woods: Number 1 Peak, Number 5 Career
Sorenstam: Number 2 Peak, Number 8 Career

Let's begin with Woods. The first of his three Amateur victories earned him a spot in the 1995 Masters. By the standards of amateur rookies, he didn't embarrass himself, making the cut and shooting a four-round score of 293 to finish in a tie for forty-first. At the 1996 British Open, Woods began a streak of twenty-eight consecutive majors—extending seven years—in which he always outshot the field average.

Woods's pro debut in the fall of 1996 nearly coincided with the beginning of the period of his greatest dominance. His first major as a professional was an overpowering statement, victory at the 1997 Masters by a dozen strokes over Tom Kite. Tiger got the same production out of fewer than 93 shots that it took Kite 96 to accomplish and that it took the average player 100 to achieve. The rest of 1997 would have been considered satisfactory for any pro—certainly for any tour rookie—except Woods. He placed nineteenth in the U.S. Open, twenty-fourth in the British Open, and twenty-ninth at the PGA.

It was a solid base from which to build, and Tiger did. In 1998 he was eighth at the Masters, eighteenth at the U.S. Open, third at the British Open, and tenth at the PGA. Woods climbed to number 1 in the Official World Golf Ranking, a perch he would retain every year but one through 2009. He followed a so-so performance at the 1999 Masters by placing fourth behind Payne Stewart at the Pinehurst U.S. Open, claimed seventh place at the British Open at Carnoustie, and then defeated Sergio Garcia by 1 shot at the PGA at Medinah. His 277 four-round total that week translated to a Z score of −2.53, a performance level that ought to be reached less than 1 percent of the time. Tiger would exceed it four more times in majors before the end of 2002.

The PGA victory also set the stage for the phenomenal 2000 season. It opened pedantically by Tiger's standards and his alone, in fifth place behind Vijay Singh at Augusta. Two months later at the Pebble Beach U.S. Open, he mounted his memorable one-man show against the wind, sea, and nature, winning by 15 shots at 272. Against the field average of 296, this amounted to a Z score of −4.12, making it the best performance in the history of major tournament golf to that date. When he added the British Open a month later by 8 shots, it came as that rarest of things on tour, a foregone conclusion. His 269 score translated to a Z score of −3.33. The PGA fell in another month with a −2.27 Z score that seemed almost unexceptional by comparison with his recent efforts. Woods's average Z score in majors during the 2000 season was −2.77, the best one-season Z score in major tournament history. Here's how it compares to the best years of some other fellows:

Tiger Woods	2000	−2.77
Ben Hogan	1953	−2.58
Bobby Jones	1930	−2.23
Arnold Palmer	1964	−2.22
Sam Snead	1949	−2.14
Jack Nicklaus	1973	−2.05

Woods's 2001 Masters victory—climaxing the "Tiger Slam"—highlighted what for him was a disappointing season. His −0.95 average Z score for that year's majors failed to exceed −1.00 for the first time since he turned pro. In other words, his average effort was only about 1.67 times as good as his fellow pros rather than twice as good. Victories in the 2002 Masters and U.S. Open—both with Z scores better than −2.50—restated his continued dominance.

In 2003 and again in 2004, Woods's numbers moderated, although hardly pushing into the realm of "worrisome." He won both the 2005 Masters and the British, making that year his best since 2000. He hit age thirty in December and after a frustrating 2006 put together his fourth exceptional season in 2007. Entering 2008, so high were expectations that even Woods talked openly about completing a calendar Slam. It didn't happen, as we all know. He placed second in the Masters, three strokes behind Trevor Immelman, and then won that astonishing playoff victory over Rocco Mediate in the U.S. Open at Torrey Pines. Treatment followed for the fractured leg that sidelined him during the rest of 2008. He returned in 2009, placed sixth in the Masters and U.S. Open, and then came in second at the PGA. Although he had failed to win a Masters, it was a good year for Woods, his only flub coming at the

British Open, where he had failed to make the cut. In the other three majors, all top-ten finishes, his Z score ranged from –1.1 (at Augusta) to –2.0 in the PGA. He appeared to be fully recovered . . . until that Thanksgiving weekend.

Since the infidelities surfaced and the injuries followed, Woods's performance has been decidedly more sporadic and less impressive.

There was a point not so long ago when Woods was on pace to overtake Jack Nicklaus on the career list. But the years since his 2008 U.S. Open victory have not been kind to that goal. Beginning in the spring of 2010, his record in twenty contested majors shows a best finish of third (in the 2012 Brit), four fourths, one sixth, nine placings outside the top ten, and five missed cuts. He also failed to get to the post a dozen times through 2017. A word about those nine placings outside the top ten: between his professional debut in the majors in 1997 and 2009, Tiger had just eighteen placings outside the top ten. He also had fourteen victories.

Were one to run a peak rating for Tiger Woods from 2011 through 2015, his decline is obvious. The average Z score of his ten best majors during that period is –0.65—in short, on the good side of mediocre. His place on the career chart has also eroded. At the end of the 2013 season, he ranked second, behind only Jack Nicklaus, for career value. Entering his 2018 comeback attempt he had fallen to fifth, and the only thing that kept him from falling further appeared to be his inability to play. His performance in the 2018 season's first major, the Masters, resulted in a tie for thirty-second, damaging his career Z score by another 0.40.

Woods has always been viewed as an exceptional driver of the golf ball. Certainly, that aspect was rarely if ever a weakness. The Strokes Gained data conclude that in 2005 and 2006, Woods picked up 0.8 and 0.9 of a stroke per round respectively off the tee. But it also suggests that, at least beginning in 2004, the true strength of his game lay in the breadth of his skills. Here are Woods's annual Strokes Gained slash lines for 2004 through 2007:

Skill	2004	2005	2006	2007	Average
Off the tee	0.32	0.90	0.80	0.62	0.66
Approaching the green	0.87	0.86	2.07	1.65	1.36

Around the green	0.34	-0.02	0.11	0.10	0.13
Putting	0.85	0.66	0.46	0.71	0.67
Net	2.38	2.40	3.43	3.08	2.82

This relatively orgasmic profile shows a player generally deriving nearly half of his prodigious 2.82 stroke advantage over the field via his accuracy from the fairway, not his abilities off the tee or on the green. Not that those represent weaknesses. In fact, if Woods near his peak— there aren't actually Strokes Gained data for Woods at his peak—had any weakness, it lay in his play around the green, where his margin against the field generally was minimal.

To a degree, one can also use the Strokes Gained data to analyze the reasons behind Woods's decline. Those data exist for only two of his postdominant seasons, 2012 and 2013. They show a player whose abilities off the tee had declined into the average to low-average range but whose approach skills remained strong. His pitching and chipping skills, never strong, remained midpack. By 2012 and 2013, Woods was a less dominant but still slightly above-average putter, generally retaining about half his previous advantage in that aspect of play.

On to Sorenstam. Like, it seems, three-quarters of successful golfers past and present, she credits her parents for spurring her interest in the sport. Certainly, it's a family trait, as evidenced by the fact that her sister, Charlotta, was also an LPGA Tour member. At sixteen Sorenstam qualified for the Swedish National Team. Even then she had leading-lady ability.

What she did not have—or at least she wasn't sure she had—was championship desire. That changed with the 1988 victory of fellow Swede Lisolette Neumann at the U.S. Open. However much Neumann's victory did for Neumann, it gave Sorenstam a role model and motivation. A participant in the World Amateur Golf Team Championships in both 1990 and 1992, she won the championship in that second effort.

By then Sorenstam had come to America and immersed herself in the profound experience that is college golf. At the University of Arizona, she became the first foreigner and first freshman to win the NCAA individual championship. She came close to dominating the amateur headlines in 1992, winning the Pac-10 Championship, being named to the All-American team, finishing second in the voting for National Player of the Year, and also finishing second at the Women's Amateur, to Vicki Goetze. She qualified for the U.S. Open but found the competition a bit stout, finishing in a tie for sixty-third.

Following graduation in 1993, Sorenstam operated mostly on the European tour, getting a limited taste of U.S. tour play via sponsors' exemptions. Her first full season here was 1994, and she lived up to expectations, winning the Rookie of the Year Award, although failing to win any of her eighteen starts. She remained winless entering the 1995 Women's Open in mid-July, but she wasn't winless leaving it. Five strokes behind veteran Meg Mallon entering Sunday play, Sorenstam recorded a final round of 68 to take the $175,000 first prize by a single shot.

If the golf world was surprised by this young foreigner's success, Sorenstam forced a quick attitude adjustment. In 1996 she repeated her Open victory, this time by a persuasive 6 strokes. That came atop a runner-up finish at the Nabisco Dinah Shore. By the time of her Open encore, the twenty-five-year-old Sorenstam was already working on her second golf fortune, having passed the $1 million mark in career earnings a month earlier when she finished fourteenth at the McDonald's event. During the season, Sorenstam won three times and won her second straight Vare Trophy for lowest season scoring average. Six wins followed in 1997, and then four more in 1998, when she became the first woman in LPGA history to record a stroke average below 70. Meanwhile, the official money poured in. By 1999 she had topped $6 million in career earnings. Nor had Sorenstam peaked yet. In 2000 Annika began a streak of six seasons in which she posted at least five tournament victories a year. That streak included the 2001 Nabisco, seven more victories, and probably Sorenstam's most famous round, a 59 she recorded in the Standard Register Ping.

Statistically, Sorenstam's peak performances in the LPGA majors didn't even begin until 2002, a season in which she made twenty-five starts and won thirteen times. Sorenstam was fully capable of hijacking the biggest events. Between 2002 and 2006, she posted a score more than 2 standard deviations below the field average in nine of the twenty majors that were played. She won six of those twenty, and the intimidating factoid is how many more she might have won with garden-variety fortune.

At the 2002 U.S. Women's Open at Prairie Dunes, a course that yielded a field average of 291, Sorenstam posted a 278, a total nearly 3 standard deviations below the norm. Shoot 3 standard deviations below the field average, and you almost always win. But Juli Inkster went Sorenstam 2 strokes better, reaching 3.4 standard deviations below the field average, the eighth most dominant showing in the history of the LPGA Tour. Sorenstam was stuck with second place.

The same thing happened at the 2003 Kraft Nabisco. Sorenstam shot a four-round total of 282, a score that was 2.26 standard deviations below the field average of 296. Of the 276 women who completed four rounds of major tournament competition in 2003, only one posted a score that was more than 2.26 standard deviations below the field average. That golfer was Patrice Meunier-LeBlanc, whose 281 beat Sorenstam by a stroke.

Again in the 2004 Women's Open, Sorenstam went inordinately low. Her 276 was 2.28 standard deviations outside the field average of 290. Of the 291 golfers completing four rounds of major competition that year, only 3 beat Sorenstam's 2.28. The best was Sorenstam herself, with a score 2.99 standard deviations below the field average at the LPGA. One of the others was Meg Mallon, whose 274 consigned Sorenstam to second place in that Open.

Generally speaking, though, Sorenstam made the women's tour boring. In 2006 she won the U.S. Women's Open again, her tenth major title, tying her for the third most wins of all time. That victory pushed her over the $19 million mark in career earnings, a record.

Based on correlatable data, Sorenstam's profound edge lay in her exceptional ability to hit greens in regulation. Sorenstam was the poster child for the value of this skill. During her peak seasons, between 2002 and 2006, the average margin by which Sorenstam's performance in GIR exceeded the field average was 2.68 standard deviations, never falling below 2.02. In fact, during the eleven-season period between 1996 and 2006, Sorenstam's average GIR margin of excellence was 2.59, an extraordinary period of extended execution at the game's most sensitive skill. Across those eleven seasons, Sorenstam reached 76 percent of her greens in regulation; her competitors averaged 63 percent. No contest.

Sorenstam retired in 2008 with a career Z score of –59.16. Whether she ranks as the greatest golfer—or at least the greatest female golfer—of all time can be reasonably debated. But based on her record, Annika's name has to be in the discussion.

Woods in the Clubhouse

Tournament	Finish	Score	Z score
1998 British Open	3rd	281	−1.95
1999 U.S. Open	T-3	281	−2.07
1999 PGA	1st	277	−2.53
2000 U.S. Open	1st	272	−4.12
2000 British Open	1st	269	−3.33
2000 PGA	1st	270	−2.27
2001 Masters	1st	272	−2.21
2002 Masters	1st	276	−2.55
2002 U.S. Open	1st	277	−2.71
2002 PGA	2nd	278	−2.30

Note: Average Z score: −2.60. Effective stroke average: 68.15.

WOODS'S CAREER RECORD (1997–2016)

Masters: 18 starts, 4 wins (1997, 2001, 2002, 2005), −24.40

U.S. Open: 17 starts, 2 wins (2000, 2002), −16.38

British Open: 17 starts, 3 wins (2000, 2005, 2006), −12.84

PGA: 18 starts, 4 wins (1999, 2000, 2006, 2007), −11.00

Total (70 starts): −64.62

Year	Z
1997	−1.15
1998	−1.06
1999	−1.58
2000	−2.77
2001	−0.95
2002	−1.99
2003	−0.61
2004	−0.60
2005	−2.28
2006	−1.02
2007	−1.88
2008	−1.94
2009	−0.06
2010	−0.98
2011	0.33
2012	−0.68
2013	−0.75
2014	2.25
2015	1.97

Tiger Woods

Sorenstam in the Clubhouse

Tournament	Finish	Score	Z score
2002 LPGA	3rd	284	-1.95
2002 U.S. Open	2nd	278	-2.94
2003 Kraft Nabisco	2nd	282	-2.26
2003 LPGA	1st	278	-2.14
2003 British Open	1st	278	-2.33
2004 LPGA	1st	271	-2.91
2004 U.S. Open	2nd	276	-2.28
2005 Kraft Nabisco	1st	273	-2.99
2005 LPGA	1st	277	-2.68
2006 U.S. Open	1st	284	-2.37

Note: Average Z score: -2.49. Effective stroke average: 68.31.

SORENSTAM'S CAREER RECORD (1994–2008)

Kraft Nabisco: 14 starts, 3 wins (2001, 2002, 2005), -19.87

U.S. Open: 15 starts, 3 wins (1995, 1996, 2006), -11.80

LPGA: 14 starts, 3 wins (2003, 2004, 2005), -21.66

du Maurier: 6 starts, 0 wins, -2.33

British Open: 8 starts, 1 win (2003), -3.50

Total (57 starts): -59.16

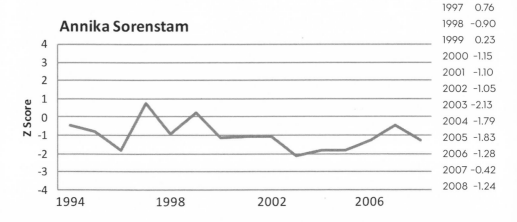

1994	-0.44
1995	-0.81
1996	-1.81
1997	0.76
1998	-0.90
1999	0.23
2000	-1.15
2001	-1.10
2002	-1.05
2003	-2.13
2004	-1.79
2005	-1.83
2006	-1.28
2007	-0.42
2008	-1.24

Phil Mickelson

Number 17 Peak

Through the 1990s and several years into the twenty-first century, Phil Mickelson piece by piece constructed a reputation as a great player—except when it really mattered. In regular tour events, his was a record to envy. As a college student in 1991, he won the Tucson Invitational. Turning pro the following season, he needed only four starts in 1993 to win again, this time the Buick Invitational. In 1994 he beat the tour's best at the Mercedes. Through 1998 Mickelson never failed to reach the winner's circle at least once.

By the spring of 2004, Mickelson had won twenty times on tour and finished in the top five on more than forty other occasions. Yet none of those aspects of his career identified Mickelson in the public mind. This one did: no majors.

It hadn't been for lack of contending. In a dozen years as a pro, Mickelson was often perceived as a major contender and not just because his left-handed game, length off the tee, flowing curls, and college-hero (at Arizona State) background made him stand out. In the 1994 PGA, the twenty-four-year-old came home third, although 7 strokes behind champion Nick Price. At Shinnecock in 1995, he stood just a stroke off the pace after three rounds but succumbed to the pressure applied by a hard-charging Corey Pavin on Sunday. Mickelson shot 74 and Pavin posted 68 and won by 3, Mickelson consigned to a tie for fourth.

That round marked Mickelson as a guy who made the big one a tribulation. In 1996 he won four times and was positioned to take advantage of Greg Norman's epic collapse at the Masters. Instead, he posted a pedestrian 72 for third place, while Nick Faldo shot the winning 67.

At the 1999 U.S. Open at Pinehurst, Mickelson added real-life melodrama to his usual golfing version. He arrived at the course packing a cell phone so his wife—expecting their first child literally any day—could summon him off the course in the event she went into labor. Mickelson shot an opening 67 to tie for the lead. He followed with rounds of 70 and 73 to stand one stroke behind Payne Stewart and one ahead of Tiger Woods as the final Sunday began. For one of the game's frontline figures, positioned to capture his first major, there was a story line: Which Mickelson would deliver first? When Stewart holed a fifteen-foot putt on the final hole to beat him by a stroke—and with Mickelson watching him do it—skill averted fate. The next morning, Mickelson became a papa. Had a playoff been necessary, he said he would have forfeited it.

The 2001 majors were Mickelson's most consistently successful but also in many ways his most frustrating. He finished third to Woods and David Duval at the Masters and tied for seventh at the Open at Southern Hills. As at Shinnecock in 1995 and Pinehurst in 1999, it wasn't that simple. His first three rounds had consistently improved: a 70, then a 69, then a 68. He stood fifth but just 2 shots behind an unimposing leader board that nowhere included Tiger Woods, Vijay Singh, or Ernie Els. Then on Sunday Mickelson ballooned to a 75 and fell to a tie for seventh. As it turned out, a 69—his average round for the week to that point—would have put him in a playoff with Retief Goosen and Mark Brooks. Two months later at the PGA, Mickelson fired three consecutive rounds of 66, followed by a 68. Nice, but not nice enough. David Toms beat him by a stroke. He was third at the Masters in 2002, second to Woods at the 2002 Open at Bethpage Black, and second again at the 2003 Masters. Mickelson had become a self-parody: Mr. Close.

He put that identity to rest at the 2004 Masters, holding off Ernie Els's final-round charge to win by a stroke. Freed from his goblins, Mickelson did not exactly run off on a long-delayed tear, but he did follow up. He turned in statistically his best performance at the 2004 Open, although finishing runner-up to Goosen. At the British Open, a Sunday 68 barely missed getting him into a playoff in which Todd Hamilton upset Els. Mickelson finished sixth at the PGA but won the event the following year. He added a third major, his second Masters, in 2005.

Mickelson turned forty-seven midway through the 2017 season, but that has not slowed him down. He added a third Masters in 2010, won the 2013 British Open, and has landed seven top fives. None were more dramatic than his July 2016 battle with Henrik Stenson for what would have been Mickelson's second British Open. He opened with a record-tying 63 and finished 17 under par. Although losing to Stenson by 3 strokes, Micklelson at least had this. His –3.07 Z score was the third best in major tournament history by a nonwinner, trailing only 1966 U.S. Open playoff loser Arnold Palmer (–3.42) and Jack Nicklaus (–3.23) in his 1977 loss to Tom Watson at Turnberry.

Mickelson's reputation as a long driver is well earned. During seventeen of his twenty-four pro seasons between 1993 and 2016, the standard deviation of his performance off the tee exceeded +1.0; never in that time did it go negative. Since turning forty-two in 2012, however, his average Strokes Gained score has turned slightly negative. Since we've already affirmed that age is hell, this may not come as a surprise. Most of Mickelson's average 1.11 Strokes Gained advantage since 2012 has come on the green (0.44) or in his approach shots (0.43).

Mickelson in the Clubhouse

Tournament	Finish	Score	Z score
2001 Masters	3rd	275	–1.69
2001 U.S. Open	T-7	282	–1.28
2001 PGA	2nd	266	–2.64
2002 Masters	3rd	280	–1.76
2002 U.S. Open	2nd	280	–2.21
2003 Masters	3rd	283	–1.81
2004 Masters	1st	279	–2.10
2004 U.S. Open	2nd	278	–2.36
2004 British Open	3rd	275	–2.14
2005 PGA	1st	276	–1.98

Note: Average Z score: –2.00. Effective stroke average: 69.03.

MICKELSON'S CAREER RECORD (1993–PRESENT)

Masters: 24 starts, 3 wins (2004, 2006, 2010), –14.22
U.S. Open: 22 starts, 0 wins, –6.80
British Open: 21 starts, 1 win (2013), +4.40
PGA: 24 starts, 1 win (2005), –7.14
Total (91 starts): –23.76

Phil Mickelson

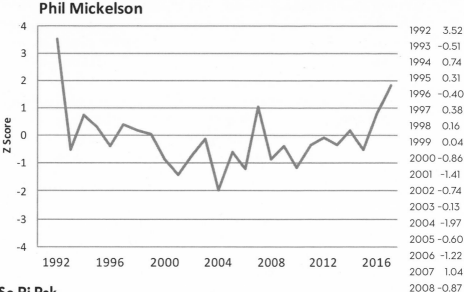

1992	3.52
1993	-0.51
1994	0.74
1995	0.31
1996	-0.40
1997	0.38
1998	0.16
1999	0.04
2000	-0.86
2001	-1.41
2002	-0.74
2003	-0.13
2004	-1.97
2005	-0.60
2006	-1.22
2007	1.04
2008	-0.87
2009	-0.36
2010	-1.15
2011	-0.34
2012	-0.07
2013	-0.35
2014	0.16
2015	-0.51
2016	0.77
2017	1.83

Se Ri Pak

Almost without exception, Asian players at the top of modern LPGA leader boards cite Pak as the role model spurring them to greatness.

It couldn't have been easy for Pak, the only Korean on tour when she arrived as a twenty-year-old rookie who spoke little English in 1998. She had one thing going for her: a work ethic. Growing up in Korea, her routine had consisted of rising every day at five thirty and then running up and down the fifteen flights of stairs in her apartment building, forward and backward. That was followed by winter and summer daylong sessions at the driving range.[1] The discipline soon helped her fashion an impressive résumé that included six victories on the LPGA of Korea tour.

Her initial efforts on the U.S. tour were undistinguished: a tie for thirteenth in her first competition, a missed cut, and a few finishes in the mid-40s. Pak arrived at the McDonald's LPGA Championship that May having won about $40,000 in nine starts, putting her on nobody's radar screen as a contender.

Yet an opening-round 65, followed with two more rounds in the 60s, led to an 11-under-par finish, 3 shots clear of the field.

That victory was initially looked upon as a fluke, in part because Pak followed it with finishes no higher than twenty-sixth in the next four tournaments. For the fifty-third edition of the U.S. Women's Open July 2 at Blackwolf Run in Wisconsin, Pak was in the familiar position of nameless, faceless part of the pack expected to futilely chase tournament favorites Annika Sorenstam, Laura Davies, and Karrie Webb.

Instead, Pak shot an opening 69 to tie for the first-round lead, followed with a 70, and then held on as Blackwolf Run chewed up the field. Surprisingly, Pak's toughest challenge came from none of the favorites but from amateur Jenny Chuasiriporn, another twenty-year-old making her first public splash. Playing one group ahead of Pak, Chuasiriporn holed a forty-foot birdie putt on the final hole to tie Pak for the lead and force an eighteen-hole Monday playoff. The two unknowns battled through all eighteen of those holes and more before Pak sank an eighteen-foot birdie putt on the twentieth hole to claim the trophy. She became the youngest woman ever to win the U.S. Open, the youngest ever to win two majors, and an idol in Korea.

Her stunning debut—victories in the first two majors in which she competed—made Pak the obvious choice as Tour Rookie of the Year, and with more than $870,000 in official winnings she finished second on the money list behind only Sorenstam. Pak followed up with a victory in the 2001 Women's British Open and added a second LPGA title in 2002 and a third in 2006, defeating Webb in a playoff. By 2007 she had qualified for induction into the World Golf Hall of fame; she was just twenty-nine, the youngest honoree in the hall's history.

Pak's most profound legacy—the hordes of young Asian players who modeled their games after her—was just starting to show itself. Those players included Inbee Park and Na Yeon Choi, both of whom cited Pak as their inspiration. At the 2007 U.S. Open, when Pak and Park tied for fourth place, her Asian-born prodigies claimed thirteen of the top-twenty-one placings. By then the tour had a generic name for them: Se Ri's Kids.

In her prime, Pak's game was a template for success on the LPGA Tour. Between 1998 and 2002—her peak seasons—Pak averaged 255 yards off the tee, 1.45 standard deviations (14 yards) longer than her competitors. She also hit greens at a 71 percent rate, 1.7 standard deviations (9 percentage points) better than the LPGA field. As she aged, Pak's advantages in those two areas shrank to about half their peak sizes, although they never evaporated entirely. What did evaporate was Pak's ability to find the fairway. Between 1998 and 2003, the standard deviation of Pak's accuracy with the driver was +0.11; from 2004 onward it was −0.76.

Pak largely scaled back her competitive schedule after 2014. Yet by inspiring her fellow Koreans to LPGA success, Pak's contribution extended far beyond the course. In a 2008 review of her career to that date, Eric Adelson said Pak "changed the face of golf even more than . . . Woods."[2]

Pak in the Clubhouse

Tournament	Finish	Score	Z score
1998 LPGA	1st	273	−1.79
1998 U.S. Open	1st	290	−2.44
2000 U.S. Open	T-15	293	−1.53
2000 du Maurier	T-7	289	−1.26
2001 Nabisco	T-11	287	−1.15
2001 U.S. Open	2nd	281	−1.74
2001 British Open	1st	277	−2.05
2002 U.S. Open	5th	285	−1.37
2002 LPGA	1st	279	−2.77
2002 British Open	T-11	279	−1.22

Note: Average Z score: −1.73. Effective stroke average: 69.43.

PAK'S CAREER RECORD (1997–PRESENT)

> Kraft Nabisco/ANA: 17 starts, 0 wins, −10.07
> U.S. Open: 19 starts, 1 win (1998), +3.64
> LPGA: 16 starts, 3 wins (1998, 2002, 2007), −0.41
> du Maurier: 3 starts, 0 wins, −2.08
> British Open: 9 starts, 1 win (2001), −5.86
> Evian Masters: 2 starts, 0 wins, −1.23
> **Total (66 starts): −14.78**

Se Ri Pak

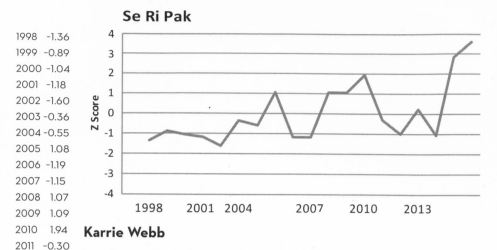

Year	Z Score
1998	-1.36
1999	-0.89
2000	-1.04
2001	-1.18
2002	-1.60
2003	-0.36
2004	-0.55
2005	1.08
2006	-1.19
2007	-1.15
2008	1.07
2009	1.09
2010	1.94
2011	-0.30
2012	-0.99
2013	0.25
2014	-1.02
2015	2.82
2016	3.62

Karrie Webb

Number 6 Peak

Who was the best female golfer of the past twenty years? Don't jump too quickly to what may seem like the obvious answer . . . at least not until considering the credentials of a talented Australian whose arrival on the LPGA Tour was as impressive as it was meteoric.

For a substantial portion of those years, Karrie Webb may have been better than Annika, Lorena, Inbee, or any other women you can think of. It would be hard to top her debut. A fledgling pro of nineteen making her way on the European women's tour in July 1994, Webb rocked the British Open with rounds of 69, 70, 69, and 70 to finish 6 strokes ahead of Sorenstam, her closest pursuer.

Despite that victory, the LPGA Tour required Webb to earn her playing card, which she did while playing the qualifying rounds with a broken wrist. She finished second in her American debut, won her next start, and finished second, seventh, fourth, and fifth in the next four. Take that, America. Webb won four times that rookie season, won three more (with four runners-up) as a sophomore, and added two more victories in her third year, 1998. By the time she was twenty-five, she had a second at the du Maurier, a third at the Nabisco, a fourth at the U.S. Open, and a fourth at the LPGA. In 1999 alone, Webb collected six tour titles, finished second another six times, finished in the top five sixteen times in twenty-five starts, and won more than $1.5 million

Then she got good.

Between 2000 and 2004, Webb was every bit the match for Sorenstam in her prime. Annika won five majors, but so did Karrie. Annika had seven other finishes in the top five; Karrie had four. Annika had thirteen top-ten finishes in the twenty women's majors contested during that period; Webb had a dozen.

Webb probably exploded into the American consciousness—which is, after all, what's important—when she won the highly visible Nabisco tournament (now the ANA Inspiration) by 10 strokes in the spring of 2000. Ten strokes is putting the field to shame, and the performance deserves more than passing mention. Webb's 274 was 20 strokes below the field average for the week, translating to a –3.77 Z score. In any bell curve set of data, a result 3.77 standard deviations below the norm will occur about one time in a thousand. You can look through all the pages of major tournament competition, and you will find just three golfers who've done better: Cristie Kerr, Woods, and Yani Tseng.

She wasn't done. At that summer's U.S. Open, Webb staged a second rout, winning this time by 5 strokes over Kerr and Meg Mallon. She tied for second at the 2001 Nabisco—losing to Sorenstam—but made up for it by winning the LPGA by 2. At the 2001 Open, Webb distanced herself from runner-up Se Ri Pak by 8 strokes with a four-round total of 273. This time she produced a –3.24 Z score, the tenth-most-dominant effort in the history of the LPGA Tour. For the eight LPGA majors contested from March 2000 through August 2001, Webb's average Z score was –2.14.

She claimed her fifth major in three seasons and completed the career Grand Slam, at the 2002 British Open, her margin a mere 2 strokes over Michelle Ellis and Paula Marti.

During her peak seasons—2000 through 2004—Webb's skill set lacked any gaps. The superiority of her advantages in driver distance, driver accuracy, and greens in regulation all ranged from 1 to 1.9 standard deviation better than the field average; her putting skills registered three-quarters of a standard deviation better than the field. As she aged, Webb's advantage in length receded; by 2016 the forty-one-year-old was averaging 251 yards off the tee, slightly below the tour average. Yet at that advanced stage of her career, she remained above average in other skill areas, hitting fairways and greens and making putts at rates that were respectively two-thirds, half, and one-quarter of a standard deviation above the tour average.

On the scorecard, Webb declined gracefully. She won the 2006 Kraft Nabisco, defeating Ochoa in a playoff, and lost that season's LPGA to Pak only in a second playoff. Then in 2007 she lost the LPGA to Suzann Pettersen by one stroke. Since 2007 she has added nine more top-ten major finishes.

Webb in the Clubhouse

Tournament	Finish	Score	Z score
2000 Nabisco	1st	274	**-3.77**
2000 LPGA	T-9	284	-1.40
2000 U. S. Open	1st	282	**-2.56**
2001 Nabisco	T-2	284	-1.62
2001 LPGA	1st	270	**-2.44**
2001 U.S. Open	1st	273	**-3.24**
2002 LPGA	T-4	285	-1.78
2002 British Open	1st	273	**-2.11**
2003 British Open	T-3	280	-1.98
2004 Kraft Nabisco	3rd	279	-1.87

Note: Average Z score: –2.28. Effective stroke average: 68.62.

WEBB'S CAREER RECORD (1996–PRESENT)

Kraft Nabisco/ANA: 22 starts, 2 wins (2000, 2006), –17.57
U.S. Open: 22 starts, 2 wins (2000, 2001), –0.19
LPGA: 22 starts, 1 win (2001), –10.13
du Maurier: 5 starts, 1 win (1999), –3.52
British Open: 16 starts, 1 win (2001), +3.40
Evian Masters: 5 starts, 0 wins, +2.88
Total (92 starts): –25.13

Karrie Webb

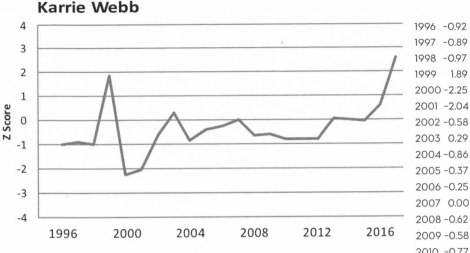

1996	-0.92
1997	-0.89
1998	-0.97
1999	1.89
2000	-2.25
2001	-2.04
2002	-0.58
2003	0.29
2004	-0.86
2005	-0.37
2006	-0.25
2007	0.00
2008	-0.62
2009	-0.58
2010	-0.77
2011	-0.77
2012	-0.79
2013	0.06
2014	0.00
2015	-0.04
2016	0.60
2017	2.60

Lorena Ochoa

Lorena Ochoa walked away from tournament golf as close to the height of her ability as it is possible to imagine.

Ochoa competed for seven seasons, plus part of her eighth, before calling it quits in May 2010. She was twenty-eight and less than a month removed from a fourth-place finish in the Kraft Nabisco. But, she said, the constant demands on time and family that the tour imposed had burned her out. "After two or three days of being in Thailand . . . I didn't want to be out there," she said, referencing a mid-February tournament halfway around the world from her home in Mexico. "There are so many other things I want to do. I am at peace."[3]

So Ochoa retired, committing her efforts to a family-run foundation with a broad focus. Golf is part of it: Ochoa designs courses, operates an instructional academy for youngsters, and sponsors her own tournament. But it doesn't stop there. The foundation also sponsors an educational center for hundreds of elementary and middle school children near Guadalajara. She has conducted clinics targeted toward senior business executives and has testified in Washington in support of fitness legislation.

It's an interesting résumé for someone who might, had her heart been driven in a different direction, be thought of today as the greatest female golfer of all time. In retrospect, however, that was never in her grand plan. In fact, a young Ochoa foreshadowed her departure from the scene during a 2002 interview with *Golfweek*. "I want to be remembered for things I did outside the golf course," she said at the time. "Not for winning tournaments. That is very clear to me."[4]

The product of parents who lived on a golf course and could afford to educate her at a private Mexican school, she early on acquired both a love of golf and a sense of commitment to the needs of her community. Unlike Lee Trevino, Ochoa didn't need a way out of the barrio; she needed a way to contribute. Golf provided that way. Since arriving on tour full-time in 2003, her success has ratcheted upward. Playing in her first full season, she chased Patrice Meunier-LeBlanc and Annika Sorenstam to the finish at the 2003 Kraft Nabisco, eventually finishing third. She played in two dozen events that first full season and failed to win any of them. But she did earn nearly $825,000.

Ochoa broke through at the 2004 Franklin Morgan Mortgage Championship, although that win could have been viewed as tainted by the absence of several of the tour's stars, among them Sorenstam. But that victory as well as another later in the season at the Wachovia—combined with nine more top-ten finishes—drove Ochoa's earnings beyond $1.4 million.

Ochoa won six more times in 2006, positioning herself to supplant Sorenstam as the game's top player. She picked up nearly $2.6 million in the process. She did not, however, win a major, missing her best chance when Webb beat her in a playoff at the Kraft Nabisco. It took until the final major of 2007, the British Open, for Ochoa to erase that debit mark on her report card, beating Jee Young Lee and Maria Hjorth by 4 shots. Given that it was one of seven Ochoa victories in 2007 alone, and the thirteenth of her professional experience, the prevailing attitude in the galleries was "What took you so long?"

A second major came quickly, the 2008 Kraft Nabisco falling to her by a telling 5 strokes over Sorenstam. Her third-place finish at the LPGA followed a runner-up showing at the 2007 U.S. Open and the British and Kraft Nabisco victories. It also marked her seventh consecutive top-ten finish in a major.

Yet it was already evident to those who looked closely that Ochoa was losing her competitive edge. In 2009, for the first time since she turned pro, Ochoa failed to record a top-ten finish in any of the majors. Her official winnings, more than $4.6 million in 2007, fell to $2.7 million in 2008 and then to $1.5 million. To outward appearances, her fourth-place finish in the 2010 Kraft Nabisco looked like the old Ochoa, but Lorena had already checked out mentally.

The on-course résumé she walked away from needs no burnishing. Nonetheless, a glance at the correlatable skills data is enlightening. Between 2004 and 2008, Ochoa averaged 267 yards off the tee, 2 standard deviations (19 yards, or two clubs) superior to the field average. She hit greens at a 73 percent rate, another 2 standard deviations (9 percentage points) superior to the field. Her putting measured 1.14 standard deviations better than her competitors. As became evident on the scoreboard, that constituted a tough skill set to beat. Ochoa's average annual Z score in the majors only once exceeded 0. As for additional honors, Ochoa simply did not feel the need to chase them.

Ochoa in the Clubhouse

Tournament	Finish	Score	Z score
2004 British Open	4th	276	–1.48
2006 Kraft Nabisco	2nd	279	–2.27
2006 LPGA	T-9	283	–1.41
2006 British Open	T-4	285	–1.71
2007 LPGA	T-6	280	–1.41
2007 U.S. Open	T-2	281	–2.05
2007 British Open	1st	**287**	**–2.43**
2008 Kraft Nabisco	1st	**277**	**–2.98**
2008 LPGA	T-3	277	–1.81
2008 British Open	T-7	277	–1.30

Note: Average Z score: –1.89. Effective stroke average: 69.19.

OCHOA'S CAREER RECORD (2003–10)

Kraft Nabisco: 8 starts, 1 win (2008), –12.29

U.S. Open: 7 starts, 0 wins, –4.45

LPGA: 7 starts, 0 wins, –8.40

British Open: 7 starts, 1 win (2007), –4.05

Total (29 starts): –29.18

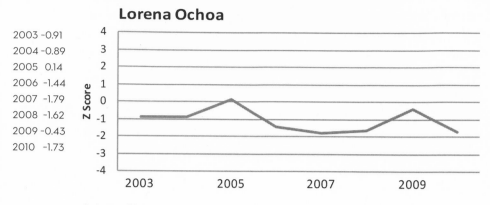

Lorena Ochoa

2003	-0.91
2004	-0.89
2005	0.14
2006	-1.44
2007	-1.79
2008	-1.62
2009	-0.43
2010	-1.73

Cristie Kerr

Number 18 Peak

During one astonishing week in 2010, Cristie Kerr authored the most dominant performance in the history of major tournament golf, men's or women's.

That June Kerr played the Locust Hill Golf Club in Rochester, New York, site of the LPGA, in rounds of 68-66-69-66 for a winning total of 269. That colorless description does not approach doing justice to Kerr's feat. She not only won her second major championship and the $337,500 that went along with the trophy but also defeated her closest pursuer by a dozen strokes.

Not that the 6,506-yard course was in lay-down mode that week—at least not for most of the competitors. Among the seventy-three who completed four rounds, the stroke average was 290.99, about 3 over par. Only thirteen managed to break the par of 288, and only four finished as many as 5 strokes below par. Kerr came home at –19.

Kerr failed to post the day's low round every day of the tournament only because Morgan Pressel managed a Saturday 68, 1 stroke better than her. She needed only 92 percent of the field average number of strokes and, perhaps as remarkably, needed just 96 percent of runner-up Song-Hee Kim's total. She beat Kim by as wide a margin as Kim beat the tournament's forty-seventh-place finisher.

It all translated to a Z score of –4.21, the best in the nearly 160-year history of the majors. Tiger Woods may have separated himself from the field at Pebble Beach in 2000, but even he only managed a -4.12 Z score. When Jack Nicklaus played the game with which Bobby Jones "was not familiar" at the 1965 Masters, his Z score only reached -3.50. Kerr's showing was so remarkable that as early as the morning of the final round, her chief competitors had done something they almost never do in major events: they had given up. "Forget about [Kerr], she's too far ahead," remarked eventual runner-up Song Hee Kim of her Sunday game plan.[5]

A thirty-two-year-old veteran who joined the tour in 1996, Kerr had struggled through six largely unremarkable seasons—a runner-up showing at the 2000 Open being the highlight—before finding her game in 2003. Kerr beat the field average in all four of that season's majors, winning a personal-best $86,000. Her first trophy came in 2004—the Takefuji Classic, followed by the Shoprite and State Farm—and her earnings rose again, this time to $115,000. A tie for third at the 2005 Kraft Nabisco preceded top tens in the Women's Open and British Open.

It all constituted a decent turnaround to that point, but Kerr had yet to hit her stride. That occurred with her 2-stroke victory over Angela Park in the 2007 U.S. Open. She finished sixth on the money list that season, tenth in 2008, second in 2009, and third in 2010.

Even setting aside her performance at the LPGA, 2010 was Kerr's pinnacle season. Her twenty-one starts included two victories, nine top fives, and two other top tens. She tied for fifth at both the Kraft Nabisco and the British Open. Her average Z score in that season's four majors was -2.01, the best on the women's tour for the second consecutive season.

Kerr was thirty-nine at the end of the 2017 season—old by LPGA standards but not debilitatingly so. Indeed, her correlatable skills had not by that point deteriorated. This may be because Kerr was solid but not spectacular in all of those areas. Across her career, she drove the ball at a rate just under 1 standard deviation better than the average, although by 2017 that figure had deteriorated only to 0.4 a standard deviation better. In 2017 she also hit greens at a rate about 0.4 of a standard deviation better than the norm, below her career-long 1.11

standard deviation advantage but still good. She compensated for those declines by enjoying the best putting season of her career, requiring just 28.89 per round. That was fifth best on tour and 1.92 standard deviations better than the tour average, substantially improved from her 0.65 career advantage.

So dominant was Kerr that magical week in Rochester that it inevitably biases her peak rating, although perhaps *biases* isn't the correct word; she did, after all, do it. Had Kerr merely won in normal fashion—say, with a –2.0 Z score—her 2007–11 peak rating would today be –1.78. But Kerr did score that unprecedented rout; she did post a –4.21. The result is a peak rating of –2.00, the eighteenth best by any player in the history of major tournament golf.

Kerr in the Clubhouse

Tournament	Finish	Score	Z score
2007 U.S. Open	1st	279	**–2.43**
2008 British Open	6th	276	–1.48
2009 Kraft Nabisco	T-2	280	–2.04
2009 U.S. Open	T-3	286	–1.70
2009 British Open	T-8	291	–1.20
2010 Kraft Nabisco	T-5	284	–1.40
2010 LPGA	1st	269	**–4.21**
2010 British Open	T-5	282	–1.81
2011 U.S. Open	3rd	283	–1.94
2011 LPGA	T-3	280	–1.77

Note: Average Z score: –2.00. Effective stroke average: 69.03.

KERR'S CAREER RECORD (1996–PRESENT)

Kraft Nabisco/ANA: 18 starts, 0 wins, –9.41
U.S. Open: 21 starts, 1 win (2007), –5.64
LPGA: 21 starts, 1 win (2010), –2.83
British Open: 16 starts, 0 wins, –7.17
du Maurier: 4 starts, 0 wins, +7.28
Evian Masters: 5 starts, 0 wins, +4.57
Total (85 starts): –13.20

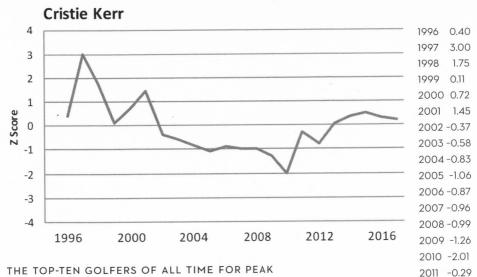

Cristie Kerr

1996	0.40
1997	3.00
1998	1.75
1999	0.11
2000	0.72
2001	1.45
2002	-0.37
2003	-0.58
2004	-0.83
2005	-1.06
2006	-0.87
2007	-0.96
2008	-0.99
2009	-1.26
2010	-2.01
2011	-0.29
2012	-0.80
2013	0.05
2014	0.37
2015	0.49
2016	0.31
2017	0.20

THE TOP-TEN GOLFERS OF ALL TIME FOR PEAK
RATING AS OF THE END OF THE 2000 SEASON.

Rank	Player	Seasons	Z score	Effective stroke average
1.	Arnold Palmer	1960–64	-2.31	68.57
2.	Jack Nicklaus	1971–75	-2.302	68.59
3.	James Braid	1901–10	-2.18	68.76
4.	Tom Watson	1977–81	-2.17	68.78
5.	Ben Hogan	1950–54	-2.13	68.84
6.	Bobby Jones	1926–30	-2.11	68.87
7.	Walter Hagen	1923–27	-2.10	68.88
8.	Sam Snead	1947–51	-2.07	68.93
9.	Mickey Wright	1958–62	-2.06	68.94
10.	Harry Vardon	1896–1904	-2.03	68.98

THE TOP-TEN GOLFERS OF ALL TIME FOR CAREER
RATING AS OF THE END OF THE 2000 SEASON.

Rank	Player	Seasons	Z score
1.	Jack Nicklaus	1962–80	-104.55
2.	Walter Hagen	1913–40	-73.79
3.	Patty Berg	1935–68	-73.21
4.	Sam Snead	1937–62	-68.69

5.	Louise Suggs	1948–72	–60.31
6.	Mickey Wright	1954–84	–59.67
7.	Gene Sarazen	1920–51	–58.09
8.	Ben Hogan	1938–62	–53.09
9.	Byron Nelson	1933–60	–44.88
10.	Jim Barnes	1913–32	–44.58

THE TOP-TEN GOLFERS OF ALL TIME FOR PEAK
RATING AS OF THE END OF THE 2010 SEASON.

Rank	Player	Seasons	Z score	Effective stroke average
1.	Tiger Woods	1998–2002	–2.60	68.15
2.	Annika Sorenstam	2002–6	–2.49	68.31
3.	Arnold Palmer	1960–64	–2.31	68.57
4.	Jack Nicklaus	1971–75	–2.302	68.59
5.	Karrie Webb	2000–2004	–2.28	68.62
6.	James Braid	1901–10	–2.18	68.76
7.	Tom Watson	1977–81	–2.17	68.78
8.	Ben Hogan	1950–54	–2.13	68.84
9.	Bobby Jones	1926–30	–2.11	68.87
10.	Walter Hagen	1923–27	–2.10	68.88

THE TOP-TEN GOLFERS OF ALL TIME FOR CAREER
RATING AS OF THE END OF THE 2010 SEASON.

Rank	Player	Seasons	Z score
1.	Jack Nicklaus	1962–80	–104.86
2.	Walter Hagen	1913–40	–73.94
3.	Patty Berg	1935–68	–73.21
4.	Tiger Woods	1996–2010	–71.91
5.	Sam Snead	1937–62	–68.69
6.	Louise Suggs	1948–72	–60.31
7.	Mickey Wright	1954–84	–59.67
8.	Annika Sorenstam	1994–08	–59.16
9.	Gene Sarazen	1920–51	–58.09
10.	Ben Hogan	1938–62	–53.09

12 Still on the Course

Something has happened to the face of the best professional golfers since the emergence of Tiger Woods. It has gotten younger. For three decades, roughly between 1970 and 2000, experience counted heavily on both the men's and the women's professional circuits. Not so much anymore.

A study of the prime performance period of the best PGA and LPGA pros shows a clear pattern. For decades, as both tours matured, the ages at which the game's greatest reached their peak declined. The decline has been slow but inexorable. If we group the approximately two hundred players whose careers were examined for this book generationally, the trend is clear.

The peaks of twenty-four occurred prior to 1920. The average age of those twenty-four at midpeak was 30.5 years. Between 1920 and the end of World War II, another twenty-six players peaked. Their average age at mid-peak was 30.8 years . . . not substantially different.

From 1946 through the 1950s, the average age of the twenty-five most successful players rose, to 34.8 years. But this was an aberration, created in some measure by World War II—which probably postponed the primes of Snead, Hogan, and Mangrum—and also by the emergence of the women's tour. Patty Berg, to name one, hit stardom at an older than usual age because there had been no stardom to hit a decade earlier. In any event, the average reverted to 31.4 years for forty stars whose midprimes occurred during the 1960s and 1970s. During the 1980s and 1990s, forty-two stars hit midprime, and they did so at an average age of 34.0 years.

The arrivals of Woods and Se Ri Pak, just 20 when she came out of nowhere to win the U.S. Open and LPGA in 1998, appear to have marked turning points on both tours. Since 2000 forty-four of the game's most dominant men and women have entered primes. The average age at prime of those forty-four was just 27.1 years, a full 7 years younger than the parallel group from the 1980s and 1990s. Among those forty-four, the primes of twenty-six have begun since 2010; their average age is just 25.9 years. That precocious list includes Jordan Spieth, Jason Day, Lydia Ko, Inbee Park, and Rory McIlroy.

The genius Tiger Woods showed at such an early age is almost taken for granted today. He was 22 years old when he entered into the best five-season stretch of his career in 1998, and perhaps some perspective is in order on that fact. Prior to Woods, the last nine true PGA Tour stars—Vijay Singh, Paul Azinger, Davis Love, Nick Price, Greg Norman, Nick Faldo, Ian Woosnam, José María Olazábal, and Payne Stewart—were all 30 or older when they hit their prime performance periods. No player had done so before age 25 since Ben Crenshaw, who was 24 when his prime began in 1976. In all of golf history, only thirteen stars—men or women—entered their primes before age 21. Eight of those thirteen began their golfing maturity within the most recent two decades and six within the most recent decade. That poses a tantalizing question: Are we now passing through the greatest era of golfing talent in the measurable history of the game?

If by that question we seek to measure the cumulative peak performances of the stars, the answer might be yes. Woods (number 1 all time in peak rating), Sorenstam (number 2), Tseng (number 5), and Webb (number 6) give the current or recently retired generation four players in the top seven.

One way to get a feel for whether any particular generation of star players was superior to others is to calculate the average peak Z score of each "generation" of the game's greats based on the midpoint of their peaks. We can easily do that for the players on whose records this book is based. The results graph as follows.

Strength by Generations

Average peak Z score by period in which rated players' peaks began

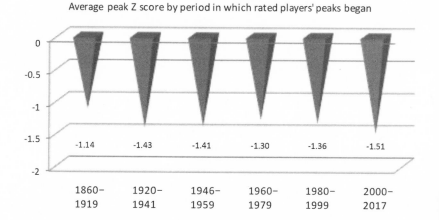

	1860–1919	1920–1941	1946–1959	1960–1979	1980–1999	2000–2017
	-1.14	-1.43	-1.41	-1.30	-1.36	-1.51

The data illustrate that at least in terms of the top-ranked players, the present crop may indeed represent the apex of superstardom on the links. At –1.51, the average peak Z score of the modern players included in the ranking represents the best performance of any generation. And since some of those modern stars remain in their peaks, they could still improve on that average.

One clear implication of the peak-score graph is that stars are stars in any generation. With the exception of pre-1920 stars, the average peak Z scores for all generations don't vary by much.

The present generation is nowhere near tops for producing career value. With an average career Z score of –20.70, that honor rests with the dominant players who reached the physical prime between the world wars. In fact, the average career Z scores of all generations since 1960 are positive. Why? The answer is likely money. With far richer pots to play for, modern-era players are hanging around several years after their predecessors packed it up and went home. In doing so, they are making big bucks but also driving their career Z scores from exceptional toward average.

Here's a graph of the career performance totals by decade.

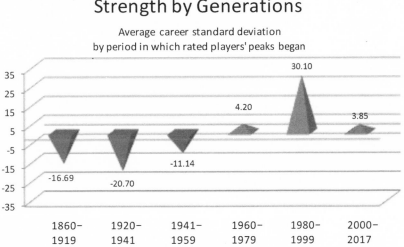

Strength by Generations

Average career standard deviation
by period in which rated players' peaks began

A second factor influencing the career totals of all players is the raw number of tournaments played. Unlike peak value, which in most cases represents the 10 best tournaments from a player's defined five-season peak period, career totals are cumulative and poor results are counted. For the game's early stars, it's virtually impossible to build up substantial career totals. Together, Old Tom and Young Tom Morris only played in 20 major tournaments (excluding those Old Tom played in when he was past his prime). That's only about one-quarter Tiger Woods's total and fewer than a fifth of Jack Nicklaus's total.

Most of the modern pros, however—those who aren't Tiger or Jack—have the opposite problem. Nick Faldo is a good example. Between 1976 and 2006—his functional career—Faldo teed it up in 93 majors. He did pretty well, too, winning 6 of them, placing second in 2 others, and landing 24 top 10s. But Faldo also missed 18 cuts, and those undermined his career Z score by about 3 points per missed cut. Like a lot of his compatriots, the lure of large paydays caused Faldo to stay at the party long enough to damage his career rating. Fifteen of his 18 missed cuts came when Faldo was in his forties. In fact, if Faldo was scored solely on his career accomplishments between 1983 and 1996, he'd be among the top thirty all time for career performance, at –32.18. Instead, his career rating is +7.32.

Let us not leave the impression that playing in a lot of majors is and always must be a bad thing. Jack Nicklaus played in 111 of them between 1962 and 1989, and he leads the career list. As with life itself, the number of opportunities is less important than what one makes of them.

Could anyone playing today eventually surpass Tiger on the peak-value list or Jack in career value?

The easy emotional answer is "Sure, that could happen." Several emerging talents could do it. Rory McIlroy, Jordan Spieth, Jason Day, and Dustin Johnson are all candidates. But the emotional answer is, of course, not always the proper answer. Woods set a monumental standard between 1998 and 2002. The fact that he leads players of the stature of Sorenstam, Palmer, and Nicklaus should give fans of Spieth, McIlroy, and a cohort of women pause.

Let's look at each of the peak and career scores through 2017 of several modern male and female stars.

Rory McIlroy

McIlroy functionally arrived in 2009, announcing his presence by tying for third at the PGA. That was the tournament when Y. E. Yang famously de-pantsed Tiger by 3 shots. But McIlroy's true peak period began in 2011 with his dominating victory in the U.S. Open. That 8-stroke win at Congressional translated to a Z score of –3.07. His win at the 2012 PGA—again by 8 strokes—brought another minus –3 Z score. McIlroy's two 2014 victories at the British Open and PGA were less dominant but still generated Z scores in the range of –2.0 and –2.4. The 2015 season brought top-ten finishes in the Masters and U.S. Open.

Four scores of –2.0 or lower in five years constitutes a pretty good start toward a memorable peak Z score. But McIlroy's performances in other tournaments have been only marginally as impressive. Among his ten best tournaments between 2011 and 2015 were also a tie for twenty-third in the 2014 U.S. Open and seventeenth at the 2015 PGA. In 2016 he mixed top tens at the Masters and British Open with missed cuts at the U.S. Open and PGA, offsetting that—in his bank account, if not his Z score—by winning the FedEx Cup. His average score in the eight 2016–17 majors is a pedestrian +0.60, including three missed cuts. With that uneven record, McIlroy failed to improve his five-year peak from its 2011–15 average of –1.66.

Given the mediocrity of McIlroy's 2016 and 2017, he would need to average about –1.75 through the 2018 season in order to improve his peak rating. The math varies, but generally a –1.75 score translates to a top-three finish. So what are the odds of McIlroy finishing among the top three in four consecutive majors?

There are three methods of speculating on future performance: past performance, historical comparables, and statistical projections. Unfortunately, none of them is notably reliable. For whatever they are worth, two can easily be applied to McIlroy.

Aside from his four championships, entering 2018 McIlroy has not produced a –1.75 score. McIlroy's five-year forecast tells the same tale. It projects average annual Z scores on the mediocre side of average. In short, Rory is a significantly less viable candidate for climbing the peak-rating ladder than he was a couple of years ago.

The same can be said of his prospects for advancing on the career-rating chart. Through the 2017 season, it stands at –10.19, well outside the top thirty. Two years ago, however, McIlroy's career score was –14.94. Those three intervening missed cuts are something dominant players are not supposed to do. Prior to his inauspicious 2016–17 stretch, McIlroy had been averaging about –3.00 per season, meaning that in the event he regains his prior form and plays consistently over the next decade, he could expect to improve his career score by about 30 points. If that occurs, McIlroy would probably find himself ranked among the top fifteen all time. That, however, is something beyond difficult, as his performance at the 2018 Masters demonstrates. He placed fifth, but produced only a –1.28 Z score. His forecast suggests that McIlroy is likely to add to, not subtract from, his career total in the near future. Simply put, McIlroy has not shown the consistency needed to gain traction on the career-rating list: the ability, yes; the consistency, no.

McIlroy's strength has always been off the tee. Since first playing enough PGA Tour events to generate a qualifying statistical base in 2010, McIlroy's Strokes Gained rating off the tee has averaged 1.02. That's more than half of his overall 1.88 average Strokes Gained. His weaknesses—perhaps *mediocrities* is a better qualifier—intensify the closer he gets to the hole. All four of McIlroy's career Strokes Gained measurements are technically positive, but his measurements around and on the green are both only marginally so. He generates less than one-fifth of a stroke advantage—compared with average players—on and around the green.

Here's how McIlroy's peak scorecard looks at the moment.

McIlroy to Date

Tournament	Finish	Score	Z score
2011 U.S. Open	1st	268	–3.07
2012 PGA	1st	275	–3.02
2013 PGA	T-8	277	–1.13
2014 Masters	T-8	288	–0.75
2014 U.S. Open	T-23	286	–0.34
2014 British Open	1st	271	–2.40
2014 PGA	1st	268	–2.09

2015 Masters	4th	276	-1.72
2015 U.S. Open	T-9	280	-1.14
2015 PGA	17	279	-0.93

Note: Average Z score: -1.66. Effective stroke average: 69.53.

MCILROY'S CAREER RECORD (2009–PRESENT)

Masters: 8 starts, 0 wins, -4.48
U.S. Open: 8 starts, 1 win (2011), +4.88
British Open: 8 starts, 1 win (2014), -2.70
PGA: 8 starts, 2 wins (2012, 2014), -7.89
Total (32 starts): -10.19

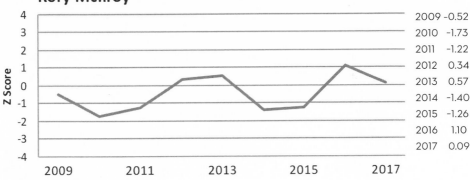

2009	-0.52
2010	-1.73
2011	-1.22
2012	0.34
2013	0.57
2014	-1.40
2015	-1.26
2016	1.10
2017	0.09

Jason Day

A superb 2015 season—victory at the PGA coupled with top tens at the U.S. and British Opens—propelled Day into the front rank of contemporary male players. A solid 2016 that included top tens in three majors led to the world number 1 rank. Beyond that, his peak rating of -1.66 entering 2017 left room to grow, since none of his ten best scores from that period came during 2012.

More than any other current young player with the possible exception of Jordan Spieth, it was fair to play the peak-value speculation game with Jason Day when he entered 2017 on the heels of four solid seasons—ten top tens in sixteen major starts. Had he maintained that performance level, his peak rating would by year's end have improved from 1.67 to

−1.80, right at the fringe of the top twenty-five all time. And he would have done so before age thirty, when most successful tour pros historically hit their stride.

To the extent that was ever a realistic forecast, it certainly is not now. It must be left to the swing analysts—or possibly the medics—to ascertain the reasons behind Day's 2017 slide. A missed cut in the U.S. Open was not fully offset by modest midpack finishes at the Masters, British Open, and PGA, the whole constituting a season that did not move Day's peak-performance needle. For a twentysomething aspiring to be counted among the greats, this is a bad trend. Compare the change between Day's ages twenty-eight and twenty-nine seasons with the same chronological seasons of the best of previous generations:

Player	Age 28-29 seasons	Age 28 average Score	Age 29 average Score
Jason Day	2016–17	−1.29	+0.57
Tiger Woods	2004–05	−0.60	−2.28
Greg Norman	1983–84	+0.11	−0.86
Jack Nicklaus	1968–69	−0.61	−0.72
Arnold Palmer	1958–59	−0.48	−1.24
Sam Snead	1940–41	−0.68	−0.21
Ben Hogan	1940–41	−0.68	−1.51
Byron Nelson	1940–41	−1.43	−1.24
Gene Sarazen	1930–31	−1.30	−1.45
Walter Hagen	1921–22	−2.00	−1.85
Average		**−0.95**	**−1.08**

If he aspires to be counted among the game's greats, plainly Day's career path took an ill-advised U-turn in 2017. Only a couple of those greats declined at all between their ages twenty-eight and twenty-nine seasons, and when they did—note Nelson and Hagen—it was a coincidental decline off a substantial season. Day's average Z score worsened by 1.87 between 2016 and 2017. In major professional golf, nothing is irreparable, but a turnaround from that sort of midcareer decline would be unprecedented.

His performance during 2017 also calls into question the future of Day's career rating. Here's the impact one season can have on projected future performance. As of the end of 2016, we would have said that had Day continued his performance pattern through 2022, his career value would have been about –47. At that level, he would be closing in on the all-time top ten. But 2017 substantially altered that projection. As of the end of 2017, Day projected to conclude 2022 with a career score around –27, making him the modern equivalent of Leo Diegel (–25.02). There is nothing wrong with emulating the career record of Diegel, the 1928–29 PGA Championship winner. But chasing Diegel is a far cry from chasing Nicklaus. And beyond that, Day's 2017 performance was so removed from his established pattern that it's hard to know whether to consider it an anomaly or a new normal. If the latter, then even Leo Diegel is out of reach.

Day's projection does at least offer this much solace. It continues negative, which is good, although not nearly at the same rate, yielding average Z scores in the –0.8 range. That, too, is Leo Diegel territory.

The Strokes Gained data provide another illustration of Day's decline. Here are his slash lines for his peak seasons:

	2013	2014	2015	2016	2017	Average
Off the tee	0.45	0.50	0.77	0.19	0.33	0.34
Approaching	0.01	0.18	0.46	0.43	–0.25	0.07
Around green	0.17	0.40	0.29	0.38	0.32	0.23
Putting	0.37	0.32	0.59	1.13	0.33	0.46
Total	1.00	1.40	2.11	2.13	0.73	

Comparing 2015 and 2016 with 2017, note particularly the sharp performance decline in Day's play approaching and on the green. Recall that an average pro's performance approaching the green correlates to his score at a 60 to 70 percent level during those seasons. Given that his 1.13 2016 Strokes Gained putting performance represents an aberration from his norm, perhaps the 0.8 of a stroke fallback in that category he sustained in 2017 represents to some degree a reversion to the norm. His overall play, however, shows a more alarming pattern. His total Strokes Gained numbers arced on what we might think of as a normal "star" pattern through the first four seasons of his prime, from 1.00 to 1.40 to 2.11 and then to 2.13. Not yet thirty in 2017, there was every reason to anticipate at least a minimal climb to 2.15, which would have put his stroke average at approximately 68.78, the best on tour and fractionally better than Jordan Spieth. Instead, he averaged 70.12 strokes, twenty-fourth best. His closest comparable was Daniel Berger. Daniel Berger is a nice player, and he had a nice season in 2017. But nobody counts him among the game's all-timers.

Here is Day's rating through 2017.

Day to Date

Tournament	Finish	Score	Z score
2013 Masters	3rd	281	–1.93
2013 U.S. Open	T-2	283	–1.80
2013 PGA	T-8	277	–1.13
2014 U.S. Open	T-4	281	–1.16
2015 U.S. Open	T-9	280	–1.14
2015 British Open	T-4	274	–2.19
2015 PGA	**1st**	**268**	**–2.70**
2016 Masters	T-10	289	–1.05
2016 U.S. Open	T-8	282	–1.16
2016 PGA	2nd	267	–2.44

Note: Average Z score: –1.67. Effective stroke average: 69.51.

DAY'S CAREER RECORD (2010–PRESENT)

Masters: 6 starts, 0 wins, –5.23

U.S. Open: 7 starts, 0 wins, –2.47

British Open: 7 starts, 0 wins, +1.50

PGA: 8 starts, 1 win (2015), –5.66

Total (28 starts): –11.87

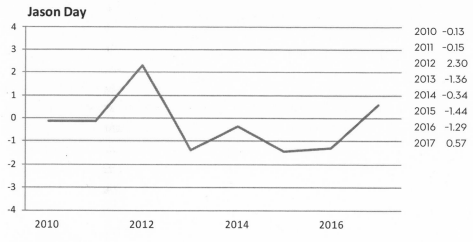

Jason Day

2010	-0.13
2011	-0.15
2012	2.30
2013	-1.36
2014	-0.34
2015	-1.44
2016	-1.29
2017	0.57

Yani Tseng

Number 5 Peak

Whatever became of Yani Tseng?

There appeared to be no limit to Tseng's ability when the Taiwanese teen defeated Maria Hjorth to win the 2008 LPGA Championship. Tseng followed that with 2010 victories at the Kraft Nabisco and British Open and then in 2011 put together the most dominant season in the history of women's major tournament competition. Tseng finished a strong second at the Kraft Nabisco, lapped the LPGA field by 10 strokes, and won the British Open by 4. Combined with a fifteenth-place finish in the U.S. Open, her −2.59 average Z score has been surpassed only by Tiger Woods (−2.77 in 2000).

In that context, Tseng's third-place finish at the 2012 Kraft Nabisco, the season's first major, looked like nothing out of the ordinary. It brought her peak Z score to −2.31, the fifth best of all time, and positioned her to threaten Woods, Sorenstam, Nicklaus, and Palmer for the top four spots. Since then, all of Tseng's momentum has evaporated. She has managed only two top-twenty-five finishes in the twenty-seven ensuing majors through 2017 and missed the cut in fifteen. Her scoring average, 69.66 strokes in 2011, rose to 71.12 in 2012, then to 71.71, 72.19 in 2014, 72.05 in 2015, and 73.47 in 2016. If one were to recalculate her peak score for the 2012–16 period, it would be +0.14, and there be no reason to be discussing Yani Tseng. Tseng's cumulative Z score for the twenty women's majors contested since 2013 is +42.53.

To date, nobody's come up with a good explanation for why the decline has occurred. If one examines the correlative data, the answer may lay in Tseng's ability to hit greens in regulation. During her peak seasons—2008 through 2012—Tseng hit greens at a rate nearly a full standard deviation better than her fellow competitors. Since 2013 she has hit greens at a rate nearly a half standard deviation worse than her competitors. On a tour with a consistent 80 percent correlation between hitting greens in regulation and scoring, that's a recipe for mediocrity. Having noted that, Tseng remains active, and as of 2017 she was only twenty-eight. So it's possible this is one of those Jack Nicklaus things—a marvelous young peak, followed by a relative decline, followed by an even greater peak, which in Tseng's case might begin next season, or five seasons from now.

If not, well, she'll always have 2008–12.

Tseng to Date

Tournament	Finish	Score	Z score
2008 LPGA	1st	276	−2.01
2008 British Open	2nd	273	−2.02
2009 Kraft Nabisco	T-17	288	−0.80
2010 Kraft Nabisco	1st	275	−2.91
2010 U.S. Open	T-10	290	−1.03
2010 British Open	1st	277	−2.77
2011 Kraft Nabisco	2nd	278	−2.70
2011 LPGA	1st	269	−4.10
2011 British Open	1st	272	−2.83
2012 Kraft Nabisco	3rd	280	−1.73

Note: Average Z score: −2.29. Effective stroke average: 68.60.

TSENG'S CAREER RECORD (2008–PRESENT)

Kraft Nabisco/ANA: 10 starts, 1 win (2010), +2.78

U.S. Open: 9 starts, 0 wins, +6.54

Women's PGA: 10 starts, 2 wins (2008, 2011), +4.87

British Open: 10 starts, 2 wins (2010, 2011), −2.91

Evian Masters: 5 starts, 0 wins, +11.95

Total (44 starts): +23.23

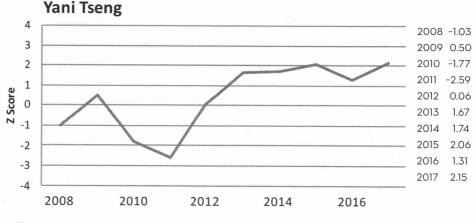

Yani Tseng

Year	Value
2008	-1.03
2009	0.50
2010	-1.77
2011	-2.59
2012	0.06
2013	1.67
2014	1.74
2015	2.06
2016	1.31
2017	2.15

Inbee Park

Number 20 Peak, Number 21 Career

Since Annika Sorenstam's retirement, the LPGA Tour has run through a series of briefly dominant players, none able or willing to rise to Sorenstam's level of performance for a lengthy stretch. From 2004 through 2008, Lorena Ochoa won two majors and finished in the top ten in fifteen. But in 2010, not yet thirty, she abruptly left the tour to pursue personal goals. The vacuum created by Ochoa's absence was quickly filled by Yani Tseng, who was brilliant for two seasons only to abruptly go AWOL from the leaderboard.

Then up stepped Inbee Park.

There are many similarities between Ochoa, Tseng, and Park. All three are foreign born—Park is from Korea—and all were in their early twenties when they arrived as stars. Ochoa and Tseng both functionally disappeared before age thirty. Park was twenty-nine in 2017.

Starting with her emergence in 2011, Park had five seasons among the LPGA's leaders, and her victories at the 2014 and 2015 LPGA, the 2015 British Open, and the 2016 Rio Olympics suggest she's not going anywhere soon. But her injury-plagued performances in 2016 and 2017 argue otherwise. Following a perfectly credible tie for sixth at the 2016

ANA Inspiration, Park missed her first major cut in eight seasons at the Women's PGA and then fought a hand injury that sidelined her for the remainder of the pro season. In 2017 she missed a fourth major of her last eight—the Evian Masters—and failed to make the cut at the U.S. Open. Beyond that, there has been speculation that Park may imitate Ochoa in another meaningful way: leaving the tour in a year or so to concentrate on her family.

In her 2016 absence, a veritable host of potential new stars divided the spoils: Brooke Henderson at the Women's PGA, Brittany Lang at the U.S. Open, Ariya Jutanugarn at the British Open, and In Gee Chun at the Evian. They along with Lydia Ko, nineteen, and Lexi Thompson, twenty-one, are not in awe of what Park accomplished when they were in high school.

Park knows that feeling. She turned pro in 2007, when she was nineteen. Her career score through 2017 is −36.80, heady stuff for a woman in her twenties. At a comparable stage of his career, Jack Nicklaus's career score was −27.60.

On the other hand, Nicklaus accumulated −71.06 career Z score points between twenty-nine and forty, an age when the best women pros of the past two decades—Sorenstam, Ochoa, Pak—have not kept pace. Park's 2016 and 2017 cumulative scores have been easily her two worst since 2009. Her five-year projection is consistent but only modestly negative, yielding annual Z scores that hang around −0.50. That would improve her career rating to about −47 by 2022. But the forecast does assume something not necessarily in evidence, namely, that Park maintains her 2014–17 form rather than her 2016–17 form. Those are two different things. Her playoff loss at the 2018 ANA Inspiration, which generated a −1.88 Z score, gave fans some reason for hope. Still, it would take a level of faith in Inbee Park ascribable only to her own mother to imagine her challenging Nicklaus's career standard.

The correlatables continue to portray Park as one of the tour's masters of the precision game. In 2017 she hit 73 percent of greens, 1 standard deviation better than the 68 percent tour average. She needed just 28.94 putts per round, sixth best overall and 1.8 standard deviations better than the 29.9 field average. Her driving stats have never ranged far outside the LPGA norm.

Following are Inbee Park's peak and career charts to date.

Park to Date

Tournament	Finish	Score	Z score
2013 LPGA	1st	283	-1.75
2013 U.S. Open	1st	280	-2.77
2014 LPGA	1st	277	-2.46
2014 British Open	1st	276	-1.65
2015 LPGA	1st	273	-3.20
2015 U.S. Open	T-3	275	-1.72
2015 British Open	1st	276	-2.59
2015 Evian Masters	T-8	279	-1.18
2016 ANA Inspiration	T-6	280	-1.23
2017 ANA Inspiration	T-3	275	-2.07
2017 LPGA	T-7	277	-1.26

Note: Average Z score:-1.99. Effective stroke average: 69.04.

PARK'S CAREER RECORD (2007-PRESENT)

Kraft Nabisco/ANA: 10 starts, 1 win (2013), -9.06
U.S. Open: 10 starts, 2 wins (2008, 2013), -9.87
Women's PGA: 11 starts, 3 wins (2013, 2014, 2015), -8.88
British Open: 10 starts, 1 win (2015), -8.17
Evian Masters: 3 starts, 0 wins, -0.83
Total (44 starts): -36.80

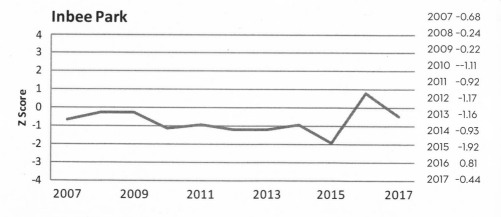

Inbee Park

Year	Z Score
2007	-0.68
2008	-0.24
2009	-0.22
2010	--1.11
2011	-0.92
2012	-1.17
2013	-1.16
2014	-0.93
2015	-1.92
2016	0.81
2017	-0.44

Lydia Ko

Prior to 2017 Lydia Ko was clearly on a path to become one of the dominant personalities in the history of major tournament golf. Having announced her presence while still an amateur by finishing second in the 2013 Evian Masters, she turned pro, won two majors, and added runner-up (at the Women's PGA) and third-place finishes (at the U.S. Open), all while rising to number 1 in the world.

More, she accomplished all that in her first sixteen professional majors, meaning that her peak rating was only then beginning to gel. It was an impressive one, hitting –1.82, within reach of the all-time top twenty-five.

Her career rating improved concurrently. Ko began accumulating Z scores at the rate of –3.75 per season. Were she to maintain that trend over the next decade, she would have hit –51 by age thirty, a total that would rank eleventh on the all-time career list.

What happened instead cannot be explained . . . at least not by me. Ko only once finished above thirtieth in 2017's five majors, posting the second- and fourth-worst performances of her still young LPGA career. Her average Z score for the year was –0.29; her average Z score one season earlier had been –1.07.

The experts lined up with theories: she had changed her caddie, she had changed her swing coach, she lacked the same mental intensity, and so on. To the extent the numbers pointed anywhere, they indicted her work on the greens. The tour's top putter in 2016 (28.31 strokes per round), she fell back to 29.14 putting strokes per round in 2017. That still ranked a solid fifteenth on tour, but it also accounted for all of Ko's 0.4 of a stroke rise in scoring average—from 69.6 in 2016 to 70.00 in 2017—and then some.

For the normal tour player, there is generally only about a 40 percent correlation between how one putts and how one scores on tour. But perhaps Ko isn't the normal tour player. Perhaps her so-so standing in the tour's other measurables requires her to putt extraordinarily well in order to succeed. Her average driving distance, around 244 yards, is about 1 standard deviation below the LPGA norm. Her accuracy is slightly above average . . . but we've already demonstrated that accuracy off the tee is the least important measurable skill for any tour pro. The *most* important skill, particularly for an LPGA pro, is the ability to hit a green in regulation. Ko improved slightly in that respect, from 70 to 72 percent in 2017. Both figures are only slightly better than the tour norm, which hovers around 68 percent.

All of the above may lead us to conclude that Lydia Ko must putt very well to win. But the data only partially support that conclusion, too. When she won the 2015 Evian Masters, Ko ranked fifteenth in the field in putting; that's good, but hardly dominant. She won that season's Canadian Pacific while ranking twentieth in putting and won the Swinging Skirts while tying for ninth in skill on the greens.

Ko's third-place showing in 2017's final major, the Evian Masters, gives fans reason for hope. Her five-year forecast paints her as a better than average but not standout player, anticipating average annual Z scores in the −0.4 range. Prior to 2017, however, that same projection line would have dipped below −1.0. Her performance on the 2018 tour will tell us a lot about her future. A strong bounce back, and 2017 will be a mere slump. A second consecutive subpar season, and she could become this decade's Yani Tseng . . . a golfing meteor. Her tie for twentieth at the season's first major, the ANA Inspiration, produced a −0.52 Z score, very much in line with the projection that she is on her way to becoming part of the field.

Ko to Date

Tournament	Finish	Score	Z score
2014 LPGA	3rd	280	−1.88
2014 Evian Masters	T-8	280	−1.18
2015 U.S. Open	T-12	279	−0.90
2015 British Open	T-3	280	−1.95
2015 Evian Masters	**1st**	**268**	**−2.91**
2016 ANA	**1st**	**276**	**−2.03**
2016 Women's PGA	2nd	278	−2.33
2016 U.S. Open	T-3	284	−1.36
2017 ANA	T-11	281	−0.94
2017 Evian Masters	T-3	205	−2.07

Note: Average Z score: −1.82. Effective stroke average: 69.29.

KO'S CAREER RECORD (2014–PRESENT)

ANA Inspiration: 4 starts, 1 win (2016), –2.46
U.S. Open: 4 starts, 0 wins, –2.96
Women's PGA: 4 starts, 0 wins, –0.73
British Open: 4 starts, 0 wins, –1.40
Evian Masters: 4 starts, 1 win (2015), –5.84
Total (20 starts): –13.92

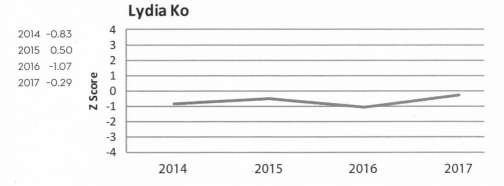

2014	-0.83
2015	0.50
2016	-1.07
2017	-0.29

Jordan Spieth

Spieth turned pro in the middle of the 2012 season, but his career path really accelerated in 2015. His victories in the Masters and U.S. Open, coupled with top tens in the other two majors, made him the 2015 player of the year with an average Z score of –2.31 in the majors. Among players who competed in at least three majors, that's the fourth-best single-season performance in history, exceeded only by Tiger Woods (–2.77 in 2000), Yani Tseng (–2.59 in 201), and Ben Hogan (–2.58 in 1953).

Spieth had competed in nineteen majors as a pro by the end of 2017, compiling a peak rating of –1.82. His record during that time provides ammunition for Spieth lovers, while leaving skeptics a few shreds to which to cling. Jordan's fans can point to his three major titles, the 2015 Masters and U.S. Open, plus the 2017 British Open. They can also cite his runner-up finishes in the 2015 PGA and 2016 Masters. They can and should note that all of the ten scores constituting his current peak rating were accomplished since April 2014, eight of them since April 2015. That gives him ample room to improve his peak rating during 2018 with no prospect of regression. (He began that process at the Masters with a runner-up finish that translated to a –1.96 Z score.) Finally, they can point to his projection, which sees him generating average Z scores consistently in the range of –1.6 to –2.5 for the near-term future. If he achieves the top end of that scale during any imminent season—the –2.5 end—it would rank with his 2015 among the elite major tournament seasons of all time.

For Spieth, the bottom line is that improvement in his current –1.82 peak is entirely plausible, possibly to the all-time elite levels. It also creates the possibility of Spieth ranking among the career all-time top ten by age thirty. Here's the bad news for that projection: it's still just a forecast.

The skeptics have a harder case to make, but they can point out that his British Open victory was Spieth's only truly exceptional performance since April 2016. They can also note that Spieth finished the 2016 major circuit by tying for thirty-seventh, thirtieth, and thirteenth in the U.S. Open, British Open, and PGA, respectively, and then largely labored through 2017 with three more major performances outside the top ten. To make much of that, of course, they would have to overlook his victory at Royal Birkdale, and to a lesser extent his runner-up finish at the 2018 Masters.

Let's assume for the sake of argument that Spieth proves his fans right and the skeptics wrong. How high up the peak and career ladder might he realistically be able to ascend? To answer that question, let's look at a few comparables:

Peak rating after nineteen professional majors
Jack Nicklaus –2.24
Tiger Woods –2.41
Jordan Spieth –1.82

Career rating after nineteen professional majors
Tiger Woods –29.90
Jack Nicklaus –25.84
Jordan Spieth –9.28

Okay, Spieth is not (yet) on track to rank with Woods and Nicklaus. Are there better comparables? The answer is: not many. If we consider the field of all PGA pros other than Woods and Nicklaus who established a peak rating better than –1.80 by their twenty-fifth birthdays, and did so within five years of turning pro, that field consists of one name: Spieth. We can expand the qualifiers to age twenty-seven and −1.60, but that only brings in one additional name: Gary Player, who had established a −1.61 peak rating by the end of the 1962 season. Player did eventually raise that rating, but only to −1.62. So going strictly by the admittedly limited number of comparables Spieth generates, it's possible that his peak rating was already more or less fully formed by 2017.

The same problem presents itself when we look at plausible career comparables. As of the end of 2017, Spieth's career rating was −9.28. Using our broader criterion of nineteen majors by age twenty-seven, only one close comparable surfaces: Johnny Miller. He had a career rating of −10.03 by the end of his 1974 season. But Miller is not an especially ideal comparable to Spieth. Most obvious, he had won only one major through 1974; Spieth had three as of the end of 2017. More serious is the problem of looking at a single, potentially idiosyncratic, comparable. Miller, eventually done in by putting problems, concluded his career with a +36.80 rating. Nobody associates Spieth with putting problems.

Analysis of the Strokes Gained data portrays Spieth as a player without a chink. Since 2013 he has averaged 1.61 Strokes Gained on the field, topping at 2.15 in 2015 and measuring 1.88 in 2017. Those gains came from every area of the course: he acquired 22 percent of his advantage of the tee, 30 percent approaching the green, 19 percent around the green, and 28 percent on the green. Five seasons' worth of data in four Strokes Gained categories produces twenty data points. In the case of Spieth, all twenty of those data points are positive, none is higher than 0.91, but only one is lower than 0.15. If one aspect of Spieth's game goes bad in a given week, he can fall back on a lot of other reliable elements.

Spieth to Date

Tournament	Finish	Score	Z score
2014 Masters	T-2	283	−1.83
2014 U.S. Open	T-17	284	−0.67
2015 Masters	1st	270	−2.79
2015 U.S. Open	1st	275	−2.03
2015 British Open	T-4	274	−2.19

2015 PGA	2nd	271	-2.21
2016 Masters	T-2	286	-1.63
2016 PGA	T-13	274	-0.91
2017 Masters	T-11	287	-0.70
2017 British Open	1st	268	-3.24

Note: Average Z score: -1.82. Effective stroke average: 69.29.

SPIETH'S CAREER RECORD (2013–PRESENT)

Masters: 4 starts, 1 win (2015), -6.96
U.S. Open: 5 starts, 1 win (2015), +0.55
British Open: 5 starts, 1 win (2017), -5.53
PGA: 5 starts, 0 wins, +2.67
Total (19 starts): -9.28

Jordan Spieth

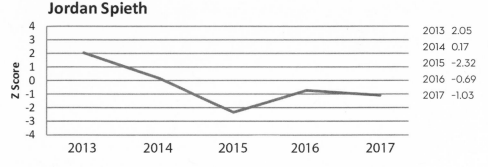

2013	2.05
2014	0.17
2015	-2.32
2016	-0.69
2017	-1.03

Worth a Few Lines . . .

JUSTIN THOMAS: His victory in the 2017 PGA Championship and his carrying home of the FedEx Cup capped Thomas's only second full season on the major circuit and constituted far and away his best showing to that date. His peak and career ratings as of the end of 2017 are identical: +0.42. That is a substantially less auspicious start than the PGA victory might suggest. To pick an obvious comparison, ten majors into his essentially parallel career, Jordan Spieth already had two major titles, and his peak and career scores had turned negative, which is good. Spieth's next ten majors included a third title and four top fives; if Thomas approximates that, he'll be fine. But that begs a question: Is Justin Thomas as good as Jordan Spieth? Despite the FedEx title, at this early stage in his career, the data are not (yet?) making that case. The average of Thomas's Strokes Gained seasonal scores is 0.97; Spieth's average for his first three seasons was 1.53. Thomas is, thus far anyway, displaying mediocrities Spieth has not shown, among them modest averages of 0.14 and 0.05 in Strokes Gained around and on the green. To date, Spieth is superior in all four Strokes Gained aspects. Thomas does have one thing going for him. His 2017 season constituted a dramatic uptick from his first two seasons, his overall Strokes Gained rising from 0.97 and 0.31 in 2015 and 2016 to 1.62 in 2017. If that trend proves more influential than the three-year average, Thomas may indeed challenge or surpass Spieth long term.

DUSTIN JOHNSON: Johnson won the 2016 U.S. Open and might have used that as a springboard to the dominance many have predicted for him. Instead, 2017 essentially became a waste season, its most memorable moment being a fall down some stairs prior to the Masters. In his five major starts since that victory at Oakmont, Johnson has missed two cuts and failed to finish higher than ninth . . . which he did once. Offsetting that, Johnson had by many standards a very nice 2017, finishing third in the FedEx Cup standings, winning three tournaments—among them two World Golf Championships—and leading the overall Strokes Gained list at 2.20. So he was to some extent a victim of this book's reliance on criteria with a long history—the majors—as a basis for its ratings. In a sense, that makes Johnson king of the 2017 nonmajors.

HIDEKI MATSUYAMA: Only twenty-five at the conclusion of the 2017 season, Matsuyama has three top-five finishes among his most recent five major appearances, so a major victory in 2018 would surprise nobody. He was one of only five players on the men's tour—the others were Matt Kuchar, Brooks Koepka, Rickie Fowler, and Paul Casey—to notch negative standard deviation ratings in all four 2017 majors. Since playing full-time on tour in 2014, Matsuyama has averaged 1.23 Strokes Gained, about 63 percent of that generated by his superiority approaching the green and another 37 percent off the tee. His problems have been with the putter, where he has on average given back 0.15 of a stroke per round. As long as he dominates off the tee and approaching the green—the two areas that most routinely correlate with stroke average—he can excel . . . but it would be nice to sink a putt now and then.

RICKIE FOWLER: Were Fowler to staple together back-to-back solid seasons, his relatively modest −1.28 peak rating Z score might be half a standard deviation better. Remember 2014, when Fowler finished among the top five in all four majors? He followed that with no top tens, only two top twenty-fives, and three missed cuts in his next nine major showings. Fowler hits age thirty in 2018, so he still has time to satisfy his legion of fans, of which this writer is one. At the same time, the 2017 major victories of Spieth, Koepka, and Thomas—all two or more years younger than Fowler—demonstrate how quickly the biological meter is running. Fowler presents a balanced game, gaining 1.00 strokes per round on the field, with roughly one-third of that coming off the tee, a second third approaching the green, and one-quarter of a stroke on the green. His relative weakness is in pitching and chipping.

BROOKS KOEPKA: The 2017 season, highlighted, obviously, by his U.S. Open win, was by far Koepka's best to date. Were he to replicate it, his −1.21 peak rating as of the end of 2017 would improve to −1.42 by the end of 2018, and to −1.57 by the end of 2019. That's not all-time elite status, but it would stand behind only Spieth, McIlroy, and Day among his contemporaries. In 2017 Koepka's Strokes Gained was about 0.90, ironically—considering his U.S. Open victory—his worst season-long performance to date. His advantages are predominately off the tee and on the greens, averaging a pickup of about 0.46 and 0.48 strokes in those areas.

LEXI THOMPSON: It takes a score of −1.95 to rank among the twenty-five best golfers of all time for peak performance. Thompson is one of only a handful of current players with a legitimate chance to reach that level. She ended the 2017 season at −1.65. A dominant 2018 featuring a couple of major victories and contending positions in the others—unlikely but imaginable—might make up the difference.

SO YEON RYU: She is five years Thompson's senior, but from a statistical standpoint they are a superb match. Ryu has two major titles to Thompson's one, and Ryu's −1.75 peak rating as of the end of the 2017 season is exactly one tick better than Thompson's. Ryu's career rating as of the end of 2017 is −24.07, giving her a decided edge over Thompson (–13.47) and Spieth (–9.28) in the race to crack that top twenty-five, where Lloyd Mangrum (–34.49) presently holds the twenty-fifth position. Ryu has gained furiously on Mangrum since 2016, adding 10.98 points to her career rating with three other top fives and five other top tens in addition to her 2017 ANA victory. If she maintains that pace, she'll put Mangrum—along with Babe Zaharias, Kathy Whitworth and Pat Bradley—behind her by the start of the 2020 season.

Afterword

We have demonstrated with mathematical certainty that at his peak, Tiger Woods was the most dominant golfer in history, while Jack Nicklaus enjoyed the most dominant career. So what? Does it, for instance, follow that in a tournament featuring the 100 best players in history, each participating in an equipment-neutral and condition-neutral setting, Woods would win?

The answer lies somewhere between "probably not" and "don't bet on it." Golf, as demonstrated in chapter 2, is simply too idiosyncratic a sport for that type of certainty.

Consider that about 140 players tee it up on the PGA Tour during any given week. Measured by effective stroke average, the difference between the best (Tiger Woods, 68.15) and 100th best (Johnny Revolta, 69.94) player whose score was calculated in the preparation of this book (which is to loosely say the best players in history) was 1.79 strokes per round. That happens to also roughly coincide with the gap between number 1 and number 56 on the 2017 PGA Tour. Based on stroke average, the best player on the men's tour in 2016 was Dustin Johnson. Yet he won just three of his twenty-three starts, and among the 20 players who won when he didn't were 9 ranked outside the top 20 in stroke average, 3 ranked outside the top 50, and 1 ranked outside the top 100. Dominance and chance.

The takeaway is that golf is a great but also idiosyncratic game. Its best in the long run may not necessarily be its best in a given tournament. With that in mind, we are left to acknowledge this: The statement that Tiger Woods—at his peak—was the most dominant player in history is both factual and measurable. But in the narrowly competitive sense, that does not make it determinative. In a condition-neutral, across-era match pitting Tiger at his peak against any of the other players featured in this book at their peak, would I bet on Woods? Yes . . . but only a friendly wager . . . a small one.

Appendix

Determining Peak and Career Ratings

1. Players are rated separately for five-year peak and for career value.
2. Unless exempted, players must have competed in a minimum of ten "major" tournaments within a consecutive five-year period. "Major" tournaments are as defined by the chief golf governing bodies for men and women. Performance in the Western Open during the pre-1958 period is used in order to offset the inability of many golfers from that era to participate in the British Open. For years prior to World War II, Z scores from major amateur tournaments are counted at 50 percent.
3. For match-play competitions, players' equivalent medal scores will be estimated using a predetermined formula.
4. A player's "peak performance" rating shall be the average of his or her ten best Z scores from up to twenty major events within a five-year period, except that every major in which the player participated during his or her peak years must be represented at least once. For post-2012 LPGA professionals who competed in up to five majors per season, peak ratings are based on a four-year window comprising up to twenty majors.
5. A player's career rating shall consist of the sum of the Z scores of his or her performances from the beginning of his or her professional career until the player turns fifty years old or announces his or her retirement from competitive golf.
6. In computing standard deviations, high-end "outliers" producing noncompetitive scores may be excluded.

Converting Standard Deviation to Stroke Average

During a normal eighteen-hole round of a PGA- or LPGA-level tournament played on a normal par-72 course, every stroke generally translates to about 0.7 of 1 standard deviation in the field performance. Assuming a field average of even par, we can use that information to create a table capable of translating a standard-deviation measurement of difference back into strokes. That's the method used in this book. At increments of 0.05 of a standard deviation, here is the resultant table.

Standard deviation	Effective stroke average	Standard deviation	Effective stroke average
-2.70	68.00	-1.55	69.69
-2.65	68.07	-1.50	69.76
-2.60	68.15	-1.45	69.84
-2.55	68.22	-1.40	69.91
-2.50	68.29	-1.35	69.98
-2.45	68.37	-1.30	70.06
-2.40	68.44	-1.25	70.13
-2.35	68.51	-1.20	70.21
-2.30	68.59	-1.15	70.28
-2.25	68.66	-1.10	70.35
-2.20	68.74	-1.05	70.43
-2.15	68.81	-1.00	70.50
-2.10	68.88	-0.95	70.57
-2.05	68.96	-0.90	70.65
-2.00	69.03	-0.85	70.72
-1.95	69.10	-0.80	70.79
-1.90	69.18	-0.75	70.87
-1.85	69.25	-0.70	70.94
-1.80	69.32	-0.65	71.01
-1.75	69.40	-0.60	71.09
-1.70	69.47	-0.55	71.16
-1.65	69.54	-0.50	71.23
-1.60	69.62	-0.45	71.31

-0.40	71.38	-0.15	71.75
-0.35	71.45	-0.10	71.82
-0.30	71.53	-0.05	71.91
-0.25	71.60	-0.00	72.00
-0.20	71.68		

Defining the Women's Majors

Over the years, there has been substantial fluctuation in the definition of a "major" tournament on the women's tour. For purposes of this study, women's majors—as defined by the LPGA—are as follows:

1930–36: Women's Western Open

1937–45: Women's Western Open and Titleholders

1946–54: Women's Western Open, Titleholders, and U.S. Open

1955–66: Women's Western Open, Titleholders, U.S. Open, and LPGA

1967: Women's Western Open, U.S. Open, and LPGA

1968–71: U.S. Open and LPGA

1972: Titleholders, U.S. Open, and LPGA

1973–78: U.S. Open and LPGA

1979–82: U.S. Open, LPGA, and du Maurier

1983–2000: Nabisco Dinah Shore (Nabisco/ANA), U.S. Open, LPGA, and du Maurier

2001–12: Nabisco, U.S. Open, LPGA, and British Open

2013–present: ANA, U.S. Open, Women's PGA, British Open, and Evian Masters

Note: The first major of the LPGA season, currently known as the ANA Inspiration, has had several names since being elevated to major status. Here is the name history: Nabisco Dinah Shore, 1983–99; Nabisco, 2000–2001; Kraft Nabisco, 2002–14; and ANA Inspiration, 2015–present.

The Top 25 Players of All Time

Based on the average of their ten best Z scores from a period of twenty consecutive tournaments or less within five seasons (four seasons for post-2012 LPGA players), unless fewer than ten tournaments were played within the five-year window in which case the window can be expanded to include ten tournaments.

Player	Peak years	Z score	Effective stroke average
1. Tiger Woods	1998–2002	–2.60	68.15
2. Annika Sorenstam	2002–2006	–2.49	68.31
3. Jack Nicklaus	1971–75	–2.302	68.59
4. Arnold Palmer	1960–64	–2.301	68.59
5. Yani Tseng	2008–12	–2.29	68.60
6. Karrie Webb	2000–2004	–2.28	68.62
7. James Braid	1901–10	–2.18	68.76
8. Tom Watson	1977–81	–2.17	68.78
9. Ben Hogan	1950–54	–2.13	68.84
10. Bobby Jones	1926–30	–2.11	68.87
11. Walter Hagen	1923–27	–2.10	68.88
12. Sam Snead	1949–53	–2.07	68.92
13. Mickey Wright	1958–62	–2.06	68.93
14. Harry Vardon	1896–1904	–2.03	68.98
15. Ayako Okamoto	1985–89	–2.02	69.00
(tie) Ralph Guldahl	1936–40	–2.02	69.00
17. Phil Mickelson	2001–5	–1.9970	69.03
18. Cristie Kerr	2007–11	–1.9974	69.03
19. Laura Davies	1994–98	–1.991	69.04
20. Inbee Park	2013–17	–1.989	69.05
21. Byron Nelson	1937–41	–1.984	69.06
22. Pat Bradley	1985–89	–1.977	69.06
23. Gene Sarazen	1929–33	–1.976	69.06
24. Nick Faldo	1988–92	–1.96	69.09
(tie) Betsy King	1986–90	–1.96	69.09

The Top 25 Players of All Time Based on Career Z Score

Player	Career years	Career Z score
1. Jack Nicklaus	1962–89	–104.81
2. Walter Hagen	1913–40	–73.94
3. Patty Berg	1935–68	–73.21
4. Sam Snead	1937–62	–68.69
5. Tiger Woods	1997–2017	–64.62
6. Louise Suggs	1949–72	–60.31
7. Mickey Wright	1954–84	–59.67
8. Annika Sorenstam	1994–2008	–59.16
9. Gene Sarazen	1920–51	–58.09
10. Ben Hogan	1938–62	–53.09
11. Byron Nelson	1933–61	–44.88
12. Jim Barnes	1913–32	–43.84
13. Sandra Haynie	1961–89	–43.61
14. Macdonald Smith	1910–37	–43.15
15. JoAnne Carner	1970–89	–43.04
16. Gary Player	1956–84	–40.86
17. Bobby Jones	1916–30	–39.62
18. J. H. Taylor	1893–1921	–38.69
19. Juli Inkster	1984–2007	–38.34
20. Harry Vardon	1894–1920	–37.88
21. Inbee Park	2007–17	–36.80
22. Arnold Palmer	1955–80	–36.67
23. Babe Zaharias	1935–56	–35.77
24. Kathy Whitworth	1959–89	–34.68
25. Lloyd Mangrum	1937-1962	–34.49

Other Scores

Here is a table of the peak and career performance scores of prominent players not featured elsewhere in this book. The players are listed in alphabetical order. The list includes their average peak Z score (Peak Z), the effective stroke average (ESA) represented by that average standard deviation (on a scale where an average standard deviation of 0.00 equals an eighteen-hole score of 71.97), the seasons constituting that peak, their career Z score (Career Z), and the seasons comprising their career.

Player	Peak Z	ESA	Peak years	Career Z	Career years
Amy Alcott	-1.59	69.63	1978-82	1.71	1975-2005
Jamie Anderson	-0.96	71.06	1869-82	-7.38	1869-88
Isao Aoki	-0.87	70.69	1978-82	30.84	1974-90
Tommy Armour	-1.47	69.81	1929-33	-16.18	1920-42
Paul Azinger	-0.86	70.70	1997-2002	52.30	1985-2006
John Ball Jr.	-0.81	70.78	1888-93	-14.08	1890-1912
Jane Blalock	-1.38	69.94	1976-80	-19.98	1969-84
Tommy Bolt	-1.24	70.15	1954-58	1.93	1950-66
Julius Boros	-1.32	70.03	1955-59	-21.62	1950-70
Gay Brewer	-1.06	70.41	1964-68	37.27	1956-81
Jack Burke Jr.	-1.40	69.91	1952-56	30.44	1940-74
Angel Cabrera	-0.89	70.66	2006-10	64.33	1997-2017
Donna Caponi	-1.70	69.47	1977-81	-15.64	1965-88
Billy Casper	-1.51	69.75	1964-68	-12.24	1956-79
Bob Charles	-1.14	70.29	1968-72	26.83	1961-76
Jim Colbert	-0.51	71.22	1971-75	37.49	1967-87
Harry Cooper	-1.72	69.44	1934-38	-22.07	1923-42
Kathy Cornelius	-0.94	70.65	1961-65	-15.96	1956-82
Henry Cotton	-1.54	69.71	1934-48	-25.02	1927-58
Fred Couples	-1.58	69.65	1988-92	22.86	1982-2009
Bruce Crampton	-1.02	70.47	1969-73	10.13	1956-76
Ben Crenshaw	-1.59	69.63	1976-80	43.47	1973-2001
Fay Crocker	-1.06	70.45	1954-58	-15.19	1954-61
Bobby Cruickshank	-1.00	70.50	1921-26	-8.75	1921-42
John Daly	-0.35	71.45	1991-95	110.05	1991-2015

Player	Peak Z	ESA	Peak years	Career Z	Career years
Beth Daniel	−1.85	69.10	1980–84	−21.57	1978–2007
Jimmy Demaret	−1.55	69.69	1946–50	−8.11	1936–58
Roberto deVicenzo	−0.75	70.87	1950–54	−15.59	1948–72
Bruce Devlin	−1.12	70.32	1965–69	8.42	1962–83
Leo Diegel	−1.60	69.62	1926–30	−28.19	1916–39
Luke Donald	−1.13	70.31	2004–8	49.08	1999–2016
Olin Dutra	−1.40	69.91	1931–35	−8.71	1928–48
David Duval	−1.36	69.97	1997–2001	56.14	1995–2015
Lee Elder	−0.12	71.79	1976–80	35.61	1966–83
Steve Elkington	−0.83	70.75	1991–95	31.57	1988–2011
Ernie Els	−1.65	69.54	2000–2004	14.52	1992–2017
Johnny Farrell	−1.40	69.91	1924–28	7.76	1922–51
Shanshan Feng	−1.47	69.81	2013–17	−7.47	2007–17
Bob Ferguson	−1.31	70.06	1868–86	13.09	1868–86
Dow Finsterwald	−1.37	69.96	1959–63	22.19	1951–76
Ray Floyd	−1.37	69.96	1974–78	1.96	1963–92
Doug Ford	−1.63	69.57	1955–59	21.74	1950–71
Rickie Fowler	−1.28	70.09	2013–17	−0.38	2009–17
Jim Furyk	−1.27	70.10	2003–7	18.17	1994–2017
Sergio Garcia	−1.27	70.10	2002–6	18.47	1999–2017
Al Geiberger	−1.05	70.43	1965–69	29.21	1961–85
Vic Ghezzi	−0.94	70.59	1940–47	9.40	1932–60
Bob Goalby	−0.68	70.97	1959–63	39.96	1957–78
Johnny Goodman	−0.46	71.29	1933–37	2.94	1929–46
Retief Goosen	−1.55	69.69	2001–5	14.99	1996–2016
David Graham	−1.30	70.06	1979–83	45.33	1970–95
Hubert Green	−1.44	69.85	1974–78	42.23	1974–96
Marlene Hagge	−1.38	69.97	1956–60	−6.04	1947–83
Beverly Hanson	−1.30	70.09	1955–59	−19.81	1950–61
Claude Harmon	−0.83	70.75	1945–49	27.22	1942–65
Padraig Harrington	−1.13	70.31	2004–8	53.66	1996–2017
Dutch Harrison	−0.86	70.70	1950–54	−7.50	1936–58
Harold Hilton	−0.98	70.53	1897–1901	−26.12	1887–1914
Jock Hutchison	−1.83	69.28	1919–23	−34.43	1908–33

Hale Irwin	−1.42	69.88	1975–79	−0.66	1971–95
Tony Jacklin	−1.29	70.07	1968–72	13.76	1963–77
Betty Jameson	−1.07	70.40	1952–56	−22.92	1934–64
Lee Janzen	−1.02	70.47	1993–97	42.37	1993–2008
Dustin Johnson	−1.38	69.94	2012–16	2.02	2008–17
Zach Johnson	−0.92	70.62	2012–16	47.08	2007–17
Ariya Jutanugarn	−0.72	70.91	2014–17	10.39	2014–17
Martin Kaymer	−0.91	70.63	2010–14	11.79	2008–17
I. K. Kim	−1.44	69.85	2009–13	1.53	2006–17
Tom Kite	−1.09	70.37	1981–85	22.72	1972–99
Brooks Koepka	−1.21	70.19	2013–17	−2.77	2012–17
John Laidlay	−0.81	70.78	1888–93	−15.32	1885–1910
Bernhard Langer	−1.33	70.01	1984–88	52.32	1984–2007
Tom Lehman	−1.41	69.90	1984–88	14.91	1992–2003
Justin Leonard	−1.21	70.19	1996–2000	50.13	1995–2016
Stacy Lewis	−1.71	69.46	2011–14	−28.86	2008–17
Brittany Lincicome	−1.16	70.26	2007–11	13.92	2004–17
Lawson Little	−0.94	70.59	1938–42	7.47	1933–57
Gene Littler	−0.84	70.73	1958–62	−9.20	1954–77
Davis Love III	−1.65	69.54	1995–99	70.65	1986–2013
Sandy Lyle	−1.11	70.34	1985–89	58.72	1977–2000
Meg Mallon	−1.60	69.62	1991–95	1.85	1986–2008
Carol Mann	−1.32	70.03	1964–68	−23.83	1961–88
Bob Martin	−1.05	70.43	1873–87	−9.68	1873–91
Hideki Matsuyama	−1.27	70.10	2013–17	−2.56	2013–17
Graeme McDowell	−1.05	70.43	2008–12	47.31	2004–17
Cary Middlecoff	−1.77	69.37	1955–59	−5.99	1940–70
Johnny Miller	−1.66	69.54	1972–76	36.80	1969–94
Mary Mills	−1.41	68.90	1963–67	−3.90	1962–83
Colin Montgomerie	−1.15	70.28	1995–99	61.89	1990–2010
Kel Nagle	−0.96	70.56	1961–65	11.94	1951–70
Larry Nelson	−1.13	70.31	1979–83	60.77	1976–91
Anna Nordqvist	−1.41	69.90	2014–17	−6.84	2009–17
Andy North	−0.55	71.16	1978–82	62.27	1975–95
Christy O'Connor	−0.88	70.68	1958–67	−11.16	1951–74

Player	Peak Z	ESA	Peak years	Career Z	Career years
José María Olazábal	-1.24	70.15	1990–94	51.46	1984–2007
Mark O'Meara	-0.91	70.63	1995–99	82.60	1980–2007
Louis Oosthuizen	-1.03	70.45	2011–16	26.17	2004–17
Francis Ouimet	-0.53	71.19	1923–29	-13.25	1913–36
Jumbo Ozaki	-0.02	71.94	1989–93	44.82	1972–97
Mungo Park	0.07	72.09	1874–86	0.55	1874–86
Willie Park Jr.	-1.14	70.29	1883–92	-13.51	1880–1905
Willie Park Sr.	-0.78	70.82	1860–70	-11.58	1860–82
Corey Pavin	-1.37	69.96	1992–96	69.15	1982–2009
Dottie Pepper	-1.54	69.71	1989–93	-31.53	1988–2004
Suzanne Pettersen	-1.76	69.38	2010–13	-3.51	2001–17
Henry Picard	-1.60	69.62	1935–39	-19.36	1932–56
Nick Price	-1.47	69.81	1992–96	31.81	1978–2006
Judy Rankin	-1.05	69.78	1975–79	1.44	1963–88
John Revolta	-1.38	69.94	1933–37	-2.18	1929–60
Chi Chi Rodriguez	-0.55	71.16	1969–73	32.85	1961–82
Bob Rosburg	-1.29	70.07	1955–59	20.01	1953–73
Justin Rose	-1.24	70.15	2013–17	33.26	1999–2017
Paul Runyan	-1.59	69.63	1934–38	-8.86	1928–57
So Yeon Ryu	-1.63	69.57	2013–16	-24.07	2010–17
Doug Sanders	-1.12	70.32	1966–70	-3.21	1957–76
Adam Scott	-1.65	69.54	2011–15	22.79	2001–17
Patty Sheehan	-1.86	69.23	1992–96	-15.23	1980–2006
Denny Shute	-1.31	70.04	1932–36	-14.54	1928–54
Vijay Singh	-1.35	69.98	1998–2002	14.89	1989–2013
Alex Smith	-1.45	69.84	1904–10	-25.76	1898–1921
Horton Smith	-1.36	69.97	1928–32	-6.47	1928–58
Marilynn Smith	-1.29	70.13	1961–65	-6.94	1950–77
Hollis Stacy	-1.31	70.00	1977–81	45.28	1974–2000
Henrik Stenson	-1.52	69.73	2013–17	9.91	2001–17
Jan Stephenson	-1.46	69.82	1981–85	20.28	1974–2001
Dave Stockton	-0.92	70.62	1970–74	37.74	1968–91
Curtis Strange	-1.24	70.15	1985–89	69.15	1975–2002
David Strath	-0.65	71.01	1869–77	-5.18	1869–77

Lexi Thompson	−1.65	69.54	2013–17	−13.47	2010–17
Peter Thomson	−1.40	69.91	1952–56	−14.15	1952–79
Jerome Travers	−0.53	71.19	1907–14	−3.87	1903–19
Walter Travis	−0.93	70.60	1900–1905	−16.89	1898–1914
Ken Venturi	−1.16	70.26	1956–1961	8.26	1956–74
Lanny Wadkins	−1.27	70.10	1984–88	29.73	1971–99
Art Wall Jr.	−0.41	71.37	1959–63	29.02	1952–73
Bubba Watson	−0.66	71.00	2011–15	28.17	2007–17
Lee Westwood	−1.50	69.76	2009–13	35.71	1995–2017
Michelle Wie	−1.18	70.23	2013–17	19.32	2006–17
Ian Woosnam	−1.16	70.26	1989–93	55.94	1982–2004
Fuzzy Zoeller	−1.19	70.22	1981–85	54.35	1976–2001

The 25 Most Dominant Major Tournament Performances in History

Rank	Player	Season	Tournament	Z score
1.	Cristie Kerr	2010	LPGA	−4.21
2.	Tiger Woods	2000	U.S. Open	−4.12
3.	Yani Tseng	2011	LPGA	−4.10
4.	Karri Webb	2000	Nabisco	−3.77
5.	Dottie Pepper	1999	Nabisco Dinah Shore	−3.57(62)
6.	Nancy Lopez	1985	LPGA	−3.57(56)
7.	Patty Sheehan	1984	LPGA	−3.56
8.	Davis Love III	1997	PGA	−3.54
9.	Betsy King	1992	LPGA	−3.52
10.	Henrik Stenson	2016	British Open	−3.50(4)
11.	Louis Oosthuizen	2010	British Open	−3.50(2)
12.	Jack Nicklaus	1965	Masters	−3.48
13.	Billy Casper (tie) Arnold Palmer	1966	U.S. Open	−3.42
15.	Juli Inkster	2002	U.S. Women's Open	−3.39
16.	Tom Watson	1977	British Open	−3.38
17.	Jack Nicklaus	1980	PGA	−3.34
18.	Tiger Woods	2000	British Open	−3.33
19.	Nancy Lopez	1989	LPGA	−3.30
20.	Tom Watson	1980	British Open	−3.26
21.	Jordan Spieth	2017	British Open	−3.25
22.	Karrie Webb	2001	U.S. Women's Open	−3.24
23.	Tiger Woods	1997	Masters	−3.20
24.	Amy Alcott	1991	Nabisco	−3.16
25.	Arnold Palmer	1962	British Open	−3.15

Note: In cases of ties, Z scores are carried out to a sufficient number of additional places to break the tie, if possible; these tiebreakers are indicated in parentheses.

The 25 Most Dominant Major Seasons in History
Based on Average Z Score (Minimum 3 Majors)

Rank	Player	Season	Z score
1.	Tiger Woods	2000	–2.77
2.	Yani Tseng	2011	–2.59
3.	Ben Hogan	1953	–2.58
4.	Jordan Spieth	2015	–2.32
5.	Tiger Woods	2005	–2.28
6.	Karrie Webb	2000	–2.25
7.	Bobby Jones	1930	–2.23
8.	Arnold Palmer	1964	–2.20(0)
9.	Annika Sorenstam	2003	–2.19(8)
10.	Byron Nelson	1946	–2.17
11.	Pat Bradley	1986	–2.16(0)
12.	Ben Hogan	1946	–2.15(7)
13.	Juli Inkster	1999	–2.15(0)
14.	Sam Snead	1949	–2.14
15.	Ayako Okamoto	1987	–2.11
16.	Ayako Okamoto	1986	–2.08
17.	Nancy Lopez	1985	–2.07
18.	Jack Nicklaus	1973	–2.05(0)
19.	Byron Nelson	1939	–2.04(6)
20.	Jack Nicklaus	1975	–2.04(2)
21.	Arnold Palmer	1962	–2.04(0)
	(tie) Mickey Wright	1961	–2.04(0)
23.	Karrie Webb	2001	–2.03(8)
	(tie) Juli Inkster	1992	–2.03(8)
25.	Babe Zaharias	1950	–2.03

Note: In cases of ties, Z scores are carried out to a sufficient number of additional places to break the tie, if possible; these tiebreakers are indicated in parentheses.

Glossary

career value: See the appendix for formula.

correlative skills: These are skills related to golf for which sufficient data exist to facilitate correlations with scoring. More than 280 such correlative skills are presently maintained by the PGA Tour alone. But because many are duplicative or ancillary, this book primarily focuses on the skills defined below.

clubhead speed: Speed on which the club impacts the ball (mph) on par-four and par-five tee shots where a radar measurement was taken.

driving accuracy: The percentage of time a tee shot comes to rest in the fairway (regardless of club).

driving distance: The average number of yards per measured drive. Drives are measured on two holes per round. Care is taken to select two holes that face in opposite directions to counteract the effect of wind. Drives are measured to the point at which they come to rest regardless of whether they are in the fairway.

greens in regulation: The percentage of time a player was able to hit the green in regulation (greens hit in regulation/holes played.) A green is considered hit in regulation if any part of the ball is touching the putting surface after the GIR stroke has been taken. (The GIR stroke is determined by subtracting two from par.)

proximity: The average distance to the hole (in feet) after the player's approach shot. The approach-shot distance must be determined by a laser and must not originate from or around the green. The shot must also end on or around the green or in the hole. "Around the green" indicates the ball is within thirty yards of the edge of the green.

putts: The average number of putts per round played.

scrambling: The percentage of time a player misses the green in regulation but still makes par or better.

estimated stroke average: A mythical figure designed to accurately translate peak Z score into an equivalent number that represents a golf score.

peak value: See the appendix for formula.

regression analysis: A mathematical tool for measuring the strength of the relationship between any two sets of numbers—for example, putts per round and strokes per round. Regression analysis thus becomes a means of answering the extent to which ability in any golf-related skill influences one's eventual score. The normal scale runs from a minimum of 0.0 to a maximum of 1.0, with 0.0 indicating no relationship and 1.0 indicating an extreme relationship. In situations where one number in the set might be expected to increase as the other declines—for instance, the relationship between driving distance and score—the correlation is expressed negatively, with 0.0 gain indicating no correlation and −1.0 indicating an extreme correlation.

The formula for calculating regression analysis for any set of numbers is as follows:

1. Find what is referred to as the dependent variable—in golf it might be driving distance, fairway accuracy, greens in regulation, or various others—for each player who has played a sufficient minimum number of holes to qualify.

2. Find what is referred to as the independent variable—for our purposes generally the score—for each player who has played a sufficient minimum number of holes to qualify.

3. For each qualified player, multiply the dependent variable by the average number for all players.

4. For each qualified player, multiply the independent variable by the average number for all players.

5. For each qualified player, multiply the result of step 3 by the result of step 4.

6. For each qualified player, calculate the square of the result of step 3.

7. For each qualified player, calculate the result of step 4.

8. Calculate the sums of the results for all qualified players of steps 5, 6, and 7.

9. Calculate the sum of the sums of step 6 multiplied by the sum of the sums of step 7.

10. Find the square root of the result of step 9.

11. Divide the sum of step 5 by the result of step 10.

standard deviation: A measure of any number relative to a "normal" set of numbers. In other words, it's a gauge of exceptionality. The bell curve is the classic illustration of a "normal" distribution of data. If golfers produce scores in a "normal distribution" pattern, then there's really no reason one can't apply standard deviation to the assessment of that data. But if they don't, one will have to find a new tool or abandon the project.

A sample of scores should suffice to test the premise. Between 2001 and 2007, more than thirty-three hundred four-round scores were recorded in major tournaments on the men's and women's tours. Relative to par, those scores ranged from a low of nineteen under to a high of thirty over. Our graph of the frequency of the occurrence of each score over that seven-year period may not be precise, because tournaments are played on different courses with different pars, and since this calculation is dealing with raw par figures, the data will not self-adjust to those differences. But allowing for some tolerance, if the graph looks like a bell curve, rock on. Following is the graph.

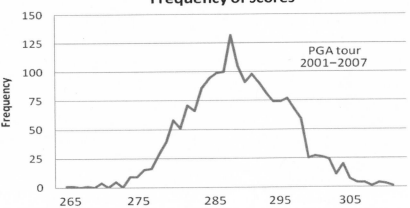

That may not be the most perfectly proportioned bell ever, but it's certainly recognizable, and the raw-score variations are reasonably attributable to the differences that relate to varying pars.

One can run the same test for various eras of the game, and for the most part the pattern will hold. There are breakdowns, especially when reaching back into the game's early eras. Those are roughly the pre-1970s for women and the pre-1920s for men. "Imperfect bell" breakdowns won't invalidate the conclusions, but they may render them more marginal. That's an official acknowledgment for the record to take the ratings of men from before 1920 and women from before 1970 as good-faith estimates but not precise calculations.

As a general proposition, one standard deviation movement away from the average in either direction will account for approximately 68 percent of all the results in a normal sample. Two standard deviations away from the mean accounts for roughly 95 percent of the data. Of course, only half of that movement will occur on the low end; the other half will be extraordinarily high. The bell has two sides, after all. A result three standard deviations outside the norm occurs only about 1 percent of the time, and again those 1 percent are split between the high and low ends. Throughout major tournament history, only about forty golfers—male and female— scored three standard deviations or better below the field average for the tournament in question. In major professional golf competition, results extending more than four standard deviations from the mean are exceedingly rare; there have been only three in the history of men's and women's major golf tournaments.

Simply put, the formula for calculating standard deviation is the average of the squared differences from the mean. Here is the more complex step-by-step formula:

1. Calculate the average for all numbers in the field.
2. Subtract each number from the average.
3. For each number, square the result of step 2.
4. Calculate the average of the squared differences. The result is the measure of one standard deviation from the field average.

Z score: Z score is a means of expressing exceptionality. It represents the number of standard deviations a given data point lies from the average. To calculate the Z score of any player in a golf tournament, begin by calculating the four-round field average and the standard deviation. Subtract the player's four-round score from the four-round field average, and divide the result by the standard deviation. For scores that are below the field average—which is to say better—the Z score is negative. In most large data sets, 99 percent of values have a Z score between −3.00 and 3.00, meaning they lie within three standard deviations above or below the field average.

Notes

Introduction

1. Charles C. Clarke, "Nauseous," *Times* (London), June 5, 1914, 14.

1. The 3 Percent Game

1. Bill Felber, "The Changing Game," in *Total Baseball*, ed. John Thorn and Pete Palmer (New York: Warner, 1989).
2. With two exceptions, the statistic in question was first kept in 1980. The tour began keeping scrambling data in 1992 and proximity data in 2002.
3. The strongest correlation between putts per round and scoring since 1980 was 54 percent in 1986; for Strokes Gained putting, the strongest correlation was 46 percent in 2010.

4. Pioneers

1. World Golf Hall of Fame.
2. Bernard Darwin, "To Underclub or Overclub," *American Golfer* (1932).
3. David Barrett, *Golf Courses of the U.S. Open* (New York: Abrams, 2007).
4. Bernard Darwin, "The Golfer's Emotions," *Atlantic Monthly*, June 1928.
5. Bernard Darwin, "Stormy Weather," *Country Life* (1961).

5. Coming to America

1. Allen Zullo and Chris Rodell, *Golf Is a Funny Game* (Kansas City MO: Andrews McMeel, 2008).
2. Bernard Darwin, "The Golfer's Cigarette," *Country Life* (1947).
3. Bobby Jones with O. B. Keeler, *Down the Fairway: The Golf Life and Play of Robert T. Jones Jr.* (New York: Minton, Balch, 1927), 33.
4. Herbert Warren Wind said Glenna Collett Vare, then a teenager, was a spectator at one of the Red Cross matches, drawing the inspiration that drove her to greatness from seeing Stirling and Jones.
5. Herbert Warren Wind, *The Story of American Golf: Its Champions and Its Championships* (New York: Callaway, 2000).
6. Wind, *Story of American Golf*.

6. Interwarriors

1. "The Golfer's Emotions," *Atlantic Monthly*, June 1928.
2. Rom Fimrite, "Sir Walter," *Sports Illustrated*, June 19, 1989.
3. World Golf Hall of Fame."
4. Fimrite, "Sir Walter."
5. Walter Hagen and Margaret Seaton Heck, *The Walter Hagen Story* (New York: Simon and Schuster, 1956).
6. Bernard Darwin, "Bad Manners in Golf," *Atlantic Monthly*, July 1938.
7. Darwin, "Bad Manners in Golf."
8. Darwin, "Bad Manners in Golf."
9. Bernard Darwin, "The Man from Titusville," in *Out of the Rough* (London: Chapman and Hall, 1932).
10. Wind, *Story of American Golf.*
11. Wind, *Story of American Golf.*
12. Wind, *Story of American Golf.*

7. Bantam Ben and Slammin' Sam

1. Wind, *Story of American Golf.*
2. Ried Hollen, "Golf's Toughest Competitor: Lloyd Mangrum," *Golf News*, December 30, 2014.

8. The King, Some Queens, and a Black Prince

1. Pat Ward-Thomas, "Palmer's Attack and Control Make Him a Great Champion," *Manchester Guardian*, July 14, 1962, 4.
2. This widely used quote has been attributed to Palmer by numerous sources, probably because Palmer himself referred to it in so many interviews. I have taken it from Mike Lupica's interview with Palmer for *Esquire*, published September 26, 2016.
3. John Stobbs, "Palm Goes to Palmer," *Observer*, July 16, 1961, 16.
4. Matt Schudel, "Louise Suggs, Hall of Fame Golfer and a Founder of the LPGA, Dies at 91," *Washington Post*, August 8, 2015.
5. Doug Ferguson, Associated Press, Aug. 7, 2015
6. Schudel, "Louise Suggs, Hall of Fame Golfer."
7. World Golf Hall of Fame
8. World Golf Hall of Fame
9. World Golf Hall of Fame.
10. Gary Player, *To Be the Best: Reflections of a Champion* (London: Sidgwick and Jackson, 1991).
11. Arnold Palmer, *My Game and Yours* (New York: Simon & Schuster, 1965).

12. World Golf Hall of Fame.
13. World Golf Hall of Fame.
14. World Golf Hall of Fame
15. World Golf Hall of Fame.
16. World Golf Hall of Fame.
17. Pat Ward-Thomas, "Lema's Magnificent Victory," *Guardian*, July 11, 1964.
18. Bill Fields, "What Might Have Been," *Golf Digest*, July 8, 2014.
19. World Golf Hall of Fame.
20. World Golf Hall of Fame.

9. The Golden Bear Market

1. Fred Byrod, *Philadelphia Inquirer*, June 20, 1971, 23.
2. Byrod, *Philadelphia Inquirer*.
3. "Nicklaus Wins Masters Title with Record-Breaking Show," *Greenville (SC) News*, April 12, 1965, 8.
4. Pat Ward-Thomas, "Jones, Hogan . . . Nicklaus," *Manchester Guardian*, July 13, 1970, 16.
5. Ward-Thomas, "Jones, Hogan . . . Nicklaus."
6. *Famous Quotes and Quotations*.
7. World Golf Hall of Fame
8. World Golf Hall of Fame
9. "Looking Back with Kathy Whitworth," LPGA, May 29, 2010.
10. Joe Passov, "Tom Weiskopf on Design Influences, Getting Sober and the Wins That Got Away: The *Golf Magazine* Interview," *Golf Magazine*, August 24, 2014.
11. Tom Weiskopf, interview by Joe Passov, *Golf Magazine*, August 25, 2014.
12. World Golf Hall of Fame
13. World Golf Hall of Fame
14. Craig Smith, "Big Momma's House," January 6, 2016, http://cascadegolfer.com/big-mommas-house/.
15. World Golf Hall of Fame.
16. World Golf Hall of Fame
17. World Golf Hall of Fame.
18. World Golf Hall of Fame
19. World Golf Hall of Fame.

10. Metallurgy

1. Gary Reinmuth, "With Norman's Gag Gift, Faldo's 3rd Masters Title a Laugher," *Chicago Tribune*, April 15, 1996, 3:1.
2. World Golf Hall of Fame
3. World Golf Hall of Fame.

11. Millennials

1. SeoulSisters.com.
2. Eric Adelson, "Bevins' Missteps Starting to Add Up," ESPN: The Magazine, September 5, 2008.
3. Lawrence Donegan, "Lorena Ochoa '100% at Peace' with Decision to Quit Golf," Guardian, April 23, 2010.
4. Beth Ann Baldry, "Lorena Ochoa: On a Mission," Golfweek, February 26, 2002.
5. Sal Maiorana, "Dominant Display," Rochester (NY) Democrat and Chronicle, June 28, 2010, D8.

Index